DEVELOPING CITIZEN DESIGNERS

DEVELOPING CITIZEN DESIGNERS

By Elizabeth Resnick

Bloomsbury Academic
An imprint of Bloomsbury Publishing Plc

BLOOMSBURY
NEW YORK · LONDON · OXFORD · NEW DELHI · SYDNEY

BLOOMSBURY ACADEMIC

An imprint of Bloomsbury Publishing Plc

1385 Broadway   50 Bedford Square
New York   London
NY 10018   WC1B 3DP
USA   UK

www.bloomsbury.com

**BLOOMSBURY and the Diana logo are trademarks
of Bloomsbury Publishing Plc**

First published 2016

BRITISH LIBRARY CATALOGUING-IN-PUBLICATION DATA
A catalogue record for this book is available from
the British Library.

ISBN: HB: 978-0-8578-5656-2
       PB: 978-0-8578-5620-3
       ePDF: 978-0-8578-5764-4
       ePub: 978-0-8578-5724-8

LIBRARY OF CONGRESS CATALOGING-IN-PUBLICATION DATA
Developing citizen designers / edited by Elizabeth Resnick.
pages cm
Includes bibliographical references and index.
ISBN 978-0-85785-656-2 (hardback)
ISBN 978-0-85785-620-3 (paperback)
1. Design—Social aspects.
2. Design—Case studies. I. Resnick, Elizabeth, editor.
NK1505.D48 2016
745.4—dc23
2015027495

Designed and Typeset by Tony Leone and Cara Ciardelli
Printed and bound in China

CONTENTS

PART 1: DESIGN THINKING

SECTION 1: SOCIALLY RESPONSIBLE DESIGN

SECTION 2: DESIGN ACTIVISM

PART 2: DESIGN METHODOLOGY

PART 3: MAKING A DIFFERENCE

FOREWORD

Bernard Canniffe

Economic realities are shifting. Small towns are disappearing, cities are faced with an aging and crumbling infrastructure and gross inequalities, and countries are struggling. People have lost faith in governments, and politicians have lost their way. Every day we are reminded that politicians are either incapable or unwilling to meet these global challenges, don't understand the relationship of local to global, and appear to only serve the needs of the few. The recent mortgage and loan debacle spun out into economic catastrophe for most people. As a result, we have witnessed many long-standing businesses disappear in the blink of an eye. If businesses and towns can disappear, and cities and countries can crumble, and if we add the possibility of a disappearing middle class, then we have to agree that there is no "there" there anymore. At the very least, none of us can predict with any certainty that long-term client relationships will continue to be something that a designer can rely on.

Student debt is crippling and prevents students from making their dreams a reality. They graduate with more debt than their starting salaries can sustain. Educators are called to fuel student aspirations and prepare them for the future. But the sad fact is that many institutions are institutionalized and the only way they understand their future is to continually raise tuition fees, while at the same time offering the same educational delivery system as they have always done. The design profession and design education must work together to address and resolve this imbalance or else we are designing ourselves into an uncertain and fragile future.

You can hold back from the suffering of the world, you have free permission to do so, and it is in accordance with your nature. But perhaps this very holding back is the one suffering you could have avoided.
—*Franz Kafka*

This quote seems more important today than it has ever been and becomes another touch point for an uncertain future. We have the choice to engage or not. We have the choice to act or walk away. If we do nothing then, sooner or later it will come knocking on our door, in one way or another, whether the knocking is from inside of us or from the outside actions resulting from our societal neglect.

We hope design can occupy this space, and we also hope that design can, for the first time, sit at the grown-ups' table. At this table, there are many experts from different fields, but they all share the same values, and see each other as equals. The seeds are already being sown and we have an opportunity. This new arena is not for the faint hearted and neither is it for those who embrace design exclusivity. The time is now, and there is both an urgency and a need for design to grow up and accept responsibility in order to meet the challenges that are set before us. We must engage in and with the world. There are a small emerging number of design educators, students, and practitioners who are rising up to meet these global challenges. They engage with and in communities, and work with healthcare providers, researchers, community activists, and civic leaders.

Design is shifting away from the service-provider model and toward the content-identifier model. Companies, communities, cities, and governments are coming to designers and asking them to help them understand who they are, and help them understand where they fit. This calls for a new breed of educator, designer, and student. This new breed of designer is a mix of community builder, designer, entrepreneur, and activist. It has many names; be it design for good social design, participatory design, or community design, these designers are helping to define and to shape a new, exciting, and much needed era of design. Many designers are reaching out to partner with social workers, business leaders, and community stakeholders, and through these partnerships, new economies are being formed and new opportunities presented.

Today, we hold Victor Papanek as a visionary, a leader, a reformer, an educator, and inspiration for everything we hold dear. He was, foremost, an advocate for social reform and saw design as an effective tool for empowerment. Yet, after he published *Design for the Real World* in 1971 he was derided and attacked, and his work was boycotted. Victor Papanek was misaligned by designers and in the name of design. Design conformity and the superficiality of design are as strong today as they were in 1971. We have to stand up for what we believe in, and protest what we know to be wrong. As educators we are called to advocate for the underserved, teach, and reach out to those who are not represented—for the disenfranchised. As designers we are charged to engage, interact, and produce that which has a societal impact.

We stand on the shoulders of giants, and Elizabeth Resnick is one such giant. I am proud to count her as a trusted friend and inspirational colleague. She has led the way by developing courses that engage with societal issues, and has curated international poster exhibitions that celebrate the role of designer as social responder. She continually advocates for design as an agent for social change, and the design world is fortunate to have her. We are all citizens of the world and we are called to use design for good. We are all citizen designers. What a wonderful picture these words conjure up! This book is a testimony to Elizabeth Resnick's passion and vision for celebrating projects that engage and inspire. It serves as a factual record that this type of work exists, and also serves as a catalyst to inspire us all that this type of work can and should be done.

Bernard Canniffe

"

The notion of 'social' design has been around at least since the early modernists pioneered the concept of good design for everyone, and not just moneyed elites. In recent decades, however, this view has been eclipsed—crushed even—by the dominant notion of design as the lubricant of consumer desire. But now the cultural climate has changed, and the 'common good' has become a concept that nearly everyone gets—even big business."

Adrian Shaughnessy, *Designer, Author,* Scratching the Surface

———

ACKNOWLEDGMENTS

As a graphic design educator employed by a publicly funded art college, it is my job to train students how to communicate using visual language. It is my responsibility to encourage them to use their training responsibly and to think beyond only serving business and commerce. They are citizens participating in a democratic society, and as such, they should be cognizant that their communication skills can be put to use as a powerful tool for social change for any number of issues they personally consider important to the well-being of the society in which they live.

This excerpt is from my previous book *Design for Communication: Conceptual Graphic Design Basics* (2003), Section 6: Visual Advocacy (p. 201). This section showcased six university-level design assignment briefs that introduced the notion of how responsible activism could be experienced in the classroom. *Developing Citizen Designers* is a direct descendant, as it seeks to expand on the notion of socially responsible design pedagogy with a dedicated book of university-level social design assignments, written in the form of case studies to educate and inspire those who would embrace this thinking and making in their classroom environments and communities.

Developing Citizen Designers is a true collaborative effort shaped by the many dedicated and talented people who believed in this book project:

Thank you to the many contributors (both published and unpublished) whose steadfast belief and lucid vision for challenging the way we practice and teach design forms the backbone of this book.

Thank you to Simon Cowell, former Senior Commissioning Editor for Design at Berg/Bloomsbury who, in early 2012, immediately understood that this book project could make a valuable contribution to design pedagogy and thinking.

I am deeply grateful to Rebecca Barden, who succeeded Simon Cowell in the position of Senior Commissioning Editor for Design in 2013, for her unwavering enthusiasm in support of this book project, and her faith in me as I embarked on the challenge of completing it in under one year; and to her editorial assistant Abbie Sharman, who provided much needed support and patience.

Thank you to Lisa Rosowsky, my faculty colleague at Massachusetts College of Art and Design for her support and expertise, as she edited all the case studies for the first round. This was no small feat, as many of the case studies were written by educators for whom English was their second language.

Thank you to Tony Leone, my book's designer, for his deft handling and impressive orchestration corralling this material into a vibrant, accessible visual form. It is also no small feat working with another designer as your client.

Thank you to my production team at Bloomsbury, Rob Brown, project manager, and Caroline Richards, copy-editor; two very accomplished professionals I could rely on and trust.

A very heartfelt "thank you" to my husband and life-partner, Victor Cockburn, who weathered my absence from our daily life with patience and understanding.

This book is further dedicated to all future citizen designers who will make a difference in our world.

WHAT IS DESIGN CITIZENSHIP?

Elizabeth Resnick

In his introductory essay for *Citizen Designer: Perspectives on Design Responsibility* (edited with Véronique Vienne in 2003), Steven Heller writes: "Milton Glaser often says, 'Good design is good citizenship.' But does this mean making good design is an indispensable obligation to society and culture in which designers are citizens? Or does it suggest that design has inherent properties that when applied in a responsible manner contribute to a well-being that enhances everyone's life as a citizen?"

The title of this book was my first introduction to the term "citizen designer," a descriptor that clearly expressed what I had been teaching my students from the beginning: that designers have both a social and a moral responsibility to use their visual language training to address societal issues either within or in addition to their professional design practice. "A designer must be professionally, culturally, and socially responsible for the impact his or her design has on the citizenry" (Heller and Vienne, 2003). And yet, the notion of what design signifies to the general public remains passively identified with aesthetics, styles, and trends when, in essence, it could promise so much more—at its best, design can change, improve, renew, inspire, involve, disrupt, and help solve the "wicked" problems of this world.

How can we encourage our students to embrace this notion of becoming "good citizen designers" when design education programs continue to train their students as passive arbitrators of commercial and client-based messages? And why do they do this? Because in an unrelenting and economically challenged vicious cycle to attract tuition-paying students, design education programs have had to cater to those students who want a job in the creative industries. And yet, it is impossible to ignore the seismic and paradigm shifts of the past decade in technology, in our environment and local cultures, in world economics and global politics that have

profoundly affected and challenged both traditional design education and professional design practice. Simply put, a change is needed.

How can design educators help students to engage in a world that is considerably interconnected and immediate, yet disturbingly more fractured, unstable, and totally disconnected from what really matters? As the fabric of our societies and cultures continues to unravel at an accelerated rate, there is both a compelling and crucial need for an unmitigated transformation of design education as we know it—design educators urgently need to revisit our ingrained methods and philosophies in order to review and reconsider how we will actually "steward" our future generations of young design practitioners.

Social Design—the practice of design where the primary motivation is to promote positive social change within society—is one possible pathway. As a discipline, Social Design[1] has experienced dramatic growth in recent years, but remains nascent in its teaching, research, and community-oriented practices. Initially inspired by the writings of Victor Papanek and others, its "social" agenda is to encourage designers and creative professionals to adopt a proactive role to effect tangible change to make life better for others, rather than to sell them products and services they neither need nor want—which has been the primary motivation for commercial design practice in the twentieth century.

Nurtured by a fervent community of international professional designers/design educators working both individually and collectively, social design pedagogy has been integrated into the traditional design curriculum by utilizing design-thinking strategies—like collaborative learning and participatory design process—to create engagements with communities or stakeholders for whom a need exists. Within these models and others, students as emerging designers can experience a more meaningful connection to, and impact on, society through their research, analysis, discourse, and creation at local, national, and, in some cases, international levels.

The backbone of *Developing Citizen Designers* is a selection of forty-two assignment-based case studies written by an engaged group of design educators who directly address the notion that design, and design education, can illuminate a pathway to effect positive change within a social agenda. Each of the case studies is illustrated with actual solutions developed by students working within the parameters of an assignment and in the context of classroom or onsite location, depending on the nature of the project involved.

I grouped the case studies into two main parts, each with three sections. The main parts and their sections reflect the general nature of the pedagogical experience: Part 1, Design Thinking, has sections on Socially Responsible Design, Design Activism, and Design Authorship; and Part 2, Design Methodology, has sections on Collaborative Learning, Participatory Design, and Service Design. Each of the six sections begins with an introductory essay designed to give context and definition to the particular subject and the subsequent case studies. Although many of the case studies could be easily "housed" under multiple sections, these classifications exist for guidance and ease of use. Included with the case studies and their introductory essays are five-question interviews with seven designers who have incorporated social design initiatives into their professional practice or teaching.

Part 3, Making a Difference, contains two sections, Getting Involved and Resources. In both sections, essays were commissioned from educators who teach in a diversity of educational programs, to address crucial aspects of teaching, learning, and putting into practice social design initiatives. The bibliography housed in the Resources section is an anthology of significant texts on the subject of social design, and resources that the case study and essay contributors have cited as important for their teaching and research.

Providing our students—and the generations of students that will follow—with the opportunity to experience making a meaningful and positive contribution to society while redefining what it means to be a designer will surely empower them to play a more empathetic role in improving the way they interact and communicate with each other and within their communities—as citizen designers. As this book illustrates, the effort is already underway.

Elizabeth Resnick
Boston, Massachusetts
June 2015

1 The field is also known as public-interest design, social impact design, socially responsive design, transformation design, and humanitarian design. From *Design and Social Impact: A Cross-Sectoral Agenda for Design Education, Research and Practice*, a White Paper based on the Social Impact Design Summit, held in New York, February 27, 2012; p. 8.

GRAPHIC DESIGN EDUCATION AND THE CHALLENGE OF SOCIAL TRANSFORMATION

Victor Margolin

Graphic design is a far more complicated practice today than it was when programs in graphic design education began to spread in the 1950s. Early programs emphasized formal qualities of layout and typography rather than the semantic problems of ensuring that whatever was to be communicated would be understood by an audience. Adding to the current complexity is the Internet, which has now become for some a more frequent means of communication than print. In recent years, design schools and programs have sought to keep up with the proliferation of new media by offering courses in web design, interaction design, and the design of moving images. Designing for the Internet has introduced issues of narrative, which derive from the ability to move through sets of links between websites and texts.

However, the greatest challenge facing design schools today, in my estimation, is contributing to clarifying and sorting out the multiple communication needs of people around the world. We live today in a world where communication between people of different cultures, nationalities, and language groups has intensified. People are also moving around the globe at a greater rate than ever before and have a great need for orientation and guidance—signage, maps, directions and explanations, place marking, instructions, and so forth. It, therefore, makes sense to teach graphic design within a global context; that is, within a context where it is presumed that communication between and movement among different peoples and cultures will continue and will even intensify.

What, then, does this mean for the graphic design curriculum of the future? First of all, it means that the graphic designer must become a cosmopolitan, someone who is comfortable moving within different cultures and absorbing social cues that indicate how to act and how to facilitate action through graphic communication. Therefore, an introduction to global culture—what characterizes it, how it operates, and how one can operate within it—is crucial. This suggests courses in global visual culture, semantic or semiotic theory, and communication theory, as well as sociology and anthropology. In short, the graphic designer of the future must understand people and their cultural milieus.

Graphic designers must also understand the range of media that people use today. They must be comfortable designing for print media as well as for the Internet. Courses in layout and visual organization must take both of these into account. While formal issues continue to be crucial, more emphasis should be placed on the most effective presentations of varied types of content. There is a greater need than ever for instruction—explanations of how to operate new and complex devices, how to fill out bureaucratic forms, how to apply for services, and how to orient one's self in a new environment. Much of this communication now takes place across cultures and care must be given to how common forms, for example, need to be designed to be understood by groups from different cultures.

Graphic designers must also learn to enter new social situations, where they can articulate communication needs. As in the design of products, graphic designers should learn to adapt to such situations and figure out what people need to know in order to function successfully in them. Reference is made here to large, complicated situations such as disaster relief, the movement of refugees, and threats to national security. More than ever, political and social agencies are seeking to communicate with large numbers of people, attempting to explain services, regulations, and guidelines. Graphic designers must be prepared to step in and facilitate such communication.

At one time graphic design was for the most part design to promote commerce, but today social communication in all its multifarious forms is the central challenge to graphic designers. This means drawing on the well-developed principles of information design, social interaction, and semantics. Whereas expertise in persuading consumers to purchase products has become highly developed, now persuasion must be applied to promoting positive social behavior such as ethnic and racial tolerance, energy conservation, and overall environmental citizenship. Promoting behavioral change has, in fact, become one of the greatest tasks of the graphic designer.

This means that the cultivation of formal judgment—the use of typography, the organization of information, the creation of symbols and logotypes—must now be taught as means of social communication rather than as pure visual techniques. This is not to give less emphasis to the typographic sophistication of classic Swiss design or the symbolic power of Polish posters, but rather to recognize that the cultivation of sophisticated visual techniques has a social purpose that calls for the graphic designer to understand the situation and audience within which and to whom he or she is communicating.

Another goal of graphic design is to assist societies to adapt languages with limited numbers of speakers to the exigencies of new electronic media. This entails a move from verbal to visual to digital—transcribing speech into alphabets and adapting alphabets to digital forms. Everyone should have access to the Internet and to be able to access it in his or her own language.

Meeting these new social challenges is essential for graphic designers and instruction in the techniques of doing so must become an essential part of graphic design education. For design schools, whether they are part of independent art academies or programs within comprehensive universities, engagement with fields of knowledge beyond design is mandatory. How this task can be converted into new curricula remains to be developed but, given the enormity of the task ahead, communication between and among design schools is essential, particularly schools that belong to different cultural milieus. The Icograda Design Education Manifesto can serve as a beacon to guide design schools toward new social ends as they reform themselves in order to meet the challenges of the global culture in which we all live.

Victor Margolin is Professor Emeritus of Design History *at the University of Illinois, Chicago. He is the author and editor of numerous books and articles on design.*

PART 1

DESIGN THINKING

"

Design and the design process can contribute to positively impacting our world and creating positive change. The process, however, is more complex than simply designing a brochure for a non-profit. It involves problem identification, targeting objectives and audiences, immersion into research, implementation of design thinking and strategy, and overall collaborative, multi-disciplinary approach to problem solving. This approach to design should not be thought of as charity, aid, or volunteerism, but a significant contribution that plays an important role in local, national, and global well-being."

Mike Weikert, *Designer, Educator, Just Design*

——

"

I believe that most designers are optimistic and passionate about what's next, not what's now or what's been. This makes them unlike politicians, religious leaders or most corporate executives who are largely acting to protect the power or resources that they already have accumulated. The future will be defined more by what we do now than what we did before. Now is the time for designers to step up and use what they know how to do to help shape a positive future for people and the planet."

John Bielenberg, *Founder, Project M, Co-founder, Future Partners*

——

SECTION 1

SOCIALLY RESPONSIBLE DESIGN

ANATOMY OF THE SOCIALLY RESPONSIBLE DESIGNER

Andrew Shea

For generations, communication designers have helped individuals and organizations give their ideas clarity, depth, and meaning in ways that have shaped public opinion and behavior. Their ability to beautify and promote products and services is undisputed. However, an increasing number of designers today are hungry to use their skills on projects that have a social cause or with organizations that align with their values. The growing number of social impact studios, academic programs, initiatives, and competitions are a sign of this trend. And while these designers might use a variety of terms to describe what they do—design for social change, design for social impact, and social design, among others—the unmistakable link between these driven designers lies in their goal of being more socially, environmentally, and economically responsible.

The seeds of this movement can be traced back to 1964 with the *First Things First* manifesto, in which Ken Garland proposed that designers prioritize helping organizations that "contribute to national prosperity" and cultural development, rather than work for organizations that are concerned with "commerce-driven projects." While many designers agreed with the manifesto when it was published, the design industry has changed very little. Seven years later, Victor Papanek published *Design for the Real World*, and stoked this movement in his preface by decrying the fact that advertising design is the "phoniest field in existence today" because it is "persuading people to buy things they don't need, with money they don't have, in order to impress people who don't care."

Many socially responsible designers share these sentiments and are responsive to the pressing needs that they see around them. An emerging set of priorities has started to define how these designers work. Many of these priorities are shared with all members of the design community, but they have become touchstones for socially responsible designers.

CULTIVATING VALUES Not all designers have a clear understanding of their personal ethics. Design educator John Kolko pointed this out at the 2013 LEAP symposium when he said that, "While designers are typically well-intentioned, many lack the ethical framework to guide their practice." However, socially responsible designers know what values drive them. They are motivated by their personal experiences, politics, morals, or other influences that compel them to seek collaborations with like-minded organizations or to promote causes they care about. They also question the effects of their work. These designers understand that they work in what Allan Chochinov called "the consequence business not the artifact business." Chochinov went on to say that, "We might be good at making anything we want, but we also need to be responsible stewards of our planet" (2013 LEAP symposium). The value-centric foundation of these designers helps them to identify potential clients and projects, and to navigate through the challenging nuances of a project.

DESIGNING WITH Socially responsible designers realize that meaningful design projects often result from authentic engagement with their clients and the target audience. In fact, many of these designers consider their clients to be partners who can help determine the success of a project by providing expert insights about the problem at hand. These partnerships focus on human-centered processes where designers build empathy with the intended audience or around the issue at hand, and engage with them to better understand their needs, personalities, and preferences. Collaborations like this ensure that the designers consider important factors like who they design for, how it will be used or experienced, what form the solution should take, whether the design will scale and at what rate, and other factors that will make the design responsive to the intended audience over time.

COLLABORATIONS ACROSS DISCIPLINES

Innovation occurs when unlike ideas collide. It can happen between a single designer and the partner around a specific issue, but many designers also look for ways to build multidisciplinary teams whose members can contribute their expertise. Expertise could include the ability to render an idea in a useful way, understand communities, or offer evidence-based insights about the challenge.

Designers also consider the group's size and demographics when looking for the right mix. A team might include members of the design professions (graphic designers, architects, planners, industrial designers), or members within the arts professions (writers, videographers, illustrators, photographers). They might also have expertise in another field (policy analysts, engineers, anthropologists, or another specialty).

Together, these teams often explore the challenges through an assortment of design processes that includes both design thinking, which helps all members understanding of the challenge, and design making, which involves repeatedly crafting prototypes, showing them to partners and the intended audience, and incorporating their feedback and insights into revisions. This iterative process allows the audience and partners to experience the content in ways that they can respond to and that helps them give useful feedback and insights to help the design to evolve.

MEASURING IMPACT One of the most exciting

challenges for designers is to show how their work affects people, organizations, communities, or causes. Some designers refer to this as "return on design," and it has become an even more critical part of the way designers talk about the value of their work. They work with their partners to define what a successful outcome would include—increased awareness, to take action on a website, a specific behavioral change, more revenue, or another project-defined goal—and how to work toward that goal.

To do this well, these designers craft methodologies that help them record conditions at the start of the project and then how those conditions changed because of their design solution. The conditions might fall into broad categories, such as economic, social, environmental, cultural, health-related, or some other category. Then they might use images, graphics, data, statistics, figures, and facts to shows the quantitative and qualitative changes that took place, whether those changes are a direct or indirect result of the design. Outlining and sharing these insights promotes the kind of open-source transparency that underlies the ethos of socially responsible design.

SHARING INSIGHTS The rise of open-source sharing

has a natural place in the life cycle of design projects. Designers eagerly share their work on their own websites, through competitions, on design hubs, and in books like this. Socially responsible designers look for ways to share more than just visuals, though. They understand the importance of compiling their work into case studies that can tell the story of their project, creating toolkits that allow others to benefit and expand on their efforts, translating what they learn into workshops or talks, and offering their insights in other ways. Their insights can help other designers navigate through the complexities of a project, especially if what they share includes reflections on what they would do differently in the future.

The community of socially responsible designers seems to grow along with our awareness of the ways design can address existing challenges and prevent new ones. While these five priorities show some of the motivations and methods of these designers, evidenced by the following projects, new priorities will evolve and will continue to demonstrate how designers can reshape the design landscape and use their skills responsibly.

Andrew Shea is a designer, writer, and educator. He is a partner at MANY, a design studio that looks for ways to add social value to the world. Shea's book, Designing for Social Change, *was published by Princeton Architectural Press in 2012 and provides graphic designers with strategies to help them work on community-based projects. To read more about his work, visit www.manydesign.org.*

FIVE QUESTIONS TO
OMAR VULPINARI

1. What were the most important influences that shaped you as a designer and a design educator?

In the late 1990s I worked with Oliviero Toscani at Fabrica, the Benetton Communications Research Center in Italy. With Toscani, my work within the social and non-profit sector went global with awareness-raising campaigns for the World Health Organization, UNICEF, Reporters Without Borders, Witness, and many more. And, thanks to Toscani, I discovered the extraordinary humanitarian impact of communication design and the multicultural bandwidth of universally disruptive imagery.

In the early 1980s I studied with, and later worked with, Massimo Dolcini (1945–2005), a champion of Italian public service communication design in Pesaro. The local governors and citizens that he serviced cherished his cultural branding and public sector posters. He often worked also for the Italian Communist Party. The social and political design scene of the Chaumont Poster Festival was his nirvana. His work was strongly illustration based, poetic and humorous but also direct and empathic. With Dolcini, I discovered the great impact of visual communication on local communities and the importance of storytelling before design.

2. Do you agree with the following statement? "Designers have a social and ethical responsibility to create and transmit meaningful forms of communication that benefit society and culture." If so, why, and how do you inspire your students to care about the society in which they live?

In order to inspire students to care about society, it's very important to help them understand the responsibility and power of change that they behold. I do this by reviewing data on dramatic global humanitarian issues with my students, while showing them "heroic" and effective design case studies. I assign in-depth readings, organize live guest testimonials from the field, and have them meet the client and audience (Skype helps). Millennial students are not pyramid hierarchy fans. They want a transparent, horizontal setting. I steward and gently nudge them toward their own learning pathway by having them engage on both real and speculative paths.

3. New roles are emerging for design professionals as their function is increasingly changing from that of generators to facilitators of ideas. How do you address this shifting paradigm in your professional practice and in your teaching pedagogy?

"Opentunity" (Openness + Opportunity) was the title of my course in Communication Design at the IUAV University of Venice in San Marino, which was dedicated to the conception and design of online creative and social participatory initiatives. Taking inspiration from today's openness culture, the students acted as both startup entrepreneurs and facilitators of collective creativity and social action.

One student group created a very effective participatory clown therapy website, titled OpenClownClinic.org, which connected child patients and parents to any hospital with qualified user-generated clown therapy free videos. Another student group created Acappellalalab.net to enable and engage people across the web to create "a cappella" (only voice) songs. Both project teams also designed and organized related live events, enabling the experiences to go from virtual to real.

1.1a–1.1b Acappellalalab poster and website.
*Design: Claudio Fabbro, Thomas Righi, Giulia Siboni,
and Giammarco Viterbo.*

4. In his 1971 book *Design for the Real World*, Victor Papanek stated: "The main trouble with design schools seems to be that they teach too much design and not enough about the ecological, social, economic, and political environment in which design takes place." What is your personal educational philosophy?
Today, this statement makes even more sense for two main reasons: first, we can no longer ignore the near-extinction crisis of the human species; and second, these issues have become very appealing to brands of all sizes and sectors because they're

good brand values for improving business. Could there be potential for a win–win situation here? Yes, certainly, and there is also space for expanding design school program offerings.

5. Today, the design community is being challenged to think beyond the omnipotent practitioner and the obsession to deliver products, objects, and things. Design is now a collaborative effort where the design process is spread among a diverse group of participating stakeholders. What advice would you give a student currently studying graphic design?
Because of the systemic complexity that embraces most communication projects today, the do-it-all-alone practitioner is simply no longer relevant. Although our job still requires the delivery of visual artifacts, in the end, these artifacts are now more similar to "components" that contribute only in part to a much larger and more complex communication effort, object, or service/experience.

My advice to a student currently studying graphic design would be to consider changing program if it's strictly dedicated to "graphic design"! Conventional graphic design has been commoditized—you can find crowd sourcing sites and agencies, online templates or apps for everything from logos to banners, from websites to brochures, posters to pictograms. Communication designers need to quickly climb the decisional ladder and get into the strategy-defining circle where they can practice an integrated approach of strategy and creativity, across channels and disciplines.

Omar Vulpinari is a cross-media creative director and academic. At Fabrica, from 1998 to 2013, he was Director of the Expanded Media area and Head of the Visual Communication department where he directed projects for the World Health Organization, UNICEF, UNESCO, and many more international nonprofit organizations. Currently he is Course Leader in Service Design Innovation (MDES) at London College of Communication, UK.

APOCALYPSIS ANTE PORTAS:
EXOTERIC CITY COMPETITION

Dóra Balla, Associate Professor, Head of Graphic
Design Department, Moholy-Nagy University
of Art and Design, Budapest, Hungary

CLIENT
ENERGIAKLUB Climate
Policy Institute—Applied
Communications in
collaboration with KÉK,
Hungarian Contemporary
Architecture Centre.

PROJECT TITLE
Apocalypsis Ante Portas—
Exoteric City competition.

DURATION
4 weeks, March–April 2014.

BUDGET
KÉK covered the expenses
of the printing, installation,
exhibition, and promotion
of the selected posters.

TEAM
Dóra Balla, project leader,
László Nagy, Adjunct Professor,
and Tamás Marcell, Associate
Professor, Graphic Design,
Moholy-Nagy University of Art
and Design, Budapest, Hungary.
Class of 16 students in the
Graphic Design 2 course.

1.2 Ways to adapt to climate change. *Design: Alexandra Bangó.*

DESCRIPTION In the twenty-first century one of the greatest challenges in art education is to encourage young designers to employ their talent and integrate their skills, knowledge, and creativity into activities that exert a positive impact on the society in which they live. Our problems are now global rather than local. We can no longer hide from the stark reality that our economies, our ecologies, and in fact our whole world are intrinsically connected, making the context of understanding more complex. This is our challenge, but it is an exciting one.

Each year, the Graphic Design department at Moholy-Nagy University of Art and Design (MOME) has the opportunity to embrace projects that require an artistic reinterpretation of existing social problems. These projects usually involve collaborative partners who seek answers to specific issues utilizing graphic design communication toolsets. We were pleased to receive an invitation from KÉK, Hungarian Contemporary Architecture Centre, to enter a large-scale info-graphic poster competition titled "Exoteric City." The competition promoted the creation of a more livable urban future and involved four organizations, among them Energiaklub, Climate Policy Institute—Applied Communications.

First-year students in our department participated in the competition. They created designs that addressed people living in cities as well as decision-making authorities. Energiaklub has been working

for 20 years to inspire the producers and users of energy, as well as political decision makers, to adopt a new approach to energy. They advocate a reasonable use of our limited resources as well as changes in consumers' energy-wasting habits by focusing on energy efficiency, renewable resources, climate protection, a return to traditional energy sources, and energy policy.

RESEARCH We received a clearly defined brief, but relatively little data. We defined our task as the rendering and visualization of our understanding of an exoteric city. Instead of using the classic methods of data visualization and info-graphics, we set out to explore a somewhat novel, different visual language. The first step was to create info-graphic elements representing the factors that influence the everyday life of city inhabitants. The brief we received detailed general problems that strongly influence the lives of citizens. The students first discussed these issues with the client, then with the leader of the project in the department, and finally among themselves. They began to shape a graphic, illustrative style to represent the issues with a uniform and easily interpreted visual language.

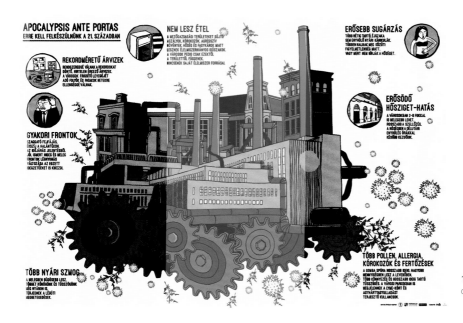

1.3 Ways to adapt to climate change. *Design: Alexandra Bangó.*

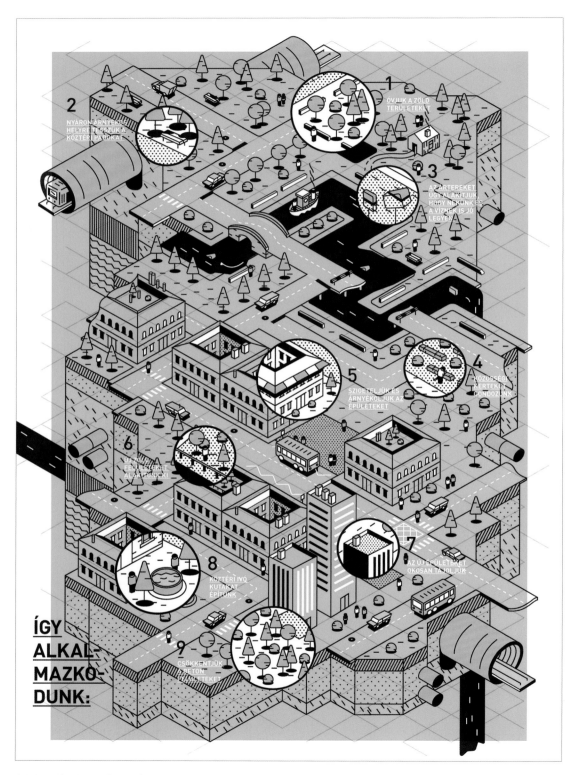

1.4 Apocalypsis Ante Portas, final version.
Design: Dávid Molnár.

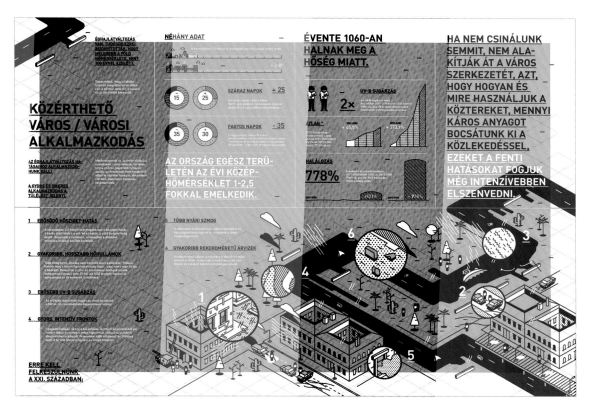

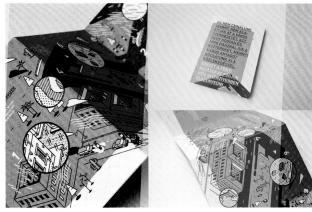

1.5 Apocalypsis Ante Portas, final version.
Design: Dávid Molnár.

1.6 Apocalypsis Ante Portas, folded.
Design: Dávid Molnár.

"

The point of the project was to present the potential outcomes of negative energy usage behavior, without resorting to the threatening messages which are so common in the visual communication of this sort."

Next, they tested their drafts within the university community, then among their families and friends. After consulting with the client, it became clear that it was of primary importance to communicate clearly to families so that parents and children could think about the future of energy together.

CHALLENGES We aimed to reach viewers of different ages through the use of professional design tools and the most up-to-date visual language. The point of the project was to present the potential outcomes of negative energy usage behavior, without resorting to the threatening messages which are so common in the visual communication of this sort. The greatest challenge was to create the image of a kind and likeable world which inspires viewers to look closer, analyze the information, understand it, and accept the necessity of the possible solutions presented.

STRATEGY Three faculty members participated in the project. The project leader, Dóra Balla, was responsible for the whole project, László Nagy supervised the creation of the illustrations, while Tamás Marcell's responsibility was to oversee the design part of the assignment. The students' task was to create info-graphic-based foldable 70 cm x 100 cm posters. The primary side of the poster incorporated the presentation of the specific issue, while the reverse side of the poster exhibited more detailed information about the issue and its potential solutions. When folded, the posters could be read as leaflets.

In the first phase of the project, students created small, explanatory illustrations, followed by the testing of others' interpretations of the images. After this, their graphic imagery was unified, and the work was presented to the professors, students, and clients, who could contribute their views and comments. In the last phase, the typography and the final visual design were completed.

Class meetings were based on discussion, rather than on following instructions. Questions were raised, and possible paths and solutions were sought together in the form of open interaction.

EFFECTIVENESS What can this type of graphic design achieve and how far can it reach? Our students observed the loss of effectiveness for the traditional print medium. They learned that digital, interactive, and interaction-provoking new media can be more effective and inspiring. As a department, we have

1.7 Students at work in the studio.
Photo: Dóra Balla.

decided to incorporate more new media strategies and tools into our future student projects. The posters were exhibited on April 29, 2014, and the winner of the competition has entered into a long-term collaboration with Energiaklub.

ASSESSMENT The assignment had a very positive effect on the students. In Hungary today, 18–20-year-olds are primarily occupied with consumption. They are open to social and societal questioning, but at the same time they are somewhat reserved. When dealing with issues that engaged their interest, they became very open and active, and looked for ways to employ their skills to achieve positive goals. They have expressed the importance of thinking responsibly and exerting influence on their environment to impact the future of their generation.

The visual language of young designers was new to our traditional client, although there was acknowledgment that contemporary design can open a gate between generations and generate integrative problem solving. The professors were the link—they mediated between the young generation and the more traditional client, while ensuring a professional quality result.

SEÑOR JOHN'S BBQ SAUCE:
FEEDING THE NATION'S HOMELESS
IDENTITY CAMPAIGN

Antonio Castro H., Associate Professor of
Graphic Design, University of Texas at El Paso

1.8 Señor John's BBQ, Marinades and Dry Rub labels, Point of purchase display, and shopping bag.
Design and illustration: Berenice Méndez.

CLIENT
John Cook, owner of Señor
John's BBQ Sauce: Feeding
the Nation's Homeless,
and former mayor of the
city of El Paso, Texas.

PROJECT TITLE
Señor John's BBQ Sauce:
Feeding the Nation's Homeless.

DURATION
8 weeks, spring semester 2010.

BUDGET
No fees were charged.

TEAM
Approximately 36 students
enrolled in the two sections
of ARTG 4306 Graphic
Design 5 course.

DESCRIPTION The former mayor of the city of El Paso,
John Cook, approached the graphic design area at
the University of Texas at El Paso to create an identity
campaign for Señor John's BBQ Sauces: Feeding the
Nation's Homeless. Feeding the Nation's Homeless,
Inc. is a not-for-profit foundation. The proceeds from
the sales of its sauces are distributed by the Feeding
the Nation's Homeless Foundation to not-for-profit
and governmental agencies that feed the needy.

1.9 Señor John's BBQ, Marinades and Dry Rub labels, shopping bag. *Design and illustration: Berenice Méndez.*

For this assignment, my advanced graphic design students were challenged to design a logo that embodied the company's core values, and apply their results to labels for a line of six different sauces, marinades, and a dry rub. Students were also responsible for the design of a stationery system, shopping bags, a point-of-purchase display, and a four-bottle package design kit.

RESEARCH The design work of students Lorena Mondragón and Berenice Méndez will illustrate this case study. Lorena's inspirations were hand-lettered cardboard signs used by homeless people across the United States, as well as old handmade BBQ signs. She researched these signs, and also researched facts about homelessness. Berenice was inspired by 1940s Americana-style graphics found in diners,

BBQ joints, and food packaging. Through her research, Berenice discovered that many homeless people are war veterans; she researched vintage military graphics as well.

CHALLENGES The biggest challenge for my students was making sure that the resulting solution to our visual challenge was in no way demeaning to the homeless community. They wanted to present a final product that would be attractive and warm-hearted, while also being educational about homelessness in America.

1.10 Señor John's BBQ Sauce and Marinade four-pack box, shopping bag. *Design and illustration: Lorena Mondragón Rodríquez. Photo: Luis Jasso.*

1.11 Señor John's BBQ Sauce and Marinade four-pack box, BBQ, Marinades and Dry Rub labels, shopping bag. *Design and illustration: Lorena Mondragón Rodríquez. Photo: Luis Jasso.*

Lorena Mondragón faced an interesting challenge. Being a vegetarian and designing for a BBQ product turned out to be a hurdle—but as the project was for a good a cause she happily accepted the challenge. I was able to point to Lorena's dilemma to illustrate to my students how often we are faced with the challenge of working on projects that we might not like or agree with, but by embracing the research and falling in love with the challenge, we could actually end up with a product that makes us very proud.

> **"**
>
> *The biggest challenge for my students was making sure that the resulting solution to our visual challenge was in no way demeaning to the homeless community."*
>
> ―――――

STRATEGY The strategy I ask my students to follow in a problem such as this is to research rigorously before moving on to the design of the logo, which is the soul of the project. Students will put the logo to work at various sizes and in different formats, creating an optimum graphic environment that later will be used in the rest of the collateral items.

EFFECTIVENESS Lorena's and Berenice's identity campaign for Señor John's was effective because their use of inviting and friendly graphics helped to illustrate an ugly problem in a very friendly way. Their designs were not only beautiful, but they were also educational and in no way demeaning to the homeless community, which was one of our biggest concerns.

ASSESSMENT As with any other project that comments on a social problem such as homelessness, I believe that the main idea or purpose is to raise awareness. First, the designer has to educate him/herself about the problem, and then come up with a compelling design that will entice the consumer to purchase the product. In this case, it was important for us to convince the consumer that they were not only buying a good product but that, in the purchasing of it, they were contributing to a good cause.

Unfortunately, as we discovered later, the former mayor of the city of El Paso hired a local advertising agency to develop the logo, label, and website even as my students were working on the project, and he chose their proposal over ours. At the end of this project, the mayor did award US$500 to the two students whose work he felt had best captured his vision. Although the mayor's decision was disappointing to some of the students, his decision helped me to illustrate that in this industry, more times than not, designers have to compete to win a piece of business, and that if their design is not selected, it should be taken as an incentive to do better the next time they are presented with a challenge.

I believe the two most important results of this challenge were that my students were able to work with a real client, and that their initial conversations helped them to understand the challenge, present their proposals in a professional fashion, and witness first-hand how clients at the end of the process agree or disagree with the designer's solution. By conducting research on a social problem such as homelessness, students were able to educate themselves about this reality that affects many people, and perhaps be less judgmental the next time they meet a homeless person.

WOMEN'S EXCHANGE

Brockett Horne, Chair, Graphic Design, Maryland
Institute College of Art (MICA), Baltimore, Maryland

1.12 Visual identity as applied to the storefront and sandwich board sign at the Women's Exchange.
Photo: Brockett Horne.

CLIENT
The project was funded by
PNC Bank, who selected
the client, The Woman's
Industrial Exchange. Part of
our solution was a name
change to Women's Exchange.

PROJECT TITLE
Women's Exchange
Visual Identity Program.

DURATION
July–August 2013. Eight
weeks divided into four 2-week
phases: discovery, ideation,
design, and implementation,
and later assessment on the
part of the faculty advisor.

BUDGET
The production budget was US
$2,000. With this seed funding
from PNC Bank, students
were able to advocate which
design objects to produce
and apportion the budget to
support their priorities.

TEAM
Faculty advisor: **Brockett
Horne.** *Student fellows:* **Crystal
Dimeler** and **Sung Mun. Megan
Miller** from MICA's Career
Development Office, who
provided project oversight; **Will
Backstrom**, our champion from
PNC Bank; **Stephanie Halley**
and **Faith Tenant**, Woman's
Exchange Executive Directors.

DESCRIPTION This eight-week design fellowship,
sponsored by PNC Bank, paired design students and
a faculty advisor at Maryland Institute College of Art
with a local non-profit in Baltimore. The fellowship
aspired to accelerate economic development in the
city through design.

For the Women's Exchange—a 140-year-old
organization that offers programs, community events,
and handmade items for sale to the general public—
MICA students produced new identity materials and
visual sets, generated a strong narrative with targeted
messages, and identified potential audiences and
future programming opportunities. The design
deliverables that were manufactured include: logo,
custom typeface, posters, storefront and exterior
signage, website skin and e-news templates, print

and digital correspondence package, and promotional materials. The resulting designs increased sales at the shop, traffic in the restaurant, and opened the client's capabilities for focusing on community events, a part of the organization's mission that was not meeting its potential. As a result, board members and constituents found a new momentum and positivity about the future of the organization embodied in the design process.

Strengthening our community is one of the five initiatives in MICA's strategic plan, demonstrating a commitment to continuing a legacy of pioneering community-engaged academic curricula, programs, and research. The college values deep commitment to community and economic development and urban revitalization. The PNC Design Fellows program promotes a culture of collaboration between the areas of design and community development by matching designers to community development organizations to allow them to explore the transformational impact of design on their practice.

The PNC Design Fellows program fulfills a critical need for selected MICA students by providing them with paid summer professional experiences in non-profit organizations in Baltimore. Students who are passionate about working in and supporting Baltimore, but are not financially able to accept an unpaid internship, often must forego summer internship opportunities that are important professional development experiences. The PNC Design Fellows program allows these students to pursue rigorous professional work, and to be recognized for the value of their services. The program will also attract the most capable and competitive design students and encourage them to stay in Baltimore for the summer rather than seek out internships in other cities.

1.13 Street banners and store signage for the Women's Exchange. *Photo: Brockett Horne.*

RESEARCH Students pursued two weeks of discovery and research. They interviewed a dozen constituents of the client: board members, interns, employees, funders, those served by the Exchange, and others. Students visited the store several times and took on a variety of scenarios: as customer, as employee, as funder. As well, visual research was a key aspect of the process: identifying peer or similar organizations and analyzing the visuals helped articulate the unique qualities of our client.

Research culminated in a 15-page text document describing communications goals, design schedule, and production plan for our project. It turned out to be a strategic deliverable for the client in considering the value of design for its long-term success.

1.14 Crystal Dimeler and Sung Mun apply new vinyl signage to the storefront window of the Women's Exchange. *Photo: Brockett Horne.*

CHALLENGES Two challenges framed this work for the faculty advisor: determining activities that were feasible given our 8-week timeline, and taking on a role different from teaching—somewhere between small in-house studio director and instructor. It was challenging to create an atmosphere for our small team that was unlike being in school, and to provide critiques that were effective and professional, but not "art directed."

Challenges for student fellows: writing was a large part of this project. Also, the experience required students to play multiple roles within our small team, from photographer to developer, to media buyer, as well as the challenge of amassing the decision makers/thought leaders in the client base and encouraging them to make swift decisions. In some cases, we designed multiple presentations for different groups, with different content, to push the ideas along.

STRATEGY Discovery Students conducted interviews, and experienced the programming of the client by attending meetings and presentations.

Ideation Students participated in three different kinds of ideation exercises:

1. Mind-mapping Students used large butcher paper to map words related to the client's area of service. We mapped different words: job development (goal of the organization), history (value of the organization), bridge (metaphor generated by students), etc. Key phrases were then highlighted and new word lists generated from them. As a result of the mind-mapping exercise, students identified three different visual directions to pursue for generating logos.

2. Thinking Wrong Students selected a single word, at random, from the dictionary, and tried to force connections between it and their preliminary ideas. This offered the chance to flex and open ideas, for whimsy and chance to enter the study. The exercise also gave way to a later idea used in the preliminary client pitch: to use names for each visual concept.

3. Speed Dating On Skype, students pitched their preliminary ideas in swift phrases to MICA alumni working in the design discipline. This gave the students a non-client response to their design work.

Design Students generated a task list from the deliverables outlined to the client and worked in teams to create solutions for presentation. We met at 10:00 a.m. every day for a status check-in and then again at 3:00 p.m. for in-progress critiques of work.

Implementation Working primarily from a Google document, we researched a variety of production options for our ideas and weighed the pros and cons of each. For example, we decided to cut and install vinyl store graphics ourselves to save money, which we used for a professionally printed stationery package. We aspired for most deliverables to be produced locally, which was more expensive than online print-on-demand services.

1.15 PNC Design Fellowship Studio at MICA, summer 2013. Left to right: Sung Mun and Crystal Dimeler.
Photo: Brockett Horne.

> **"**
>
> *Our work became a catalyst for the organization to reframe its programming and re-present itself with a fresh identity."*
>
> ———

EFFECTIVENESS The fellowship was effective in demonstrating the power of design for the Women's Exchange. Our work became a catalyst for the organization to reframe its programming and re-present itself with a fresh identity. The 8-week timeframe was effective in certain ways, but was also challenging for developing a studio and producing so many solutions, from the ground up. However, the intensity inspired the students toward design excellence. Since we hope to continue this project, we'll try to find ways to serve more non-profit organizations in the city.

ASSESSMENT All participants were surveyed at the end of the fellowship and our goals (listed above) were compared. Most responses described the experience as transformative. Outcomes exceeded our expectations: student learning outcomes were delivered, clients believed in the power of design, and PNC Bank provided immense support to the community.

As a faculty advisor, it was essential for me to see the leap the students make from the classroom to practice. This experience allowed me to witness first-hand how successfully our curriculum prepares students for the demands of real-world design. It was also essential to keep some of MICA's top talent here in Baltimore over the summer, and to inspire students to consider their career goals in relation to the needs of our local community.

THE KELABIT HIGHLANDS COMMUNITY DEVELOPMENT PROJECT

Dr. **Meghan Kelly**, Senior Lecturer, School of Communication and Creative Arts, Deakin University, Melbourne Burwood Campus, Victoria, Australia

CLIENT
Dato **Isaac Lugan**, President, the Rurum Kelabit Sarawak (RKS); Kelabit community representatives from Bario, Miri, and Kuching. The RKS is the peak organization that represents and promotes the Kelabit community's social, cultural, and economic interests. It is strongly supported by the community and works in close association with the traditional village governance system through committees of Longhouse or Village Headmen.

PROJECT TITLE
Branding Bario Region and Teripun Tauh Kelabit Highlands Community Museum.

DURATION
2010–2016.

BUDGET
This project was conducted at Deakin University as part of the curriculum, and no additional funding or budget was required.

TEAM
Dr. Meghan Kelly, Senior Lecturer, and 72 third-year Visual Communication Design students enrolled in the course, Global Design Strategies.

1.16–1.17 Teripun Tauh logo design and tote bag application. *Design: Lara Millsteed.*

DESCRIPTION In 2011, the Rurum Kelabit Sarawak contacted us through an educational consultant based in Malaysia to seek assistance with the Kelabit Highlands Community Museum development project, a museum development situated in the remote Highlands of Borneo, Sarawak. This project seeks to incorporate heritage values into local development and cultural tourism plans—a development seen to advance the social cause of the Kelabits and therefore contribute to societal gain for this community group. The potential scope of the Kelabit Highlands Community Museum development matched expertise in pertinent areas at Deakin University, including museology and cultural heritage management, sustainable architectural practices, the preservation of intangible cultural heritage through film and digital media and cross-cultural visual communication strategies.

The first phase of the project included extensive community consultation investigating the extent to which a museum concept was understood and shared by the community, and to which existing cultural capital and assets might be utilized to sustain such a museum.

The second phase was to address concepts for the built environment and create schematic representations of what the museum might look like. These concepts are currently being used to generate funding to build the museum.

Phase three of the project (the case study presented here) extended the investigation to place branding for the Bario region and also addresses the branding strategy for the Kelabit Highlands Community Museum. Students were required to create a document to demonstrate ideas around a branding strategy for the Bario region and the museum. Our aims were to make the project real and achievable in the minds of the Kelabit community, highlight the opportunities this project can offer to the local people, and provide documentation to support the community in seeking local funding. The Rurum Kelabit Sarawak specified key outcomes, which provided the framework for design outcomes.

RESEARCH Students developed their theoretical understanding of designing in a cross-cultural context with a 3-week research project prior to beginning the design process. Successful visual communication must appeal to a broad range of stakeholders and recipients with a strong emotional investment in the message; and in a cross-cultural context there is a greater possibility for interpretations to appear different from what was intended. As a result, there exists an increased potential for debate, dissent, conflict, and miscommunication. This project offered an exciting opportunity to explore our understanding of cross-cultural design practices and outcomes, analyzing themes of identity creation, representation, and communication from an interdisciplinary perspective.

Students were required to position their own design work within an understanding of cultural identity, cultural appropriation, stereotypes, place branding, and museum and tourism studies. They further were to demonstrate they had considered the complexity of a project that holds great importance for this community and, through research, had understood their obligation to respectfully visually represent the Kelabit community to a broader audience.

1.18 Teripun Tauh logo design and brochure application.
Design: Syed Mansoor Ahmed.

CHALLENGES There were significant considerations while working on a culturally sensitive project for a remote location. Students had not visited the location and that added challenges to their understanding of the project. The completed document to be returned to the Rurum Kelabit Sarawak had to be designed to fully explain, demonstrate, and validate the design direction, positioning the work within strong theoretical and observational research. Further community consultation is planned based on these initial conceptual documents.

Contact with the community throughout the project was not available. This resulted in students taking initiatives that suited their own outcomes. It was challenging for the students to reflect continually on a client that they had not met and could not consult with during the design process. It was my role to question and re-question the design decisions of the students.

1.19 Teripun Tauh logo design and brochure application.
Design: Syed Mansoor Ahmed.

This newspaper advertisement acts like a checklist to those who travel often, and attract people who want to travel to a new destination. It is attractive, represents Bario and the natural environment but remaining honest by not using over the top graphics which would not be seen in this area.

1.20 Bario product tag showing logotype design and Bario Tourism advertisement. *Design: Shanie Carnie.*

STRATEGY Students enrolled in Deakin University's Visual Communication Design third-year class, "Global Design Strategies," were each given the opportunity to participate in this project. Seventy-two design solutions were submitted. The teaching program ran for 11 weeks, divided into three phases. The first phase was spent conducting research, where students worked in teams to gather relevant information and present to the rest of the class. The second phase involved the design of two logos, one for Bario region and one for Teripun Tauh, the Kelabit Highlands Community Museum. The third phase was the development of a document drawing on aspects of the first two phases, combined with a demonstration of how the design can be applied to various outputs.

Completed documents were discussed in a consultation process within the confines of Deakin University. The best design solutions were assessed and debated through a process of peer review, and then evaluated by a panel of Deakin University representatives who had met the Kelabit community and previously visited Bario. Based on the outcomes of this extensive evaluation process, the 10 strongest design submissions were emailed to representatives of the Bario community for feedback. Hard-copy examples were also mailed.

The most important reason for branding the Bario region is to put it on the map, in terms of tourism, and to promote their handmade products. Craft items require a tag application in which the Bario style is evident and have the correct information being identifiable by customers and tourists. Because this item will be taken away from Bario, a tag is one of the only applications where the full logo would be used, as the branding elements are more recognisable in other forms.

1.21 Bario product tag showing logotype design and Bario Tourism advertisement. *Design: Shanie Carnie.*

> " *Students were required to position their own design work within an understanding of cultural identity, cultural appropriation, stereotypes, place branding, and museum and tourism studies.*"

As anticipated, patterns emerged within the design submissions: a designed version of the landscape with a focus on Batu Lawi, the mountain feature seen as you fly into Bario; the building structure of the proposed museum; and skills of the community such as weaving and beading. The brief offered us the ability to discuss and highlight the method by which designers approach complex design problems and the sometimes limited options available to them.

The results were excellent within the confines of Deakin University, and satisfied the criteria of the brief. Community comments were positive as they thought that the results were impressive bearing in mind the students had never been to Bario and were required to research the Kelabit culture, region, and history themselves, before translating this into a communicative design. No comments were made on specific design submissions.

EFFECTIVENESS The peer review process identified a core number of submissions that were impactful and effective. Deakin University representatives and the grading process identified the same designs. Comments from Deakin University representatives noted the success of students in capturing the essence of the location and drawing on what was important to the community. There was concern, however, that some of the designs were young and edgy and not reflective of an aging, isolated community, and, therefore, they might not be well received by all stakeholders.

ASSESSMENT Students considered the project challenging. It taught them a great deal about the larger impact of design—moving beyond the client–designer relationship and considering a broader range of stakeholders. The students understood these concepts, but they found them difficult to apply in their design practice. There was concern about whether the designs would work effectively in the Bario environment, were acceptable to the client that they were serving, and were reflective of the subtle aesthetics of the region.

RESOURCES Sweet, J. and Horman, T. (2012). "Museum development and cross-cultural learning in the Kelabit Highlands, Borneo." *Museums Australia Magazine*, 21(1): 23–26.
Sweet, J. and Kelly, M. (2013). "Consultation unlocks interdisciplinary resources: A community museum evolving the Kelabit Highlands, Malaysian Borneo." *Museums Australia Magazine*, 22(2): 27–29.

FUNDACIÓN MARK

Gustavo Morainslie, Instructor, Universidad Tecnológica de México campus Atizapán, Mexico City, Mexico

CLIENT

Fundación Mark [Mark Foundation], Mexico City Fundación Mark is a Mexican foundation that was established in 2006 as a private institution operating several programs to entertain children and teenagers undergoing cancer treatment— making them stronger, more joyful and optimistic through play and entertainment. The foundation provides hospitals with special games rooms filled with toys, books, and portable video-game stations; it also organizes activities, workshops, and parties as well as publishing valuable information to help patients and families better understand their cancer treatment.

Mark's personal experience during his illness awoke in him a desire to look for ways to help kids in the same situation: every child undergoing cancer treatment should be able to learn, have fun, and enjoy life. With a lot of enthusiasm and joy, he planned his own foundation. Mark has since passed away, although he left a large footprint to both inspire and define the guiding principles that shape the foundation today. "Mark continues at my side and I connect to him through the kids, the foundation and my dreams where I can see him again, talk, play and kiss him. We can't decide how much time we are going to live, but we can decide how we are going to live. A great example for us is the mission that Mark had despite his young age" (**Sonia Zuani**, Mark's mother, founder and president of Fundación Mark).

PROJECT TITLE

Illustrations for a social cause: Helping Mark.

DURATION

9–12 months projected project duration, 2014.

BUDGET

None.

TEAM

Instructor: **Gustavo Morainslie**. *Students:* **Sandra Macias, Diana Cortés, Gabriela Mondragón, Abraham Salcido**. *Founder and president of Fundación Mark:* **Sonia Zuani**. Illustration for Graphic Design 2, course in Graphic Design B.

1.22 "Doctors" illustration: Diana Cortés. *Photo: Gustavo Morainslie.*

1.23 Sonia Zuani briefing students in the classroom at Unitec campus Atizapán, Mexico City. *Photo: Gustavo Morainslie.*

1.24 Sandra Macias holding her illustration. *Photo: Gustavo Morainslie.*

DESCRIPTION The last project in the Illustration for Graphic Design course focuses on the responsibility of graphic designers to address social issues and work for non-profit organizations. The objective is to inform students of the possibilities of social design. As an instructor I act as a mediator, helping to develop a scheme in which the students and the organizations involved could benefit. Students build their portfolios and gain experience, while the organizations receive the valuable resource of pro bono graphic work.

The client, Sonia Zuani, visited the classroom and shared her experience as founder and president of Fundación Mark. Her current design needs consisted of illustrations for a small storybook text aimed at both raising awareness of and spreading information about the struggles that families and children undergoing cancer treatment have to face every day.

RESEARCH Students were encouraged to research the subject for a time period of 3 weeks. Personal interviews with cancer patients were suggested to gain a better understanding of the assignment.

CHALLENGES One of the biggest challenges for some of the students was to overcome a lack of emotional connection and sensitivity; they missed the point of the assignment and approached it as another "must do" homework. Many of my students were working in a rush and produced very poor solutions. Once I had selected the best assignments, I found it challenging to establish an effective communication protocol to follow up on the process between students and the foundation.

STRATEGY

- The client visits the classroom.
- Introduction and project briefing occurs.
- Student research.
- Brainstorming session, concept revisions.
- Sketching of selected concepts.
- Development of final illustration and character designs.
- Meeting between client and instructor to choose the best assignments and suggest revisions.
- Further meetings (in person and online) between the team to finish the project and to discuss ideas for new collaborations.

1.25 "Mark" illustration: Abraham Salcido. *Photo: Gustavo Morainslie.*

1.26 "Hope" illustration: Gabriela Mondragón.
Photo: Gustavo Morainslie.

1.27 "Mark" character design: Sandra Macias.
Photo: Gustavo Morainslie.

EFFECTIVENESS Four students from a class of twenty developed outstanding projects and were selected to continue to work directly with the foundation. Sandra Macias was assigned to illustrate the main text storybook for kids; Diana Cortés was assigned to illustrate a secondary text storybook aimed at teenagers; Abraham Salcido's illustration was selected for an upcoming foundation's magazine cover; and Gabriela Mondragón's illustration was chosen for a flyer and poster design.

I consider this project successful because a new generation of students had an opportunity to understand both the importance and the potential of social design thinking within a school course collaboration. Many school programs and assignments lean toward the commercial and business side of design, leaving little space for pro bono or low-budget projects.

In contrast, I was disappointed that such a low percentage of our students were emotionally connected or motivated to develop this type of project. For future assignments, I will consider

providing more time for the project, while avoiding the final evaluation and holiday timeframes. I would also embed activities to provide a deeper connection with the client: for instance, having students visit patients at the hospital would, I believe, result in more robust student commitment and work quality.

ASSESSMENT This project continues to have a positive impact on everyone involved. In addition to the original assignment for the book illustrations, new ideas have emerged, such as painting a joyful mural in one of the hospitals, an idea which has been received with great enthusiasm by patients and their families. Students, the instructor, and patients' family members will take part in painting the mural. We hope this class assignment experience will be just the beginning of many opportunities to continue our collaboration with Fundación Mark.

GREENING THE MIND (MATARKISTA REYKJAVÍKUR)

Massimo Santanicchia, Course Director, Iceland Academy of the Arts, Reykjavik, Iceland

CLIENT
Community project for the urban neighborhoods of Reykjavik.

PROJECT TITLE
Greening the Mind (Matarkista Reykjavíkur).

DURATION
6 weeks, spring semester 2014.

BUDGET
US$300 for all design work and project management costs.

TEAM
Instructors: **Massimo Santanicchia**, course director, and **Thomas Pausz**, course co-director, Iceland Academy of the Arts; and faculty members **Lóa Auðunsdótti**, **Sigrún Birgisdottir**, **Garðar Eyjólfsson**, **Birna Geirfinnsdóttir**, **Dóra Isleifsdottir**, and **Katrín María Káradóttir**.
Students: **Brynja Guðnadóttir** (group leader), MA student in Design; **Anja Kapschütz**, BA exchange student in Graphic Design; **Auður Inez Sellgren**, BA student in Product Design; **Helga Birgisdóttir**, BA student in Product Design; **Heiðar Samúelsson**, BA student in Architecture; **Hjalti Guðlaugsson**, BA student in Architecture; **Jón Pétur Þorsteinsson**, BA student in Architecture; and **Susanne Fellner**, BA exchange student in Graphic Design.
Local agents: Skafthall biofarm; Dill restaurant; Frú Lauga food store.

1.28 The posters were hanging on the kitchen, and the shelves were full of different plants and herbs. Student Auður Inez Sellgren by the kitchen. *Photo: Hjalti Guðlaugsson.*

DESCRIPTION Iceland is responsible for the largest environmental footprint in the world; this is due to our consumerist behavior as the world's biggest oil users per capita. How can we change this situation and green up our minds? We believe our relation to food is of pivotal importance.

In the old days, people were dependent on the land for their survival. They had to live in harmony with nature and respect both the visible as well as the invisible forces of life. Today "local" has been replaced by "global," causing us to become alienated from nature. We need to learn to appreciate the "local" to become more sustainable consumers.

Our project's goal was to encourage people to take a closer look at their surroundings and discover all the edible greens that exist. We often call these greens "weeds," and generally consider them bad, as they are a threat to our tamed environment. But how can a nutritious edible plant that spreads quickly and requires no labor on our part be our enemy? These plants have been served as food and have also been used for medical purposes throughout the ages.

During April and May 2014, we searched the city of Reykjavik for edible greens, foraging for wild food resources. We tried food experiments with dandelion, sweet cicely, angelica, and chervil. To our surprise, food can be collected at the end of April just outside our doors and the variety only increases as the summer gets closer.

For our project we built a travel kitchen to educate people about the importance of food self-sufficiency. During spring 2014 we cooked for pedestrians in public spaces in Reykjavik, and drew attention to the edible vegetation that grows in the city; above all, we encouraged people to take their own steps toward a more sustainable lifestyle.

RESEARCH We started researching permaculture, global warming, collaborative design, and composting, recycling, and urban psychology. We also met with local agents, such as the biodiverse farm Skaftholt, the local farmers' market store Frú Lauga (which is trying to restore the bond between farmers and consumers), and Dill, a restaurant that is a part of the Nordic food revolution specializing in locally farmed and locally foraged food. As this research progressed it became clear that some major changes need to be made to our food systems. Food waste as well as food transportation is a big problem in the modern world. We explored ideas about growing in an urban context, setting up a food stand with food recycled from supermarkets, making use of food waste, and making a food composting station in the urban areas for Reykjavik's inhabitants.

Design Process To begin with, we visited various local agents who are working on different ways to improve our food system and society. For inspiration, we painted the profile of a head on a wall, painted the brain area with a brown muddy mixture that with time grew into moss-graffiti. We found it to be a perfect symbol for the process that we were going through.

We made a 66-second video teaser showing students foraging for wild plants, cooking with Icelandic plants growing in our surroundings, which led to the creation of a 3-minute video reflecting the process and the outcome. We also made a WordPress website for the project onto which we uploaded photos and text about our food experiments and other information about the herbs and our project.

We held a food event at Lækjatorg Square in Reykjavik, where we took our travel kitchen to a public space and cooked for pedestrians. The event was very successful and the 15 liters of northern dock and tomato soup we made went quickly. We were able to get flyers out to the public with information about our website and to educate people about foraging.

In the final presentation we showed our 3-minute video and brought prepared food—then we made some northern dock pesto on the scene, which we served to the audience. After the final presentation we served snacks for 60 students, which we made out of local plants, along with two kinds of pesto. People were very curious to taste it all.

1.29 Here is the kitchen in all its glory that we created from mostly recycled material, with Auður Inez Sellgren serving the soup.
Photo: Hjalti Guðlaugsson.

1.30 Serving soup with greens. *Photo: Hjalti Guðlaugsson.*

"

At the beginning of the process we speculated about what 'greening the mind' meant for us, and the importance of greening up our mind to make a positive input as designers."

———

CHALLENGES The primary challenge was how to divide the work among the students and find out what skills each student had to offer. This meant that research into food and foraging was primarily in the hands of product designers, communication in the hands of graphic designers, and building in the hands of the architecture students. The main challenge then became experimenting and developing recipes out of the local flora that would actually taste good. The recipes we explored didn't always turn out delicious or even really edible.

The nature of the work was provocative, as it challenged the ideas people have on what is food and what isn't. So what we saw as we engaged with the community was that some people were reluctant to set aside their prejudice and taste the food. But seeing others try it convinced almost everyone that this might actually be something worth exploring further.

1.31 We made some delicious northern dock pesto on site.
Photo: Hjalti Guðlaugsson.

STRATEGY At the beginning of the process we speculated about what "greening the mind" meant for us, and the importance of greening up our mind to make a positive input as designers. We divided reading material between us about the food system in Iceland, permaculture, biodynamics, recycling in design, foraging, biodiversity, etc. To help students visualize and construct their ideas, three major assignments were developed through the course. The first assignment was making a poster, the second was the video teaser, and the last was the video documenting the whole experience.

EFFECTIVENESS What worked? The outcome of the project seemed to have its intended effect on our clients—the pedestrians. The cooking performance caught their attention and curiosity. Most stopped to ask what it was about, seemed inspired when we explained the project, and did not hesitate to give it a try. We started collecting weeds at the end of April when there is not much green to be seen but enough to do some testing. To our surprise, spring came very rapidly and in only 2 weeks there were plenty of weeds to cook!

What did not work? The sharing of roles and the interdisciplinary collaboration made the work more effective, but in the end the roles of each group became too isolated. It would have been much more interesting if the designer of the kitchen and the food designers had collaborated more. Also, we could have advertised the event better if one person in the group had been in charge of communication. Communication between group members was lacking at times due to language differences, which led to some misunderstandings.

What did you learn? We learned much about collaboration, how to conduct research and visualize it. This was just the beginning of a project that can be developed much further with the aim of finding a sustainable operational form. And, as with all learning, we learned how little we know. There is so much more to be discovered and we have just scratched the surface.

ASSESSMENT The project showed that there are a lot of weeds/food that can be collected within the urban area of Reykjavik. This is the kind of food supply that is not bound to supermarkets. Collecting weeds, cooking them, and bringing them to the public is a way to educate ourselves and others who are curious about this way of cooking. The project affected us by revealing the possibility of a little independence from food stores, the simplicity of growing food, and spreading new (and reviving old) food knowledge. By showing other people our results, we shared our knowledge and taught them to be curious again about nature and the world we live in. In return, visitors let us know their thoughts and gave us advice about how we can continue with our project.

ADDITIONAL INFORMATION
Matarkista Reykjavíkur–Greening the Mind video by Audur Sellgren https://www.youtube.com/watch?v=TFhc_b9stdU

TOGETHER+:
A PROJECT THAT ADDRESSES XENOPHOBIA IN JOHANNESBURG, SOUTH AFRICA

Robert Sedlack, Associate Professor of Design,
University of Notre Dame, Notre Dame, Indiana

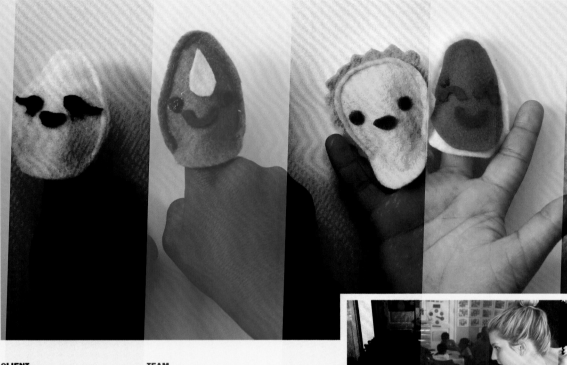

CLIENT
The project serves
neighborhoods in
Johannesburg,
South Africa.

PROJECT TITLE
together+.

DURATION
The students began the
project in the fall semester
2011; it continues today.

BUDGET
US$24,000 for the eight-
person trip to Johannesburg.
US$50,000 Sappi Ideas that
Matter grant to produce
the various materials.

TEAM
Professor Robert Sedlack.
Faculty: 11 undergraduate
students (eight undergraduate
students continued the project
in the spring semester 2012);
Paul Horn, who lives and
works in Johannesburg, was
a key contributor as he had
access to several organizations
with whom we needed to
connect; Kgosi Neighbourhood
Foundation; the University
of Notre Dame, Indiana;
Pellegrino Collaborative and
Notre Dame's Center for
Social Concerns.

1.32a In addition to creating the book, we also created
supplementary materials to support the instructor, including
finger puppets of the seeds and hand puppets of the flowers.
We employed mothers of current students to help create
these. In many instances, these mothers were unemployed
and learned sewing skills in the process.

1.32b Student Amelia Bernier shares the concept
and initial images of the *Blooming Together* book with a
teacher at Wings of Hope School.

DESCRIPTION In May of 2008, riots occurred in Alexandria, located in northeast Johannesburg. South African citizens attacked migrants, killing two people and injuring many others. This incident spawned further attacks, which spread throughout South Africa. These xenophobic attacks had economic and cultural motivations. Tension is still high and there are strong concerns that further attacks will break out in the future.

Kgosi Neighbourhood Foundation, the University of Notre Dame, Pellegrino Collaborative and Notre Dame's Center for Social Concerns have joined forces to develop together+, an educational and promotional campaign to reduce fear and build connections and community in neighborhoods where both South Africans and refugees compete for scant resources. The campaign focuses on the communication of diversity as a positive outcome. Materials include the *Welcome to South Africa* guide and map that explains refugee and migrant rights under the South African Constitution, 10,000 copies of which have been distributed by Jesuit Refugee Services to migrants and refugees entering South Africa at border posts, as well as refugees and migrants in South African urban centers; and the *Blooming Together* children's book and curriculum which was produced for distribution in South African elementary schools.

Blooming Together is the story of seeds blown by a continental storm to a garden in Johannesburg. The story portrays the message of unity through diversity. Other teaching materials, including finger puppets, have been developed to accompany the book; a multilingual poster series (in seven different languages) and a pamphlet explaining medical rights were produced for distribution to health clinics and non-governmental organizations; and a mural project using the together+ identity to be executed by community members. The mural is designed to build solidarity, unify the diverse groups of migratory peoples, and provide a sense of hope for all neighborhood residents living in poverty. Each project seeks to ignite positive change and unity in South Africa, one neighborhood at a time. together+ seeks to address xenophobia in South Africa by educating schoolchildren about the challenges faced by migrants and refugees. The project also seeks to empower refugees and migrants who are unsure of their legal rights and immigration procedures within South Africa.

RESEARCH The students spent time researching the reasons for the xenophobic attacks. Additionally, weekly Skype sessions with Paul Horn were also very informative. I also brought to class three experts on refugees and Africa. The most enlightening research was done during the trip to South Africa, where students were able to talk directly with people affected by the xenophobic attacks. During their time in South Africa, the students were able to share mock-ups of each of the projects with their target audience, which led to some major changes.

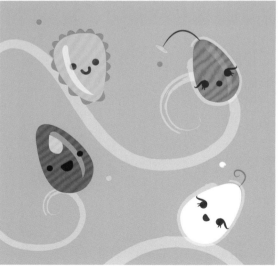

1.33 Pages 32–33 from *Blooming Together*.

1.34 Pages 36–37 from *Blooming Together*.

1.35 In addition to creating the book, supplementary materials were created to support the instructor, including finger puppets of the seeds and hand puppets of the flowers. Mothers of current students were employed to help create these. In many instances, these mothers were unemployed and learned sewing skills in the process.

CHALLENGES The most formidable challenge was that we were half a world away from our target audience. While English is spoken widely in South Africa, not everyone we met with was fully fluent in the language. The challenges that the clients faced had primarily to do with their status as refugees. There was some hesitancy on the part of many refugees to talk openly due to the discrimination they faced. For me, the biggest challenge was not to know what the end-of-project deliverables would be; I placed great faith in the students and their ability to create viable solutions. The most important step we took to sort out many of these challenges was traveling to South Africa and engaging with the target audience directly.

STRATEGY The students individually developed ideas to address the issue of xenophobia, and the most viable four ideas were selected. After that, students were clustered into teams and worked on each project. The weekly Skype sessions with Paul Horn were crucial as he was able to make suggestions based on his own thoughts and the thoughts of others in the community. In spring semester, eight of the students enrolled in a special studies program with me, allowing each project to fully develop. Prototypes of three of the four projects were taken to South Africa and shared with many refugees, which produced critical information that led to alterations in three of the projects. The fourth project was the mural painting.

EFFECTIVENESS The community wall painting was paired with a cookout, and was a fabulous success. Members of the local community, including refugees and native South Africans, came together and repainted a graffiti-covered wall. The people who were involved came from a variety of economic backgrounds. This event was meant to be replicable, but to date it is the only one that has occurred. Ten thousand *Welcome to South Africa* guides, explaining refugees' rights in detail, were printed and distributed. Initially, this book was titled *Refugee Rights*, but we were advised that this was a bad idea, hence the change in title. Five thousand *Blooming Together* children's books were printed. Currently they are being used in 10 second-grade classrooms. We are in discussion with 60 other schools interested in the book. One thousand posters were printed but have yet to be distributed.

These are to be posted in hospitals and clinics, although we are skeptical as to whether they will last because healthcare is an area where discrimination is rampant. The learning curve was a steep one, and students gained great knowledge from the face-to-face interactions.

1.36 Book cover for *Blooming Together*, a children's story about acceptance.

1.37 Because South Africa has such a diverse population, the healthcare posters had to be created in seven different languages.

ASSESSMENT It was clear that the students became more aware of the notion that design is not just about selling products, but can inspire, engage, and inform. While it is probably true that most of these students will not pursue a "social model of design" after graduation, they will keep these kinds of projects in mind during their lives as professional designers. It would not be surprising if some of them encouraged their employers to donate time to worthy causes.

The *Welcome to South Africa* guides were also a huge success because rights are often denied to refugees who do not fully understand all of their entitlements. The children's book and the accompanying materials that were also produced (including puppets) are gaining great traction in the schools that have included them in their curriculum. As an educator, my trust in the students' ability to address and solve challenging problems has increased dramatically. In fact, as difficult as it was, I did not make any concrete suggestions for the outcomes. This meant the weight of the entire project was on the shoulders of the students, who rose to the occasion. Additionally, I realized that assigning a project that addressed issues in countries far away was a viable option.

Six International Summer Service Learning Project (ISSLP) students and 24 graphic design students have participated in the project and conducted research in Johannesburg, South Africa since 2011. Design solutions have expanded from class projects such as this one that addresses xenophobia to senior research thesis projects addressing rape, sexual abuse, and the empowerment of young women.

ADDITIONAL INFORMATION Financial support for the trip came from a variety of sources, including several institutes on campus. Without this, the projects would not have come to fruition. Additional resources included access, through Paul Horn, to refugees, schoolchildren, and native South Africans during our trip.

In September 2012 the *together+* campaign was awarded a $50,000 Sappi Ideas that Matter grant. This award is considered to be the industry's highly respected grant program aimed at helping designers create and implement print projects for charitable causes. In 2012 the winning projects reflected the grant program's "on-going commitment in the design community to utilize design in combination with innovative thinking to solve social problems." The video created for the students' project can be found here: http://news.nd.edu/news/34737-nd-design-students-project-results-in-50-000-sappi-ideas-that-matter-grant/.

WOMEN OF ISTANBUL THROUGH TIME:
WOMEN'S MUSEUM ISTANBUL

Başak Ürkmez, Assistant Professor of Graphic Design, Mimar Sinan Fine Arts University, Department of Graphic Design, Istanbul, Turkey

CLIENT
Mimar Sinan Fine Arts University, Istanbul, Turkey.

PROJECT TITLE
Women of Istanbul through Time: Women's Museum Istanbul.

DURATION
Fall mid-term, November 2013–February 2014.

BUDGET
All design work and project management was completed without cost. These concepts will be produced with the help of donations.

TEAM
Başak Ürkmez, Instructor; Illustration 2 Module students, Graphic Design department; Women's Museum Istanbul, project partners.

1.38 Yaşar Nezihe (1882–1971), the first female poet to write a poem about May 1st, Labor Day. *Illustration: Abdurrahman Pala.*

DESCRIPTION The Women's Museum Istanbul (IKM) is an urban women's museum. The permanent exhibition focuses on the biographies of women who have broken new ground in the artistic and cultural life of a city that was built in 660 BC. Originally named Byzantium, Istanbul acquired the name Constantinople in AD 330, and was then known as Kustantiniye, Kostantiniye, and Istanbul after 1453, and was officially recognized in 1930 as Istanbul. For the Women's Museum Istanbul, the term "groundbreaking" is by no means a static concept. Included in the collection are works by ground-breaking artists who were born in this city or who moved here from elsewhere, spent part of a lifetime here and in so doing enriched urban women's memory of Istanbul, both culturally and artistically. In light of all the information collected through academic research into women's history, the museum conducts biographical studies of those women who lived in Istanbul and produced innovative works in their respective fields, thus rediscovering women who, sometimes deliberately, were forgotten in the annals of history. The museum also opens new channels of communication between different identities that constitute the city, creates possibilities for intergenerational interaction, and instills in urban dwellers the sense that they are also a part of the city's history.

The underlying purpose of the Women's Museum Istanbul is to create a place of homage and a resource center that will strive to keep the subject of women's history on the current social agenda, and thus contribute to the construction of a collective women's memory. Hoping to set a worldwide standard in contemporary museum development, the museum is still searching for an exhibition space that will allow visitors physical access to the collection. At the moment, it can only be visited virtually.

Out of nearly 90 biographies within the museum's online collection, the students were asked to pick one biography they found most appealing and to create a set of illustrations in a technique of their choosing. The Illustration 2 class is workshop-based. The students are expected to take risks and dare to make mistakes without ignoring the fundamental objectives and principles of visual communication. The project progressed in four stages. In the first stage, students analyzed their personal choice and designed a character page. Next, they illustrated the woman in her authentic environment, and the time period in which she lived. In the third stage, the students were asked to respond to the following question: How would this character take shape if she had lived in a time period of your imagination? This prompted the students to illustrate the woman in a new historical and geographical context, building a different dialogue with their character. In the fourth stage, the students were asked to design a storyboard for a short story in which their character was the protagonist. This storyboard had to be comprised of at least four and no more than 10 frames.

RESEARCH A meeting was held with the team of the Women's Museum Istanbul in which they expressed their wish for the institution to be managed as a professional organization in keeping with worldwide standards and criteria for a contemporary museum. The team also addressed the issues they faced throughout the construction phase of the museum, and also their views for its long-term future.

1.39 Yaşar Nezihe (1882–1971), the first female poet to write a poem about May 1st, Labor Day. *Illustration: Abdurrahman Pala.*

1.40 Semiha Es (1912–2012), the first female travel and war photographer for the Turkish press. *Illustration: Eray Zengin.*

1.41 Leyla Gamsız Sarptürk (1921–2010), a pioneering woman painter who combined abstract and traditional trends in art. *Illustration: Kutay Akbas.*

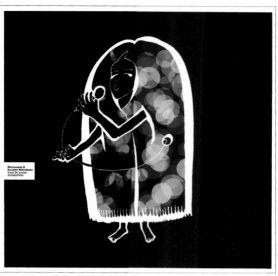

1.42 Tülay German (1935 –), the first female representative of Anatolian pop. *Illustration: Sanat Deliorman.*

At the beginning of the project the students were asked to come up with a draft consisting of short biographical notes based on the museum's website. The recommendation was to adopt an approach targeting an intergenerational, intergendered, and intercultural dialogue. The project proceeded as outlined in the brief and students' selections were reviewed.

CHALLENGES The biggest challenge in the project was the question of how far the characters based on the women's biographies should resemble the actual appearances of their role models. The scarcity of visual resources in many of the biographies complicated things even further. And yet the situation proved inspirational for some of the students who conceived the idea of illustrating the characters as hyperreal heroes.

STRATEGY The project's aim was to create informed awareness through its contribution to the building of a collective women's memory based on research into the role models in women's history. The project focused specifically on the artistic and cultural aspects that constitute only a part of the vast legacy that is women's memory of Istanbul. The project aimed to present the biographies of those women who chose to pursue a lifestyle that defied the established norms and expectations of the dominant cultural and artistic trends in Istanbul—women who were creative and enthusiastic, who were open to new experiences, who made courageous and determined efforts in their chosen paths, and shone with the brilliance of their originality. Illustration, within the limits of its own visual vocabulary and through its own technical means, was used in this project to bear witness to the history of Istanbul in a given time period and space.

1.43–1.44 Maryam Şahinyan (1911–1996) Turkey's first professional Armenian woman photographer.
Student name: Huseyin Burak Yel

1.45 Halet Çambel (1916–2014), the first female archeologist to have developed the "conservation on the site" model by establishing Turkey's first outdoor museum.
Illustration: Ferhat Akbaba.

> **"**
>
> *The project's aim was to create informed awareness through its contribution to the building of a collective women's memory based on research into the role models in women's history."*
>
> ——

EFFECTIVENESS This project fictionalized characters taken from real life and offered its audience new views of the world enriched by the behavior and perspectives of these characters. Abstract concepts used most often in the daily lives of these characters, and the ways they contextualize these concepts, were focal points in this project. They also functioned to guide and influence the students by displaying the ways in which the characters were transformed as a result of shifting social dynamics.

ASSESSMENT A project assessment can lead us to the following conclusions. The project increased the level of interest in the subject of urban women's memory and reminded the students of the true value and significance of "herstory." Efforts were made to honor all contributions to women's history without any discrimination between time period and cultural orientation, and, in considering their long-term effect on our contemporary life, the valiant endeavors of all these women of the past were remembered with respect.

An opportunity for dynamic interaction was opened up, enabling the growth of interest in the subject of urban women's memories, while the students were encouraged to show a deeper interest in the lives of these outstanding individuals.

Other important aims of this project was to build a visual portfolio of the academic studies conducted on the subject of women's history in Istanbul; to keep urban women's history of Istanbul on the current social agenda and make it accessible to a wide variety of audiences; to open channels of exploration into the original significance of a cultural legacy and what it means to us today. Toward the realization of these objectives, the project collaborated with a non-governmental organization in order to introduce a practical aspect to the theoretical dimension of urban women's memory studies, to share the outcomes of the research with a wider audience, and to encourage further studies in the field.

RESOURCES The Women's Museum Istanbul's website was utilized to access the reference sources and biographies: http://www.istanbulkadinmuzesi. org/en. The ultimate aim of this project is to continue and expand it with the further inclusion of more outstanding women characters.

SECTION 2

DESIGN ACTIVISM

WHAT DESIGN ACTIVISM IS AND IS NOT:
A PRIMER FOR STUDENTS

Natalia Ilyin

It is my experience that design students come in three basic varieties of cat. The first backs into design because she is actually an artist but her parents will agree only to pay for an education in "something that makes money with her talent." Of her we shall speak no more, for she has a difficult and twisting road ahead. The second student has found in himself a love of pattern, paper, or fabric— texture, color, type, or line—and lives to see and feel the ways these things rub together. He is happy. We shall leave him alone. The third may have begun her design life as an artist or sensualist, but, when off on her own, alone, finds herself thinking about how much better the world could be. Rather than retreating from its complex problems, she realizes that she can use her design skills to make life better. This third student brings her brain and her talent to becoming a design activist.

WHAT DESIGN ACTIVISM IS NOT First, let's do away with the popular misconception that design activists prance about with large signs, bellowing for immediate social change. Some do. A certain amount of signage happens. Contentious claims for change can do some good, in that they disrupt the status quo and create a moment in which average people look up from their iPhones and think briefly about the government or about Monsanto. But instigation is only a small part of the work of a design activist. Look-at-me "interventions," though valuable in certain situations, are not the complete story.

A smoke-filled melee in the streets may topple this or thrash that. But wild-eyed excitement can hurt as many people as it tries to help. The kind of designing that creates smooth transitioning toward long-time goals—though less of a momentary rush—is the kind of design that helps people in the long run. Revolution is not all it's cracked up to be for the people caught in the cross-fire. Real, positive, long-term, world-

changing activism is not showy. It frames issues publicly, true, but it brings its audience along with it. This kind of design works with people: it does not alienate its audience by claiming moral superiority.

WHAT DESIGN ACTIVISM IS Design activists work for people who do not have access to the design tools, strategic thinking, or knowledge of communication systems they need to advocate for themselves or their causes. They work for people, animals, and environments that do not benefit from the demands of the current economic system. They work for causes sidelined because they are not politically advantageous, because of their social complexity, or because they center on people that are not "players" on the world stage.

Design activists design for the public good. They can save the Yoruba language from oblivion. They can create summer camps that teach girls math and software engineering in Utah. They create their own programs, or they support people who have spent their lives learning how to deliver humanitarian aid but know nothing about designing a website.

In this way, designers can effect significant change. They can change societies. They can change who's in power. They can change which trees are cut down, and for what reason. Because they are trained in the tools of persuasion, they can tell the tale of the other side, of the "underdog," of the endangered species. They can get attention for people who cannot get attention, and can play a large part in political, environmental, and social innovation.

DESIGN ACTIVISTS AS PROPAGANDISTS To many, the word "propaganda" is a tainted word. It ushers in thoughts of Soviet and Nazi posters. It reminds us of all the times we've been duped by governments into going to war or killing people, or believing things about people that turned out not to be true. But the word "propaganda" only started to get bad associations after World War I. Before then, it was perfectly fine to call someone a "propagandist," meaning that that person was working to broadcast a particular ideological stance with which she agreed—a particular view, shared by many.

A person representing her own view is not a propagandist. A person representing the view of a group, an institution, or a "dominant order" is. That's why a lone psychopath's personal manifesto is not propaganda, but Hitler's *Mein Kampf* is. The lone psychopath has no followers and sells no books, whereas 10 million copies of *Mein Kampf* circulated in Germany by the end of World War II.

Advertising is often seen as propaganda, because, taken as a whole, it represents the cause of the "dominant order" of capitalism. Although each individual ad agency does not salute the flag of commodification every morning, they all agree on the tenets of our economic system, and believe that convincing people to buy things through behavior-modifying messages and strategies is the way to keep that system going.

Design students who have not studied the prompts and motivations of propaganda risk being tricked into using their talent to support causes and empires not of their own choosing. As you learn the science—for it is a "soft" science—of convincing, you begin to see how propaganda has affected your own life. You become able to parse societal messages, rather than repeating them. And you choose which messages you will produce and reproduce. This is personal agency.

With the graphic design diploma comes a license to persuade. Whether you design materials for a big corporation or for a social cause, you're often designing propaganda. My father, a former Cold War propagandist, used to say, "Don't point a gun at a man unless you intend to shoot him." Don't use the tools of graphic design—powerful tools of manipulation, tools of convincing—unless you know exactly what messages you are sending, and to whom.

AND THAT BRINGS US TO ETHICS It is impossible to become a design activist without finding yourself in many conversations about ethical choices. What is "good" in one designer's world may be anathema in another's. We all know the phrase, "One person's terrorist is another's freedom fighter." And, similarly, one designer's "empowered sexuality" is another's "evidence of the commodification of the Self." One

designer may be fine with making dog food labels as a career—after all, he likes dogs. Another would find a life of designing dog food labels an agony—a personal myth of Sisyphus.

In order to focus your talents on social issues, you must first have the opportunity to sort out what it is that you believe, what it is that is important to you—and find a "good" good enough to spend your time and talent supporting. Experiments that help you sort out your moral stance are crucial to your development as a citizen designer. Study ethics.

ACTIVIST AS SLEUTH Just as ethical decision making is part of design activism, so is learning to think in a larger way. In your rush to do good you might ignore the signs that an organization may not be what it says it is. Is it a real non-profit? What does it really do with the money it collects? Who supports it? Who funds it? What is the background of the executive director? In every class I teach, when it comes time to choose a non-profit to rebrand, at least one student finds herself realizing that the "do-good" organization she had planned to work with is actually a front for another, less savory, institution or cause.

When designing for activism, your thinking shifts from aesthetics to sleuthing. Do I believe that the actions this organization is taking are right? Does its actions mirror its mission? Does it do what it says it is going to do? Or does it require the people it is "helping" to adhere to a particular ideology, give up something, alter their behavior?

Listen like a spy listens. Listen to the people you are trying to help. The most valuable design activism supports ideas and projects initiated by the community itself and not by the designer. Avoid charging in, deciding the villagers need a well, spending design work, time, and resources building a website to get them the money for a well, and then patting yourself on the back for being such an activist designer. Those villagers didn't need a well. If they had needed a well, they would have told you. How would you like it if someone came in and infantilized you in that way?

Natalia Ilyin is Professor of Design at Cornish College of the Arts in Seattle, Washington. She is also Founding Faculty in Graphic Design at Vermont College of Fine Arts, a low-residency MFA program. Natalia's most recent design book is Chasing the Perfect: Thoughts on Modernist Design in Our Time, *for Metropolis Books.*

FIVE QUESTIONS TO
HARRY PEARCE

1. What were the most important influences that shaped you as a designer?

My college years were a very nascent time. I felt quite lost in relation to the design world—I was adrift. Yet looking back, and seeing what was actually going on around and within me, the seeds for my whole creative life to follow were being sown.

Two external tutors at Canterbury (UK), Andrzej Klimowski and Ian Beck, brought a wonderful clarity to my outlook. Andrzej opened my eyes to the power and grit of Polish poster design. Ian drew me into Cassandre's expressive typography. I also finally understood the vision of Duchamp—primacy of the idea—and Breton—*The Communicating Vessels*, a vision of living in two realities, waking and dream. Somehow typography and surrealism was a doorway for me, toward an approach. Also, at that time, I was recording my dreams and had been reading Jung since my late teens.

I met Peter Gabriel at an African art show in Bath, England. His balance of social conscience and creativity had a huge influence, epitomized by his song *Biko*, and the Donald Woods book of the same title, which I then read.

I have always been drawn to the East. Spiritually, I moved away from Europe and organized religion. I now realize that this period was actually my foundation. Somehow, in my last year at college so much fell into place—I've always remained a searcher. If I look back across my career, these were the foundations, and they are still running through my work today.

2. Do you agree or disagree with this statement: Designers have a social and ethical responsibility to create and transmit meaningful forms of communication that benefit society and culture? Why?

Leading a creative life is a great privilege and equally a great responsibility. I find it sad that so few designers realize they are having such an effect on our culture and the world at large. The power of ideas is limitless. They can elevate or impoverish our world, and we as designers hold that power daily in our hands. It's a simple choice, made constantly every time we consider our next creation. Years ago I had a moment of real clarity when I found a beautiful 500,000-year-old stone hand tool. It was perfect, in form and function, and it made me realize we are in a long stream of human endeavor; we owe it to our time, our past, and our future to give the best we can creatively. We are what we create.

3. WITNESS is an international non-profit organization that trains and equips people to use video in their fight for human rights. You are a member of their advisory board, working with Peter Gabriel for more than 21 years. Can you talk about your initial involvement with WITNESS and why it is important for you to stay involved and do this type of work?

As I mentioned, I met Peter back in the early 1980s. I knew of and loved his work, especially the balance between his creativity and social conscience. Later, in 1990, I heard of Peter's idea of giving cameras to the oppressed around the world to allow them to make films and to get their stories out and effect change—the brilliant notion of "little brother watching big brother." I saw the short WITNESS introductory film he made with Chiat/Day, and I was determined to help. I hoped that I could bring integrity to the design work; get them noticed, help them to be taken seriously.

1.46 DVD covers for WITNESS. *Design: Pentagram.*

5. What advice would you give a student studying **visual communication toda**y to help them prepare **for contemporary professional practice?**

- Design from the heart.
- Hunt relentlessly for a truth in your work; realize that you are constantly affecting the world and don't take it lightly.
- Believe in your intuition for it takes you to the core; over-intellectual guff leaves you at the periphery.
- Let the ideas find you; if you're open, they will.
- Design and its potential are limitless, so dream there should *not* be the possibility of indifference.

Harry Pearce, Pentagram partner, part-time optimist, photographer of schisms, human rights activist, dream diary keeper, graphic designer, and accidentist. He joined Pentagram's London office as a partner in 2006 after having co-founded and grown Lippa Pearce to become one of the UK's most respected design agencies over the previous 16 years. His work touches many disciplines, from spatial design and identity to print, packaging, and posters, while encompassing the public and private sectors, local and global charities, and commercial enterprises.

I made a commitment to WITNESS and Peter, and 21 years later we are still working together. It is often part of the daily life of my design team. We integrate it into our business and have never charged a penny. It's my balance, my "thank you" for the privilege of being able to live by my creativity. I sincerely hope I can continue indefinitely.

4. New roles are emerging for design professionals **as their function is increasingl**y changing from **that of generators to facilitato**rs of ideas. Can you **comment on this?**

Stefan Sagmeister is a shinning example of this, and he's really led the way. The design world has become ever more fluid, and wonderfully so. I really don't care if lines are crossed or where one discipline begins and ends, so long as the pursuit is enriching for receiver and transmitter alike. Where this all fails is when it gets self-indulgent, and it so often does. If egos can be left behind, and our collective endeavors are delivered with true feeling, illuminating and life enhancing, then so much the better. The quality of our thought is the quality of our future—how, when, or where that happens or by whom, matters nothing as long as it's of worth.

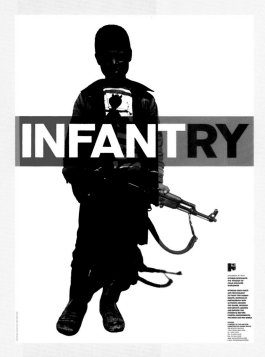

1.**47** Poster for WITNESS on the subject of children being forced to become soldiers. *Design: Pentagram.*

DESIGN ACTIVISM AND SOCIAL CHANGE WORKSHOP

Gülizar Çepoğlu, Associate Senior Lecturer, Graphic and Media Design, London College of Communication, University of the Arts London, UK

CLIENT

Emre Senan Design Foundation, Izmir, Turkey. The ESD Foundation is a non-profit organization based in Yahşibey near the town of Dikili, Izmir. It was co-founded by **Mr. Emre Senan** and **Professor Ayşegul Izer,** Turkish designers/design educators in 2006.

PROJECT TITLE

Life is a Protest! Communication design as a political and social act.

DURATION

July 15–30, 2014.

BUDGET

The Emre Senan Design Foundation is a non-profit organization. No fees were levied to attend the workshop. Participants funded their own travel and daily personal expenses.

TEAM

Project leader: **Gülizar Çepoğlu,** London College of Communication.
Assistant: **Cleber de Campos,** MA Graphic Design, London College of Communication.
Guest workshop leaders:
Tzortzis Rallis, design activist;
Sarah Snaith, design writer;
Joseph Bisat Marshall, designer.
Student team: **Roxanne Bottomley, Freya Smith, Emily Todd,** and **Ryan Young:** BA (Hons) Graphic and Media Design, London College of Communication (LCC); **Dilşad Aladağ:** Architecture Faculty, Istanbul Technical University; **Ferhat Akbaba, Gizem Cansu Horoz,** and **Şevval Ceylan:** Graphic Design, Mimar Sinan Fine Arts University, Istanbul; **Görkem Işme:** Graphic Design, **Dokuz Eylül** University, Izmir.

1.48 "Gezi Park and the trees were the center of social resistance. Our heart is the center of our life. If you sever all the blood vessels, life is over. Therefore, we have to resist to live."
Design: Görkem Işme.

DESCRIPTION Yahşibey Design Workshops Project is an international educational design workshop initiated by ESD Foundation in Izmir, Turkey. The ESD Foundation invited me to be the project leader for the 34th Yahşibey Design Workshop in their purpose-built venue in the village of Yahşibey, Izmir. Following my interest and research on the visual language stemming from the recent protests in Turkey, I decided to organize a workshop on design activism.

The riots in Gezi Park demonstrated how creativity could be harnessed for effective protest by uniting people using visual communication strategies that included social media designed to span across national, cultural, and linguistic barriers. Taking the Gezi Park protests in Istanbul as my inspiration, my aim was to bring together a small group of international design activists, writers, educators, and students for a workshop centered on communication design as a social and political act. The workshop lens would be focused on the role and responsibilities of designers during a period of social unrest.

By employing a design process that encouraged participation, this design activism workshop was intended to challenge and provoke the students into advanced levels of critical thinking and creativity while instilling awareness of the social responsibility of the graphic designer to generate powerful messages that transcend language. To do this, as four different designers and educators, we ran workshops investigating how meaning is constructed, communicated, and disseminated during protests, and why design activism is important as students and designers practice.

RESEARCH Before the workshop, the students carried out wide-ranging research into different protests around the world. They were asked to prepare presentations on their reaction to Turkish and world politics. To help them with their research, the students were given a comprehensive reading list. The 10 students examined alternative media and reflected on how activists currently use verbal and visual language.

CHALLENGES The first challenge was the language barrier between the Turkish and English students. Throughout, the students proved creative, open-minded, and tenacious in their efforts to overcome the language barriers between them. While the Turkish students strived to explain their experience of the recent Turkish upheavals, the British students focused on translating the political slogans to understand the core issues, and to develop messages for a wider audience.

Working together to overcome the language difference was invaluable when it came to the second major challenge of constructing visual languages that would be globally understood with limited resources and facilities.

The third challenge was limited Internet access. This prevented the immediate dissemination of the messages to a wider audience via social media as a way of testing the work produced.

STRATEGY Tzortzis Rallis' workshop focused on words and slogans at the outset, to allow the students to articulate their political stances verbally and, then to produce visual messages and images while referencing contemporary political and agitational graphics through a practice-based approach. This enabled students to collaboratively map out the slogans from recent events and to create visual messages as socially responsible designers in a series of posters in two languages advocating a global awareness of current social, political, and economic issues.

1.49 Turkish newspapers were used to create the word "Lies" in the slogan "We Choose Our Lies." People should have the right of ownership/authorship of their own news and truths. *Design: Freya Smith.*

In the second and third part of the workshop a *critical design* approach was used. To quote Anthony Dunne and Fiona Raby from their book *Design Noir*: "Critical design takes as its medium social, psychological, cultural, technical and economic values, in an effort to push the limits of lived experience, not the medium." Students were asked to apply an awareness of their own experience to free themselves critically from the clichéd use of graphic design thinking, processes, and tools. They were encouraged to use materials from their immediate environment, interact with local people, and leave computers aside while collectively developing messages in which meanings are as important as materials.

In the second part, design writer Sarah Snaith and designer Joseph Bisat Marshall provoked the students into conveying their feelings about political unrest through the medium of everyday objects. Each student was challenged to talk briefly about a decisive moment in their lives that engaged them in activism, and was given square spaces on the studio floor in which to build a three-dimensional (3-D) representation of their experience. The group was divided into pairs to interview each other about a topic they felt strongly about—human rights, ecological issues, democracy—and produced a written article which was incorporated into the cut-and-paste design of a magazine spread.

> "
>
> *The workshop revealed the power of communication design as a political and social act. Students designed for positive social, political, and environmental change. It also enabled participants across the board to investigate powerful participatory design approaches and develop a toolkit for activists and designers alike."*

I started my three-and-a half-day workshop by having students analyze various expressions of contemporary and historical design activism. We also briefly viewed different writing systems such as hieroglyphs, ideograms, and pictograms, and discussed the impact of digital technologies on image and text dichotomy and on our writing and reading systems.

The students were then challenged to develop their own revolutionary glyphs, icons, dingbat fonts, and GIF files, as an outlet to express their own political stances without reference to a rule-bounded system such as an alphabet. In this way, they collected a canon of existing work and from it created new, inspirational visual narratives that clearly demonstrated how far they had developed as "informed critical thinkers."

The workshop closed with an exhibition of the work produced, including posters, animated GIFS, text and images, and 3-D installations. Following a formal presentation, the students received Certificates of Participation in the workshop from the eminent Turkish guest designers and academicians.

1.50 Turkish flag installation symbolizing the chemical pain inflicted when Turkish police sprayed pepper gas on protestors. The ideogram conveys "Resist Turkey!" *Design: Ferhat Akbaba.*

1.51 Two facing fists convey "Resist Istanbul!" The image visually suggests land masses on either side of Istanbul's Bosphorus Strait. *Design: Ferhat Akbaba.*

1.52 Poster created on the concrete studio floor using black tape. *Design: Roxanne Bottomley.*

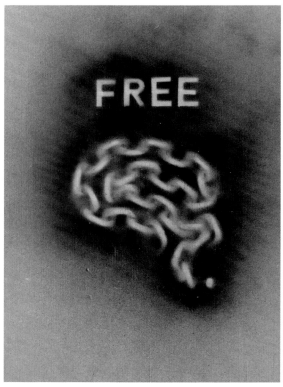

1.53 "Be free!" Unchain your brain! *Design: Görkem İşme.*

EFFECTIVENESS The workshop revealed the power of communication design as a political and social act. Students designed for positive social, political, and environmental change. It also enabled participants across the board to investigate powerful participatory design approaches and develop a toolkit for activists and designers alike. An e-book that displays the presentation, work, and images from the exhibition is available on Yahşibey Design Workshops' website: http://yahsiworkshops.com/eng/yahsibey.html.

ASSESSMENT A final presentation was prepared for the guests in both languages. All participants gave feedback, clearly articulating what they had achieved with clarity of purpose, evidencing an awareness of the use of appropriate materials, techniques, and methods. An exhibition was successfully curated displaying the myriad of work produced.

Throughout the workshop the students autonomously made good decisions and collectively overcame complex and unpredictable situations. The group took risks, openly discussed, succinctly criticized, and clearly communicated ideas. Once this level of interaction was reached the group collectively demonstrated a strong sense of motivation and enthusiasm and was committed to long working hours despite the Aegean heat. A valuable outcome of the workshop was that this method of working enabled students to reflect, plan out of necessity, and conduct relevant evaluation of their self-progress.

LCC students participated in this workshop as an educational event for which they will now be credited toward their Diploma in Professional Studies. Upon their return they handed in a written report about their experience, together with an evaluation report from the workshop leaders.

AMEN:
SUPPORTING MALE VICTIMS OF DOMESTIC ABUSE

Brenda Dermody and **Clare Bell**, Lecturers,
Dublin Institute of Technology, Dublin, Ireland

Her new heels
certainly made an
impression on me.

046 902 3718
amen.ie

AMEN Supporting male victims of domestic abuse ♥Cosc

@amensupportservices

1.54 Amen: Shoes. *Project team: Lauren Flynn, Michelle Geoghegan, Deividas Dvylaitis, Ben Salveta, Joseph Egan, Alan Harbron, Orla Flanagan.*

CLIENT
Amen Support Services Ltd.

PROJECT TITLE
Amen: Supporting male victims of domestic abuse.

DURATION
8 weeks, spring term 2014.

BUDGET
Amen is funded by Cosc, the National Office for the Prevention of Domestic, Sexual and Gender-based Violence in Ireland. Cosc allocated a total of €15,000 to Amen to fund 48 sheet billboards, bus shelter ads, and a regional radio campaign. All design work and project management was done at no cost as it was part of the students' coursework.

TEAM
Project coordinators and tutors:
Brenda Dermody and **Clare Bell**
Students Learning With Communities (SLWC) coordinator: **Dr. Catherine Bates**
Student team: **Lauren Flynn, Joseph Egan, Michelle Geoghan, Alan Harbron, Ben Salveta, Deividas Dvylaitis, Barry McCabe, Orla Flanagan**
Members of Amen Support Services Ltd.
Design industry consultant:
Ciarán ÓGaora, Zero-G design consultancy
Visiting lecturer: **Professor Elizabeth Resnick,** of Massachusetts College of Art and Design, provided constructive guidance on the development of a conceptual framework with which to identify and clarify the design problem.

DESCRIPTION Amen Support Services Ltd. is a voluntary group that provides a confidential help line, support, and information services for male victims of domestic abuse. It is the only service in Ireland specifically addressing the needs of men suffering silently and alone in abusive relationships.

All too often, domestic abuse against men is a hidden issue, with victims too ashamed to come forward for fear of being disbelieved or ridiculed. The male victim is stigmatized for not being able to protect himself. Added to this, statistics show that when a woman is violent and abusive in a relationship, it is not necessarily assumed that this violence extends to her children or that she is an unfit mother. The law in Ireland almost always presumes that the children are better off with their mother. Therefore, the only option for men seems to be to put up with the abuse or to leave the family home, since under the law they receive no real protection.

Most men react by staying silent. Very often they remain in an abusive relationship for the sake and protection of their children. Men who choose to leave the family home frequently experience difficulty in obtaining regular and meaningful contact with their children. The net effect is that men are treated as perpetrators rather than victims.

Amen approached The DIT Programme for Students Learning With Communities (SLWC) office seeking to collaborate with students on the creation of an awareness campaign. The two primary goals of the campaign were to increase societal awareness of the issue of domestic abuse against men and to promote the services offered by Amen regionally and nationally. The target audience included men who find themselves in a domestic abuse situation and also the families and friends of victims who need information on how best to support a male friend or relative who is in an abusive relationship.

The aim of the project was to develop a new brand strategy for a given community partner and indicate how this might be rolled out across a range of applications. The project also aimed to encourage students to explore how graphic design contributes to, and reproduces, cultural meanings that have an effect on social issues and practices, thereby becoming more aware of, and accountable for, graphic design's social impact and responsibility.

As the starting point for this project, students were asked to explore design's social function: the way it is determined by our culture and the link between our choices as designers and the sort of culture to which we wish to contribute. The project asked students to consider how visual communication can be used to highlight an important social/educational message.

The designs selected were an amalgamation of ideas and approaches from a number of students and were completed by the project team. Of particular importance to the Amen project was the art direction, photography, and copy.

Week 1: Client Briefing Sessions Ciarán ÓGaora launched the project with an initial presentation on branding that focused on campaigns and design for social good. In the first phase of the project students were asked to evaluate the community partner's existing brand strategy—if one existed—and to devise a new brand strategy based on and stemming from their findings. At this point the students also developed a design brief and strategy which they presented to the client for approval and sign-off. They also began to create initial visuals of their ideas.

1.55 Amen logo. *Project team: Lauren Flynn, Michelle Geoghegan, Deividas Dvylaitis, Ben Salveta, Joseph Egan, Alan Harbron, Orla Flanagan. Concept and design: Deividas Dvylaitis.*

1.56 Amen: Shoes. *Project team: Lauren Flynn, Michelle Geoghegan, Deividas Dvylaitis, Ben Salveta, Joseph Egan, Alan Harbron, Orla Flanagan. Concept and design: Lauren Flynn. Photography: Michelle Geoghegan.*

1.57 Amen: Jersey. *Project team: Lauren Flynn, Michelle Geoghegan, Deividas Dvylaitis, Ben Salveta, Joseph Egan, Alan Harbron, Orla Flanagan. Concept: Ben Salveta. Layout: Lauren Flynn. Photography: Michelle Geoghegan.*

Week 3: Interim Client Presentation Once the brief was agreed upon with the client partner, students developed and tested visual proposals for a refresh or redesign of the identity. They also developed visuals for a range of applications (which in this case included a rebranding of the organization and an awareness campaign). The prototypes also demonstrated how the final proposal could be adapted and grow with the organization.

Week 7: Final Client Presentation

Week 8: Project Submission

RESEARCH Students were encouraged to conduct primary research in a number of ways including context definition and field mapping through the collection and annotation of their findings. They were also asked to gather and collate material, either as mood boards or in notebooks, with which to build fluent visual vocabularies that they could draw upon. Further dialogue and interviews with the client partner, site visits, and, where appropriate, meeting with service users or other stakeholders also proved invaluable.

CHALLENGES The issue of male victims of domestic abuse is a little known fact in Ireland and is often stigmatized. Highlighting the issue of male victims without minimizing domestic abuse against women had to be negotiated carefully.

STRATEGY Amen was open to the idea of a rebrand as they felt the brand identity they had was not relevant to the brand ethos or the public image that they wanted to convey. The new logo design by Deividas Dvylaitis is based on the strong square shape of the letter "M" which represents strength and masculinity. The addition of the circular dot suggests the widely recognized male isotype. The remaining characters represent the nature of the organization with the letter "A" leaning toward the "M" in a figurative display of support. The crossbar of the "A" was removed to streamline the form and to suggest openness and inclusivity.

Initially the students worked alone, developing individual solutions to the brief. Following this, the students presented their work to Amen. Amen selected two campaign concepts, a logo and a video from students. Although the two concepts were different, they were similar enough in approach to be consolidated to create one coherent campaign. Images of everyday, innocent domestic objects found in every home were photographed to look like weapons—in particular, one of the billboards subverts the image of the high-heeled shoe as a symbol of femininity, beauty, and female sexuality, subtly depicting it as a symbol of aggression. Also, quotations from a male victim of domestic abuse ran as taglines alongside the images to express the point of view of the victim.

The advertising campaign was originally to consist of five posters all with varying content but similar design, and these were to be displayed on buses, bus shelters, and billboards around Dublin city. In the final edit, due to financial constraints, only two of the designs were actually printed and used for the campaign, one with the image of the shoe and the other with an image of a football shirt (tying in perfectly with World Cup 2014 which coincided with the campaign run). The short film also related to the World Cup as it contained references to sport. The film and the advertising posters were used for Amen's social media and online campaign on Facebook, YouTube, and Twitter.

"

The two primary goals of the campaign were to increase societal awareness of the issue of domestic abuse against men and to promote the services offered by Amen regionally and nationally."

———

Not all injuries
happen on
the pitch.

046 902 3718
amen.ie

AMEN Supporting male victims of domestic abuse · Cosc

@amensupportservices

1.58 Amen: Jersey. *Project team: Lauren Flynn, Michelle Geoghegan, Deividas Dvylaitis, Ben Salveta, Joseph Egan, Alan Harbron, Orla Flanagan. Concept: Ben Salveta. Layout: Lauren Flynn. Photography: Michelle Geoghegan.*

EFFECTIVENESS **Media launch** The media launch was a resounding success—70 people attended the event at Amen resource center, which had been set up to seat just 40. The launch was featured and broadcast on Six One News, and was reported by a number of print and online newspapers and magazines.

Print campaign The 48-sheet billboards proved to be the most successful aspect of the print campaign, gaining the highest level of recognition from clients and the general public. Since the campaign launch Amen has been contacted by the Rape Crisis Centre, the Citizens Information Bureau, and the Legal Aid board with requests to produce copies of campaign posters to place in offices and waiting rooms. The headlines that the students developed for the billboards were also adapted for a national radio campaign.

The bus shelter ads were not quite as successful, with a lower level of recognition and response. In future campaigns, along with the billboards, Amen will run the ads on buses serving local and national routes. These "moving billboards" will be a significantly more effective means of bringing Amen's message to a much wider audience.

ASSESSMENT From our community partner: "The experience of working with DIT and the student group was transformative for staff and clients at Amen in a number of ways. The affiliation with a third-level institution provided Amen with the confidence and the impetus to hold their first-ever press launch for their annual awareness campaign. A significant motivating factor behind this decision was Amen's desire to garner recognition for the students for all of the time and effort they had invested in designing the campaign."

Manager Niamh Farrell stated that the collaboration with students and the quality and variety of visual concepts produced as a result created a tangible positive energy among the staff at Amen, as well as "the courage to go on and do bigger things." Farrell also spoke of how clients of Amen attending the launch were moved by the fact that the issue of domestic abuse directed at male victims was not "mocked or ridiculed" by the students—rather it was "accepted as a real issue" by the young people working on the project.

BIRD'S EYE VIEW:
DESIGNS FOR PROTECTIVE WINDOW FILMS

Alice Drueding, Professor, Program Head,
Graphic & Interactive Design, Tyler School of Art,
Temple University, Philadelphia, Pennsylvania

CLIENT

Temple University, Temple University Office of Sustainability, Audubon Society, SurfaceCare. The project specifically served the Temple University community, but the ultimate goal was to develop a viable solution to the bird-strike problem in urban environments.

PROJECT TITLE

Bird's Eye View: Designs for protective window films.

DURATION

2011–12; 2014. The project was assigned in the first week of the fall 2011 semester. Students had up to four weeks to research the problem, followed by a 3- to 4-week period for the design process. The work was shown in a juried exhibition at Tyler in spring 2012, followed by another 6-week exhibition at Paley Library during the actual spring migration period. The winning design by sophomore Molly Denisevicz was produced in spring 2014 at the Paley Library, Tuttleman Learning Center.

BUDGET

The project budget was minimal: 13" x 19" printable acetate was purchased for inkjet printing. SurfaceCare produced and installed the winning design for a large-scale window installation in 2014 at no cost to the school. Cash awards for the competition were donated.

1.59a–1.59b Installation of window film at Paley Library test site. *Design: Molly Denisevicz.*

TEAM

Instructors: **Alice Drueding, Joe Scorsone, Abby Bennett, Dermot MacCormack, Kelly Holohan.**
Students: 96 sophomores and juniors, Graphic & Interactive Design program, Tyler School of Art.

DESCRIPTION A group of concerned faculty, students, and staff at Temple University formed an ad hoc committee to address the problem of birds striking the windows of campus buildings, particularly during the spring and fall migration seasons. Dead and injured birds are found daily in many locations around the campus. Tyler School of Art's new building on Temple University's main campus in Philadelphia is one of several locations where a significant number of dead birds are regularly found, especially at the base of the enormous glass wall that runs along the building's interior courtyard. This prompted the committee to contact Tyler School of Art faculty to see if someone there would be interesting in working on an art or design project related to the problem.

Representatives from the Audubon Society and the Philadelphia Zoo were enlisted to advise the group about possible ways to address the problem. Student volunteers and grounds staff at Temple began collecting the victims, identifying their species and determining where bird strikes were occurring

on campus. Bird strikes happen most frequently at buildings with large amounts of glass. Birds, especially those not born in urban environments, do not see the glass as an obstacle to reaching building interiors or the landscape surroundings that are reflected in windows. The results are devastating for individual birds and even entire species.

I met with the committee and learned about the extent of the problem, along with potential solutions. Among the proposed solutions were films adhered to windows that were being tested at the Philadelphia Zoo. The films were transparent, and printed with white or black horizontal 6 point rules spaced approximately an inch apart. They did not completely obstruct the view in or out of the windows, but did provide a visual "warning" to birds that the windows were there. I proposed an assignment for students to design window films that, in addition to being functional, would be both decorative and informative. The committee enthusiastically embraced the idea.

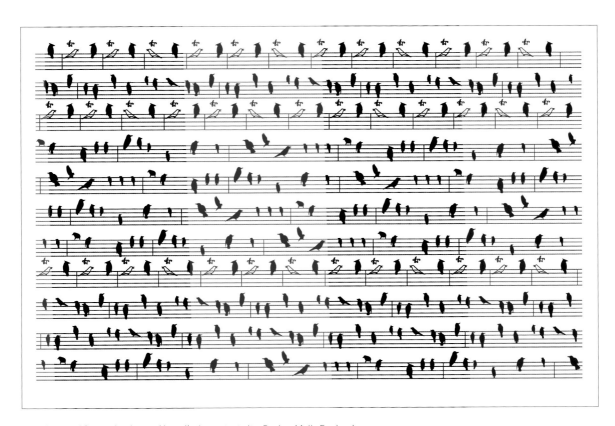

1.60 Selected for production and installation at test site. *Design: Molly Denisevicz.*

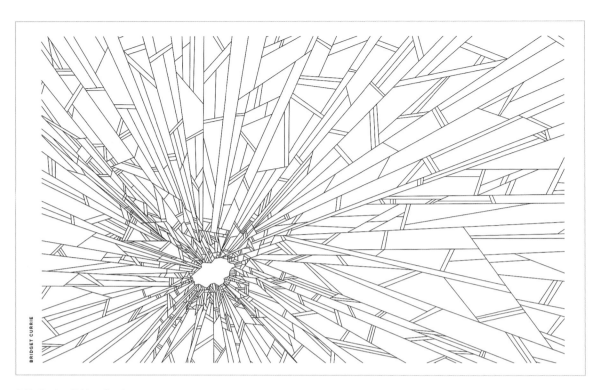

BRIDGET CURRIE

1.61 *Design: Bridget Currie.*

The project, entitled *Bird's Eye View*, was undertaken in fall 2011 with sophomore and junior classes in the Graphic & Interactive Design program. This was to be followed by two 6-week exhibitions of the work in spring 2012 at two different campus locations. The project was presented as a competition, with funding for awards coming from Temple University's Office of Sustainability, the Audubon Society, the Philadelphia Zoo, SurfaceCare (the manufacturer of the films), and the Graphic & Interactive Design program. SurfaceCare was committed to producing the winning design on film so that it could be tested in a large-scale context at a site of frequent bird strikes on Temple's campus.

RESEARCH The assignment was given at the beginning of the semester so that students would have adequate time to research the problem and, based on their concepts, any solution-related information that they would need. Students were directed to several organizations' websites as a starting point for their research, including the Cornell Lab of Ornithology.

CHALLENGES Seven different classes and instructors—nearly 100 students—participated in the project. It was essential that the large number of participants understand the problem and the requirements of the brief and work within the same timeframe. The assignment had to be appropriate and challenging enough for sophomores taking their very first design class, and juniors in their first or second semester in the major.

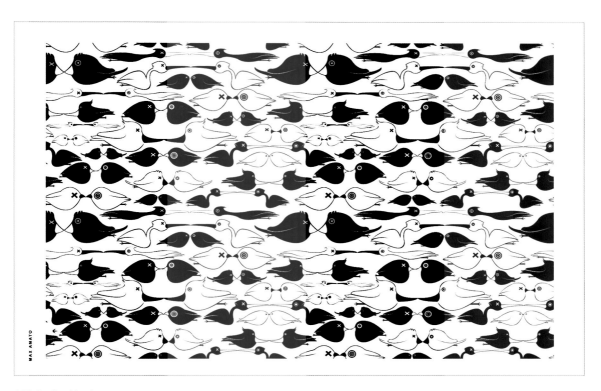

1.62 *Design: Max Amato.*

1.63 *Design: Pamela Casey.*

STRATEGY The faculty team and their students worked closely together. Student participants talked about the project outside of class and spread the word to other students at the school as well as to friends and family outside the school. This not only helped them in the development of their design solutions, but also contributed to achieving the goal of the project—raising awareness of the bird strike problem.

The parameters for the assignment were at once very narrow (color, spacing, size) and very open (a bird-related theme). Obviously, the problem was a serious and even tragic one, but students were encouraged to explore concepts that did not address the problem literally. Solutions could be educational, factual, ironic, humorous, whimsical, or poignant.

"

Bird's Eye View was a unique opportunity for students to use design to raise awareness about a large environmental problem while contributing a functional solution to that problem."

EFFECTIVENESS Students believed in the importance of the project and rose to the occasion. The balance of boundaries and freedom within the assignment kept it both manageable and interesting for students with varying levels of experience. Conceptual freedom in the approach to content, style, and message allowed for invention and self-expression. Two years after the project was given, the large-scale installation of the winning design continues to draw attention to the issue, adding to its successful outcome. Ultimately, the effectiveness of the films themselves will only be known after extensive testing. The installation at Paley Library, Tuttleman Learning Center is a valuable contribution to that effort.

ASSESSMENT The Graphic & Interactive Design program at Tyler School of Art, Temple University has long been committed to encouraging students to use their design skills for the greater good. Tyler students have participated in many initiatives and competitions focusing on environmental and social issues. Bird's Eye View was a unique opportunity for them to use design to raise awareness about a large environmental problem while contributing a functional solution to that problem. The results of the project exceeded expectations. The exhibition of nearly 100 pieces on the glass in the long hallway where so many bird strikes were occurring at Tyler, and later in Paley Library, significantly raised awareness of the problem within the Temple University community and beyond. Reports on the project appeared in several university publications and others, including the *Philadelphia Inquirer*, *Audubon Magazine*, and the environmental publication, *Grid Magazine.* The ongoing impact of this project—from the first exhibition of the work at Tyler to the large-scale installation of the winning design—is remarkable. It continues to generate interest in the plight of migrating birds on campus and beyond, and we hope it will lead to an effective way to prevent their loss through bird strikes.

ADDITIONAL INFORMATION All of the work from the Bird's Eye View assignment and exhibition can be seen here: http://tylergaid.squarespace.com/special-exhibitions/birds-eye-view-an-exhibition-of-designs-for-protective-windo/.

SUSTAINABLE__

Joo Ha, Professor, Visual Information Department, Namseoul University, Cheonan, South Korea

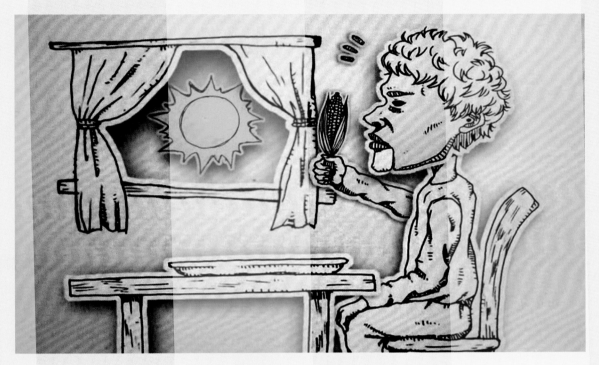

1.64 *"Reasons to Eat Less Meat,"* screen capture from stop-motion movie *Design: Hyung-Woo Ahn and Hyun-Woo Kim.*

CLIENT
Classroom project.

PROJECT TITLE
Sustainable—.

DURATION
7 weeks, fall 2009–12.

BUDGET
None.

TEAM
Instructor: **Joo Ha,** Professor; students and student teams in the Graphic Art class, Visual Information Department, Namseoul University.

DESCRIPTION Graphic Art is a studio elective course for fourth-year students in the Visual Information Design Department at Namseoul University, South Korea. *Sustainable__* was the first of two projects for the course, and it focused on global environmental issues. Within the parameter of a sustainability theme, each student was challenged to choose his/her own topic to fill in the blank, "Sustainable__," based on his/her own personal interest. Students were encouraged to produce experimental designs as there were very few limitations imposed. The final design outcome could take any form, or be produced in any medium, as long as the project successfully delivered its intended message to its target audience. Both individual projects and team projects were permitted.

Since most of the students had completed their graduation projects, they were ready to start a new project with fresh minds. Unlike many previous projects that focused on a commercial aspect of design practice such as package design, advertising design, book/brochure, and identity/branding design, students were encouraged to undertake extensive research into a variety of environmental problems for this project. The main goal of this activity was to train students as design thinkers who could successfully conceive and manifest their own idea through a design solution. In order to do that, students were expected to learn how to manage self-initiated projects by following a specified design process provided within the class curriculum.

RESEARCH Students started this project with very little knowledge of sustainability, yet they developed an enthusiastic interest during the research process, which was divided into two categories: the concept research stage and the design research stage. For concept research, students undertook in-depth research on the topic of sustainability. Once they discovered areas of interest, they would narrow these areas to very specific themes or ideas.

CHALLENGES In their fourth year, students in Korean universities start applying for jobs, with many of them being successfully hired before graduation. Many students in the Graphic Art class left to begin working. This left me with a nearly empty classroom environment, making it difficult to motivate the remaining students to stay on task. Moreover, the students who were preparing for working in commercial design industries questioned how realistic it was to pursue a career in social design.

To engage the students remaining in the class each week, I would present good examples of social design work and explain their impact in our everyday lives. Also, each student was expected to present topics concerning global issues, encouraging the class to develop design solutions to address presented topics or concerns on a weekly basis.

Getting students actively involved in rigorous research has been one of the major challenges. Students struggled to develop a concept and content throughout the research process, as they never considered research a priority in shaping ideas into design solutions—only a few minor research

examples, such as case studies and market research, had been included in former design project briefs for these students. In order to help the students become more effective researchers, a process guideline and examples of strong design solutions clearly demonstrating a variety of methods to utilize research materials were introduced during the class periods.

STRATEGY Throughout the project's timeline, each student designed, directed, and curated his/her own work. Considering that most of the students were not familiar with self-initiated projects, certain steps were provided as a guideline:

Step 1: Concept Research Choose an interesting area within sustainability, and discover various facts about the area. Narrow down the subject and shape it into particular ideas, which would be the main theme of the project. Write down specific messages to be delivered including the purpose of the project.

1.65 Screen capture of *"Are You Liar?,"* Facebook pages about false green marketing. *Design: Young-Jun Huh and Chung-Hee Kim.*

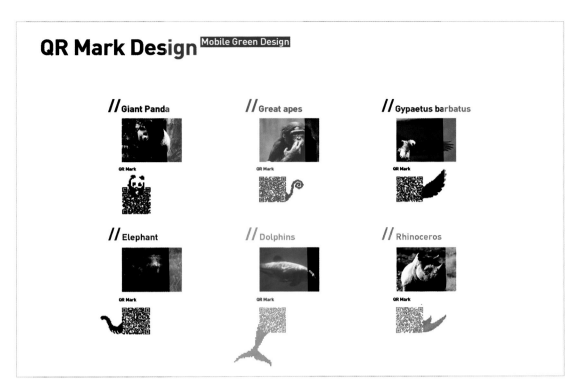

QR Mark Design `Mobile Green Design`

//**Giant Panda**

QR Mark

//**Great apes**

QR Mark

//**Gypaetus barbatus**

QR Mark

//**Elephant**

QR Mark

//Dolphins

QR Mark

//Rhinoceros

QR Mark

1.66 "What Are You Wearing?" QR code series about endangered animals. *Design: Jun-Ho Kim.*

Step 2: Design Planning Make design decisions on various items, such as visual scheme, form (size/media), target audience, and presentation methods.

Step 3: Design Execution Make thumbnail drawings for a layout, a logo, or a visual storyline. If more information is needed, additional research may be initiated.

Step 4: Documentation and Presentation Find the best way to present your design. If it was created outside of the classroom environment, document the installation.

Three design outcomes, a SNS site (social networking site), QR code series, and a stop-motion movie, were the most interesting of the student design solutions in the group. "Are You Liar?" was a SNS site, which provided a platform to share and to discuss various aspects of environmental ads. A team of two students reviewed environmentally themed advertising discovering many false or untruthful "green" ads. To reveal the lies hidden in

green advertising and marketing to the public, they created a Facebook page where they could manage the content and lead discussions about the nature of green marketing.

A series of QR code designs called "What Are You Wearing?" mediated between actual animal products and the environmental truth behind the creation of the products. The student designed QR codes to visually reflect endangered species used in the creation of fashion goods. He secretly placed the QR codes next to animal by-products in actual stores, with the intention of creating awareness for customers who wanted more information about the products. Each QR code would direct the viewer to a site about the particular endangered species for more information.

A stop-motion movie, "Reasons to Eat Less Meat," was created to reveal the environmental impact caused by meat-eating habits. To reach as many people as possible, the movie would be uploaded to YouTube and various design blogs.

피 보는 소비자는 왕따다!

소비자가 만드는 녹색 거짓말 파헤치기
아 유 라이어?

1.67 Screen capture of *"Are You Liar?,"* Facebook pages about false green marketing. *Design: Young-Jun Huh and Chung-Hee Kim.*

"

Sharing their ideas while developing various design solutions motivated student interest in environmental awareness design."

———

audiences were never fully completed. The Facebook page, "Are You Liar?" was not actively managed although it was a perfect platform to lead and create discussions with various audiences. In order to reach out to audiences more actively and effectively, extra guidance and encouragement should have been offered during and after each project's completion.

ASSESSMENT This project would be more successful if it was placed in the third year of study, when students can fully focus on the project demands. Since this project involves learning new design thinking and processing, third-year students with basic design knowledge would make a good fit to undertake such a project. Despite the students' low level of design completion, this project broadened their perspective on design practice that was previously limited only to commercial contexts. Students gained confidence and each student developed a sense of responsibility through the undertaking of a non-commercial design project.

EFFECTIVENESS Although students greatly enjoyed the first project, "Sustainable—," they were not satisfied with the design outcome. I encouraged some of the students to continue on and create different design solutions based on the same topic from the first project for the second project of the course. More rigorous design project execution was attempted, resulting in several stronger designs. For example, the first series of "Sustainable eating habits," a printed installation, became the basis of a stop-motion movie titled "Reasons to eat less meat."

Moreover, discussions every week helped students to expand on their point of view about design. Sharing their ideas while developing various design solutions motivated student interest in environmental awareness design. Students created many design ideas, which influenced actual design outcomes.

Despite interesting design ideas, many designs did not achieve a high level of completion. In particular, documenting installations and communicating with

FINDING YOUR WAY:
WAYFINDING AND ORIENTATION CONCEPTS FOR DE GROTE BEEK, EINDHOVEN

Catelijne van Middelkoop, Program Head/Coordinator, Department of Man and Communication, Design Academy Eindhoven (DAE), Netherlands

1.68 Disguised as a game whose objective is to take good care of a personalized pet, the app encourages individual clients to exercise while exploring different locations on the premises. *Illustrations and development: Jelmer den Adel and Willem van Amerom.*

CLIENT
Geestelijke Gezondheidszorg Eindhoven en De Kempen (GGzE), a mental healthcare organization located in Eindhoven, Netherlands.

PROJECT TITLE
Finding Your Way.

DURATION
The project was originally scheduled to take place during the first semester of the academic year 2012–13 but was prolonged to reach a larger audience during the yearly Design Academy Eindhoven Graduation Show held in October 2013 that attracted 30,000 visitors.

BUDGET
The GGzE is one of the "Friends" of DAE. Friends are commercial and non-commercial companies and organizations that, during a 3-year partnership with the academy, contribute to design education by enabling and supporting various practical research projects. The starting point of each research project is a mutual agreement between the organization/company and DAE that guarantees the collaboration will be mutually profitable and that it will provide both parties with added value. Friends of DAE, depending on the kind of organization, either pay in

money or in knowledge and means for the work that the students do.
Additional support for the project was granted by the City of Eindhoven as part of a local innovation program. One of the requirements was that the project would move beyond mere conceptual thinking and into actual implementation. A second requirement was that the outcome had to be innovative wayfinding that would reach far beyond traditional graphic design solutions.

TEAM
Project supervisor/critic: Catelijne van Middelkoop. *DAE relation manager on educational projects:* Tessa Blokland. Ad van Oostrum, Roelof Kleppe, and Janneke van Kessel, staff members of the GGzE who acted as external advisors. *Students:* 18 third-year undergraduate students from the Department of Man and Communication: Jelmer den Adel, Willem van Amerom, Mathilde Bindervoet, Ruben van den Bossche, Laura Cornet, Marit van den Gevel, Katja van Heugten, Rosa van Heusden, Alfiana Matulessy, Nick Meehan, Gosia Pawlak, Lenka Praxova, Saar Scheerlings, Maartje Slijpen, Paul Stümpel, Karlin Tuinte, Hannah Vischer, and Myra Wippler.

DESCRIPTION Geestelijke Gezondheidszorg Eindhoven en De Kempen (GGzE) is a mental healthcare organization in Eindhoven, the fifth largest city in the Netherlands. Although the GGzE operates from several locations within the city, the core activities and facilities of the organization are located on the premises of De Grote Beek, an estate in the northern part of town. This project sought to serve a diverse group of people, from patients (referred to as "clients") and their caretakers, relatives, and friends, to suppliers and even business-oriented visitors to De Grote Beek. All experienced one urgent design problem that needed to be addressed: the lack of both functionality and consistency in the current wayfinding system of the estate.

Permanent and non-permanent visitors of De Grote Beek often get confused about where they are and where they need to go, both literally and figuratively speaking. Throughout the years, buildings at the estate have come and gone, due to budget cuts as well as changing treatments and needs of the inhabitants. As a result, the area is now characterized by various approaches to functional architecture, housing plans, and recreational areas, connected only by a few simple signs pointing pedestrians to footpaths and visitor parking spaces. These professional signs navigate people in the right direction, but the additional well-meaning and more humanistic attempts by amateurs have not been as helpful. Therefore, the GGzE invited students from DAE to conceive of innovative new ideas to improve the current wayfinding system.

RESEARCH The research question was addressed across multiple scales. Most students first tried to tackle the design problem on a personal level by conducting interviews and researching how clients with individual needs located and accessed areas that were important to their personal care. After talking to clients and employees of De Grote Beek, and extensive visits to scope out human behavior on the premises, many students realized that, because different (mental) diseases demand different approaches, a number of related and smaller issues needed to be dealt with first before an effective overall solution could be found.

At a larger scale, several students researched the large variety of buildings on the premises and discovered that an architectural structure from, for example, the 1970s, would ask for different interior wayfinding than a building from the beginning of the last century, or one from just a few years ago. Zooming out even further, other students who focused on the entire complex tried to group exteriors of buildings that related to each other based on their function, and discovered even more design problems to address.

When some also took on the challenge of looking into possible ways to connect the premises of De Grote Beek to the world outside of this fenced community—for example, to the special GGzE ward in the local hospital or the various housing projects for clients that are spread throughout the city—a completely new and equally important issue became clear: the stigma attached to mental illness and its power to obstruct the way to acceptance and tolerance.

CHALLENGES As the project unfolded the primary challenge for the students and the rest of the team was to stay open-minded and flexible. What started as a seemingly "simple" design problem turned out to be a multi-layered investigation into stigmatism, bureaucratic decision making, and utopian thinking. Because of this, the scope of the project became much broader, more diverse and also more critical than anticipated. Aware that the project was required to move beyond mere conceptual thinking and into actual implementation, the students had to step up their game when it came to convincing the client of the urgency of exploring different directions.

Het wegdek is de weg kwijt

De route met voetstappen geeft het al aan; op Landgoed De Grote Beek komt het nogal eens voor dat er overal voetpaden lopen, behalve in de gewenste richting. Er is geen duidelijk systeem in wegen en paden te herkennen. Sommige wegen lijken alleen voor auto's bedoeld te zijn en ergens anders gaat het voetpad ineens over in een fietspad. Bij één van de drie hoofdingangen kun je zelfs niet via de stoep het terrein op komen en dat is eigenlijk best gevaarlijk.

8   Het wegdek als gids

9

Tot ziens!

Wanneer je het terrein verlaat, kijk je tegen allemaal lege borden aan. Deze ruimte zou benut kunnen worden voor het vermelden van de uitgang: Viredoord, Boschdijk, Anthony Fokkerweg of een andere boodschap.

68   Officiële bewegwijzering GGzE

69

1.69 Marit van der Gevel started out with a thorough assessment of the signage at De Grote Beek. Putting a confronting finger on some imperfections of the current system, her 144-page book became an important tool in the discussions that followed the assessment of the project. *Design and photographs: Marit van der Gevel.*

❝

Both students as well as the client discovered that even within a seemingly restricted brief, there is always room to make a project resonate on a different and unexpected level, sometimes reaching a whole new audience."

———

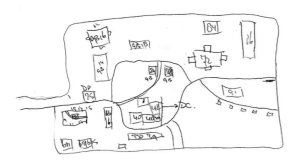

1.70–1.71 and **1.72** (opposite) As part of their initial research, students Nick Meehan and Paul Stümpel asked several people at De Grote Beek, from staff members to former clients, to draw a map of the estate. The various results were an early indication that a cookie cutter solution for the wayfinding problem would most likely not address all the needs of the local community. *Drawings: anonymous.*

Not only did this approach result in one of the students openly questioning and rewriting the original brief, the research of another student who attended church with the inhabitants of De Grote Beek for 10 weeks in a row led to her acceptance into, and better understanding of, the local community. A third student tested the boundaries of the original brief even more actively. After convincing a local housing organization to let her use an empty "normal" home elsewhere in the city of Eindhoven for a drawing experiment with locals, she took on the bigger challenge of orchestrating the same experiment simultaneously with clients of De Grote Beek and visitors of DAE's annual Graduation Show. Participants at both locations were invited to add a "crazy" touch to prints of ordinary, "normal" homes. Documented via a live feed, this attempt to visually define what is crazy and what is normal proved a challenging, extraordinary undertaking. By embracing, rather than trying to limit, all these different perspectives that the students gained during the process, the overall result and underlying message of the project became much more meaningful.

STRATEGY Instead of starting the project with the brief, the project began with a tour of De Grote Beek. The students were asked to meet at a set time and address, which happened to be at the main gate of the estate. During the tour there was no deliberate mention of the existing wayfinding issues, and the students were not told beforehand "who was who"— client or staff member, visitor, or permanent resident. This "cold read" of De Grote Beek was followed by an introduction about the history of the institution and the structure of the organization, and a lecture about different mental illnesses and treatments throughout time. The official brief followed one week later, after which the students were invited to revisit the premises for a "second opinion."

EFFECTIVENESS This strategic and open-minded introduction resulted in an enormous variety of media output. Initial fear and prejudices were overcome at an early stage and the students realized their importance as well as pioneering role in addressing the client's original needs. From nuanced spins on traditional signage to the organization of workshops, creation of awareness campaigns, educational tools,

and even an exercise app, the students interpreted the brief in such a way that they were able to tackle many issues that related to the wayfinding problem of the GGzE. Both students, as well as the client, discovered that even within a seemingly restricted brief, there is always room to make a project resonate on a different and unexpected level, sometimes reaching a whole new audience. For the client, this candid take on the brief, and the students' sometimes razor-sharp analysis of the imperfections of the current signage system at the estate, was eye-opening as well as confrontational. Although the GGzE was very pleased with the surprising results, the client was also left with the realization that one simple solution solving the wayfinding issues at De Grote Beek would not be found, not unless other issues were addressed first.

ASSESSMENT Besides a welcome opportunity for the students to work with a large variety of people, the most valuable outcome of the project was the mutual realization, by both client and students, that nothing is ever what it seems, no matter what "norms" we try to live by.

BLUE+YOU:
DESIGNING POLICE

Bernard Canniffe, Chair, Graphic Design, College of Design, Iowa State University, Ames, Iowa

CLIENT
Sarasota Police Department, Sarasota, Florida.

PROJECT TITLE
Sarasota Police Department Branding and Design Strategy, Phase I.

DURATION
16 weeks, spring semester 2014.

BUDGET
None.

TEAM
Instructor: **Bernard J. Canniffe**; nine undergraduate students; Officer **Linda DeNiro**, Sarasota Police Department Liaison.

1.73a Pre-press release photo in SPD lobby. Students (left of poster) Christian Lowell (AD), Tebllo Mosenene (AD), (right of poster) Gabriella Thompson (GD), Anna Jones (GD), Elisabeth Kerr (GD), Genesis Silva (GD), Bernard J. Canniffe (Chair), Carly Lohr (GD), Nazanin Varasteh (BOAD).

1.73b YOU+BLUE SPD/community brand identifier.

DESCRIPTION Early in 2014, the Sarasota Police Department (SPD) approached Ringling College of Art and Design (RCOAD) with the idea that design students would assist them in the development of a new website and a new identity.

The class met both inside SPD and also in a classroom on the college campus. Officer Linda DeNiro, our SPD liaison, arranged for a designated space inside the SPD building and every week the students would tour different areas of the police department as well as hear presentations by police officers. Some of the presentations were from the K-9 Unit, the Bomb Disposal Unit, and SWAT, in addition to individual presentations from senior and junior police officers and community leaders. We utilized the SPD classroom to present our creative strategies to the police officers, and the academic classroom as the space where the students developed their creative strategies, and as a presentation space to show these ideas to other design faculty and students.

RESEARCH My research is partly produced through the creation of "mind maps", I create these for every project I undertake and every community design course I lead. I also take notes at every meeting and every class. These mind maps give evidence of the visual experience and the evolution of the project, and are important tools to allow the students to understand the complicated processes they are going through. They also assist me in developing an historical record of the project.

The course was divided into four research phases. It is important to note that we included SPD and the community in every phase:

- Students completed a series of exercises that focused on using design to engage with communities.
- Students conducted research on socioeconomic, demographic, and cultural statistics about Sarasota. They also researched SPD, and other police departments throughout the world.

- Students interviewed people in the community. The questions were intended not to confront or direct, but to ascertain what community members thought about SPD, and what they would like to see improved.
- Students developed multiple creative strategies that were refined into a single strategy that was then implemented.

CHALLENGES These projects are not for the faint-hearted. You have to be part community leader, part design strategist, part design activist as well as instructing both students and client about a new way to understand and interpret design. Another challenge is that these projects are applied, and there is a risk that those in the educational institution will not understand how they relate to the institutional understanding of design education.

A major challenge to overcome was that SPD expected very specific deliverables, and these expectations reinforced their understanding of design as a service provider. I asked Linda DeNiro in our initial meeting why SPD needed a new website and identity. She explained that there was a need to reengage with the local community, and to have the community understand that the police officers were a part of their community; it was imperative that both constituents be able work together with mutual respect. SPD had a new Chief of Police who was both a charismatic leader and a visionary. I explained to Linda that the students would not necessarily produce a website or identity, but would help SPD on creative strategies to engage with the community and that a website and identity might be part of this creative strategy. The reasons for asking the client to think broadly were twofold:

- to move the client away from understanding the role of the designer as a service provider
- to present the idea to the students and the institution that design can engage strategically and not superficially.

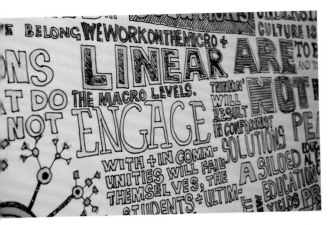

1.74 Mind.ed map: Historical and inspirational visualization of SPD and RCAD course. *Map and photo: Bernard J. Canniffe.*

Another challenge was selecting the student team. Because the project's success depended on highly motivated students who could offer a variety of skills, it was decided that students should go through a selection process. I selected nine students for the SPD project. The group was comprised of one business student, five graphic design students, two advertising design students, and one digital film student. Within the graphic design student mix, I selected students who had web, branding, and community engagement expertise. I chose the advertising students who had campaign and copywriting expertise, and the business student because of her business and entrepreneurship expertise. The digital film student was selected to document the course experience, as well as look for creative avenues to engage with the community.

STRATEGY The most effective way to engage with community projects is to embed yourself, and the most effective way to change behavior is to listen to everyone's needs and aspirations. It is in the listening that the solution will reveal itself to the designer. Our creative strategy was to bring the community and SPD together through a free movie series, and the movies would be projected on the exterior walls of the SPD building. The movies series would bring the community to the police building and the venue would provide significant touch points to engage and interact. These interactions would allow the police to present a face of SPD to the community that was human, welcoming, and not authoritative. The community would be able to come to, and understand, SPD as a place of mutual respect.

This coming together was also represented in a typographic representation entitled BLUE+YOU. BLUE+YOU is a simple and malleable logotype—it portrays SPD as empowering the community as well as reflecting the need for social change. Each is linked to the other by the "+" symbol that connects and empowers both communities as equal partners for positive change. The flexibility of the mark is based on typographic hierarchy. The community is represented by YOU and is empowered to engage with SPD. SPD is represented by BLUE. BLUE *serves* YOU, BLUE *feeds* YOU, YOU *welcome* BLUE, and YOU *help* BLUE— YOU+BLUE. BLUE+YOU was used on all promotional vehicles as well as on the new website.

Website The original SPD website was visually awkward and full of information clutter. It was difficult to navigate and the most important information was hard to find. There were crime statistics on the home page, for instance, and although most of this information was relevant and needed, it was of little interest to the community.

The students presented a SWOT analysis of the current website and this presentation included snapshots from the existing website as well as a hierarchical map that demonstrated the ineffective navigation and information clutter.

The new website embraced and supported BLUE+YOU, both aesthetically and intellectually. Its visuality was improved by employing a clean typographic approach coupled with a simplified navigational system. Community information was placed front and center with optimistic police and community stories reinforced with photographs. The website embraced the SPD and the Sarasota communities working together; it can be viewed at: www.sarasotapd.org.

1.75 SPD movie night promotional community poster.

1.76 Student interviews by local Sarasota News team. Left to right: Elisabeth Kerr (GD), Genesis Silva (GD), Gabriella Thompson (GD). *Photo: Bernard J. Canniffe.*

"

The most effective way to engage with community projects is to embed yourself, and the most effective way to change behavior is to listen to everyone's needs and aspirations. It is in the listening that the solution will reveal itself to the designer."

———

EFFECTIVENESS SPD held a press release to announce the launch of BLUE+YOU, the new website, and free movie night. Every local TV news affiliate, as well as many of the local newspaper reporters, attended this event. It is important to note that the media would help promote the upcoming movie night. The Chief welcomed, and personally thanked, each at the start of movie night. It was both a rewarding and a humbling experience to hear the SPD Chief speak so enthusiastically about our students, as well as endorsing their design strategy.

Each student wore a BLUE+YOU tee shirt, and the police handed out free popcorn, water, and soda as well as giving BLUE+YOU T-shirts. We had placed blue stickers on the underneath of some popcorn bags and those people were given a free T-shirt. This was followed by the premiere of the student documentary that featured an interview with the Chief referencing her decision to engage with an art school, and her assessment of the creative journey. The film also featured interviews with police officers, at community events, and ending with the Chief discussing the importance of the BLUE+YOU brand. Finally, the

movie was shown. There were over 150 people (off-duty police officers, their families, and the Sarasota community) who attended the free movie night. The uniformed SPD circulated through the crowd thanking everyone personally for attending.

After the course was ended RCOAD took back the projector from SPD, and decided to develop a checkout policy for the projectors. It is unclear if the movie series would continue without having access to the projectors.

ASSESSMENT The students, SPD, and the Sarasota community all had a transformative experience. They learned how design can engage socially and become a catalyst for positive change, as evidenced in the following two videos: www.youtube.com/watch?v=1528b0Ixh9E and www.youtube.com/watch?v=LpyO6TFpqUE.

COMMUNICATION DESIGN FOR SOCIAL ISSUES

Hyunmee Kim, Associate Professor of Communication Design Department, Samsung Art and Design Institute, Seoul, South Korea

1.77 Anti-fur campaign targeted to fashion design students that went viral through fashion design students' SNS network. The key to the campaign is the design of the fur hat that grabs the viewer's attention and communicates the message. *Design: Moo-sun Kim.*

CLIENT
Korean community and the world.

PROJECT TITLE
Communication Design for Social Issues.

DURATION
5-week project, fall 2013.

BUDGET
None.

TEAM
38 second-year (junior-level) students, working individually or in teams voluntarily.

DESCRIPTION "Communication Design for Social Issues" was a project assigned to junior year students in their Typography 4 course. The project had two goals. One was to allow students and young adults, to be aware of themselves in connection to their own community, to look around with critical eyes, and to understand that it is each individual's responsibility to keep his or her community and environment safe, healthy, and sustainable, and to think about the roles communication designers can play in this respect.

1.78 Anti-fur campaign targeted to fashion design students, this went viral through the fashion design students' SNS network. The key to the campaign is the design of the fur hat that grabs the viewer's attention and communicates the message. *Design: Moo-sun Kim.*

The other goal was to have them experience the strategic design process. They were required to write a design brief early on to plan the stages of their own projects with clear goals in mind. In the larger context of the program curriculum, this project prepares students for the year-long senior project by introducing possible subject matter and giving them a brief experience of strategic design thinking. Students had to identify a social issue worthy of public attention and design a message/media leading to desirable change around the subject matter. Students were given the following definition from the introduction to the book *Graphic Agitation* written by Liz McQuiston*:* "Personal Politics: Individual awareness and concern for world problems and a sense of responsibility to self, friends and family, society and the planet as a whole." Students were tasked with thinking about their responsibility as members of Korean society and as global citizens, as well as their roles as communication designers who use persuasive visual language in the public sector.

Issues presented to the students for consideration were *environmental*—recycling, habits harmful to the environment, the overuse of disposable products, etc.; *political*—human rights issues in North Korea, etc.; *social*—bullying, marginalized children, public education; and *cultural*—cultural heritage worth preserving, etc.

"

Students were tasked with thinking about their responsibility as members of Korean society and as global citizens, as well as their roles as communication designers who use persuasive visual language in the public sector."

RESEARCH Student research included a literature review and the scanning of published literature such as books, articles, theses, and video clips. They also conducted primary research such as interviewing staff members of the organizations in which they were interested, as well as interviewing their target audience. Shadowing of the target audience was also highly recommended.

CHALLENGES Korea has been a nation of people deeply rooted in Confucianism, mostly due to a high level of interest in education. The country has developed dramatically over the last 60 years, from a nation of extreme poverty to one that can help other countries. Such development within a short time span has left residual effects on many levels. Korean society is overflowing with competition and materialism, while volunteering and donating are relatively new activities.

STRATEGY For the five-week project, the "double diamond method" developed by the British Design Council was used as a guide to manage the project. Divided into four distinctive phases—Discovery, Define, Develop, and Deliver—the double diamond method is a simple way of mapping the design process:

Week 1: Discovery Phase Students search for the issues that interest them, do both desk and field research, and share the results at the first meeting.

Week 2: Defining Phase Students define the problems in communication and plan the project, culminating in writing a design brief. Design briefs include the title, general introduction, the problem, the objective of communication, target audience/users, media search and strategy, visual language strategy, schedule and timeframe, etc. Students then make a presentation to the class.

Week 3: Development Phase Students brainstorm communication ideas for solving the defined problem. From the pool of ideas students make several visual prototypes and share them with the class.

Week 4: Delivery Phase Students refine the most effective prototypes, complete them, and share the completed prototypes during the final critique.

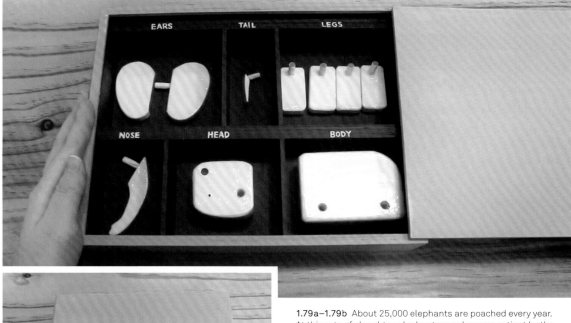

1.79a–1.79b About 25,000 elephants are poached every year. At this rate of slaughter, elephants may become extinct by the year 2025. In order to create awareness of this issue, the student designed an elephant-making wood block play kit for children. *Design: Min-hae Lee.*

EFFECTIVENESS AND ASSESSMENT First, the students were excited that what they learned could have a positive impact on society. The openness of the subject matter added to their enthusiasm, as did the acquired knowledge on a variety of issues. Discussion, and sometimes argument, revealed differing viewpoints on the same issue. Since the project choices were up to the students, they became highly motivated and displayed a willingness to compete for a smarter solution and higher quality in the final prototype. In the course of searching for the right media for each project, everyone, including the instructor, is exposed to the most up-to-date media available for maximum exposure and dissemination of the visual message.

What became evident was that the more primary research that is involved, the more feasible the solution that emerges. Some of the projects that involved the clients' participation turned out practical solutions to their problems. I would emphasize the importance of participatory design and making sure that students do their primary research for the next "Communication Design for Social Issues" project.

1.80a–1.80c Among the 15 leading OECD countries, Korea ranks first in teenage abortion rates, and also scores the lowest in teenage awareness of contraception. Although sex education is being offered in the school curriculum, ideas for other ways of education on safe sex targeted to middle school students is urgently needed. Student Hee-yeon Lee suggested a public service system where condoms can be easily acquired for free by asking at designated stores near the school. She named the service "Life Protector" and used the image of a shield as a visual metaphor for keeping life from unwanted pregnancy. The service is visualized in the touchpoints of a poster, a condom package, and information is accessible by mobile phone through a QR code on the package. The information accessed by mobile phone is designed using illustration and text for students to easily understand. *Design: Hee-yeon Lee.*

WASH CURRICULUM REDESIGN

Ken Visocky-O'Grady, Associate Professor, Graduate Coordinator, School of Visual Communication Design, Kent State University, Kent, Ohio

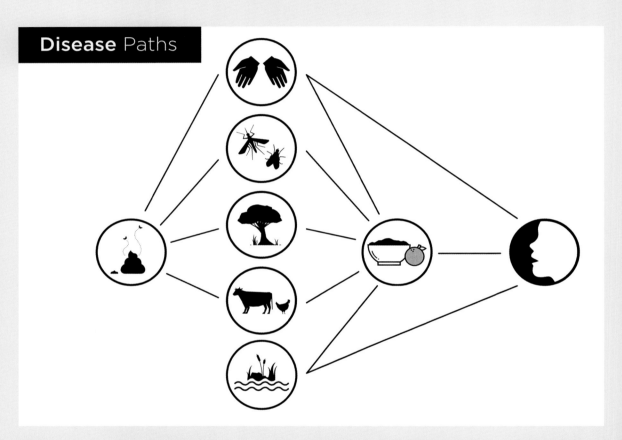

Disease Paths

CLIENT
Lifewater International.

PROJECT TITLE
WASH curriculum redesign.

DURATION
2013–14, with most of the research and initial prototypes being completed in the fall semester of 2013.

BUDGET
None.

TEAM
Instructor: **Ken Visocky-O'Grady.**
Graduate assistant: **Daniel Echeverri.**
Graduate students/Team members: **Basma Almusallam, Larrie King, Bryan Rinnert, Todd Wendorff,** and **Catherine Zedell.**
Project partners: **Justin Ahrens,** Principal of Rule29 + Lifewater International.

1.81 (above) and **1.82a–1.82b** (opposite) Hand washing instructional charts. Supporting images for the WASH curriculum, the most commonly used method for teaching basic sanitation and hygiene in developing nations.

DESCRIPTION In fall of 2013, graduate students at Kent State University's School of Visual Communication Design were tasked with analyzing WASH, the most commonly used curriculum for teaching water safety, sanitation, and basic hygiene around the world. Among rural, impoverished communities and tribal groups, the concept of hand washing is not inherently known or practiced. Aid workers in the field need ways to share concepts of clean water, sanitation, and hygiene, but are up against diseases that spread rapidly in communities with varying degrees of literacy, and which are largely without access to clean drinking water. Our partners for this project were Rule29 and Lifewater International.

Rule29 is a creative strategic firm whose approach is built on collaboration, commitment, and caring. The firm works with companies that value design thinking, that appreciate design's role in providing a competitive advantage, and that embrace teamwork.

Lifewater International is a non-profit organization that helps communities around the world to gain access to safe water, to have effective hygiene practices, and adequate sanitation. They partner with in-country organizations to gain an understanding of specific cultures and the challenges they face.

Lifewater believes that sustainable solutions are made possible through community involvement and empowerment. Lifewater shares the knowledge, skills, and inspiration people need to take responsibility for their water sources and make long-term improvements to community health. From 2011 to 2013, Lifewater has been active in Ghana, Kenya, Laos, Cambodia, Ethiopia, and Uganda.

According to Lifewater International, 1,800 children die every day from preventable water-borne disease. Impoverished communities with little or no consistent access to clean drinking water may not understand how germs and diseases spread, or the value of hygiene. Compounding communication problems related to health and science literacy, each country in which Lifewater operates may use several different languages or dialects, making it difficult to produce culturally appropriate educational material to serve each group.

Our goal for the 16-week semester was to explore improvements to the WASH program through a universal design approach rooted in research and culturally sensitive problem solving. By utilizing simple and universally understood visual solutions to augment the curriculum, the design team felt it was possible to transcend cultural barriers, without requiring much time or effort from WASH program facilitators to learn new systems.

Sad Dirty Hands

Washing Happy Hands

RESEARCH The design team had to understand the context in which the WASH curriculum is taught and the relevant issues facing both WASH facilitators and students. Various research techniques were utilized throughout the course of the project, including:

Content overview Students conducted a comprehensive review of Lifewater's current curriculum and materials, closely assessing the visual elements, to grasp its goals and understand its methods of delivery.

Literature review The team analyzed competing materials and curricula from organizations with a similar mission of promoting hygiene in developing nations to categorize commonalities and discern the intended direction of the messaging. Each system had strengths and weaknesses. The process allowed the design team to recognize the commonalities across the varied programs.

Audience To understand the audience, the team researched the countries and associated communities that Lifewater serves, establishing a standard of shared characteristics. Targeted research on the larger audiences let the team set a baseline of elements present among each group. Through this survey the team was able to identify a segment within the community—specifically children—that would have the greatest potential for long-term behavioral change. The team also made use of secondary information via tools like Flickr and YouTube to gain an understanding of what teaching conditions were like on the ground.

Interviews The team engaged in non-structured interviews with professionals who are close to Lifewater, involved in some form of missionary work, or work in kindergarten–8th grade education.

Role-play To gain a deeper understanding of the curriculum, the design team spent several days acting out the roles of facilitator or student and documenting their experiences. At the close of each session, the design team would discuss what they felt was successful or where they felt there were gaps in the experience, and how to navigate through them with future changes or new tools.

Additional methods To make sense of all of the information that they gathered during the research phase, the design team made use of personas and an experience model, mapping the experience from the user's point of view. These tools allowed the team to aggregate their data and make the information more relatable. The experience model also allowed the team to identify gaps and incongruencies from both the facilitator and student perspective.

The most substantial challenge for the design team was to understand all the factors without having the opportunity to meet face to face with people from the cultures and nations affected."

CHALLENGES The most substantial challenge for the design team was to understand all the factors without having the opportunity to meet face to face with people from the cultures and nations affected. Geographic limitations meant the students also had to rely on secondary sources for research.

It is also important to understand that these types of projects are long-term, and that the solutions developed may only lead to more questions. Overcoming the desire to solve the problem completely is itself a difficult challenge. The design team struggled with the concept of their work only being the beginning of a much longer investigation, one that may be carried out by future generations of visual communication design graduate students.

Tippy Tap Instructions: **V2**

Pierce a hole on top of the jug handle.

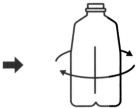

Turn the jug around so that you are facing the opposite side from the handle.

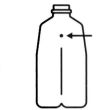

Pierce a hole in the jug on the opposite side of the handle.

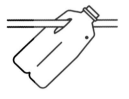

Hang the jug from a stick by the handle.

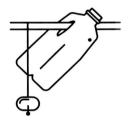

Thread a string through a piece of soap and hang that from the stick.

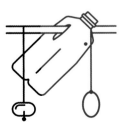

Tie a string around the neck of the bottle and make a loop at the end of the string large enough to slide your wrist through.

Fill the tippy tap with water and pull the loop to begin washing hands.

1.83 Instructions for creating a Tippy Tap. A commonly used method for creating safe hand washing stations out of found materials.

Using Soap and Water - 2

1.84 Hand washing instructional charts. Supporting images for the WASH curriculum, the most commonly used method for teaching basic sanitation and hygiene in developing nations.

STRATEGY After compiling primary and secondary research, the design team boiled down the curriculum to a simplified set of criteria for each lesson of the WASH curriculum. Their "new standard" reassembled the content and eliminated redundancies. In the new suggested plan, content was reduced significantly—from 10 learning blocks to seven and information within each block was trimmed. This was done to maximize content delivery on the part of the facilitator, and the shorter format is better suited to the attention span of the target age group. Previously, lessons could range from 20 to 30 minutes, some even as long as 50 minutes. In the revised curriculum, lessons are only 15 to 20 minutes.

The revised content developed by the team also allows for teaching through three different learning modes, with information suited to kinesthetic, auditory/verbal, and visual learners. Each lesson within the revised block makes use of materials and activities that allow for a blended, multi-sensory approach, reinforcing key information throughout the students' educational experience.

Next, the team created simplified graphic illustrations based on the new curriculum that supported learning outcomes. This more universal approach allows the curriculum to be taught in different regions without having to create customized solutions for each location in which Lifewater operates, obviating the cumbersome and costly creation of new materials.

EFFECTIVENESS Preliminary tests of teaching materials and the associated visuals indicate that a universal approach to supplemental illustrations was better understood by the target audience and helped aid workers overcome cultural barriers. This will enable Lifewater to develop one curriculum rather than customizing teaching materials based on geography, saving time, money, and resources. Dr. Pamela Crane, Director of International Programs, adds: "The culturally neutral drawings are particularly useful to Lifewater. Traditionally, we have tried to make culturally appropriate drawings for each of the contexts that we serve. Kent State's recommendation of culturally neutral drawings reduces a tremendous barrier to expanding into new countries and regions."

ASSESSMENT Lifewater plans to incorporate the visuals that students developed into all of the materials used to train people across a number of cultures, breaking down barriers and allowing the information to impact on numerous and diverse cultural and tribal groups, nations, and dialects. The tools are universal and flexible, making them easy to share, and adaptable for facilitators from any organization working toward the WASH mission.

Before Preparing Food

After Cleaning Latrine

Before Eating

1.85 All images on page: Food preparation teaching visual support.

SECTION 3

DESIGN AUTHORSHIP

EMBRACING THE NOTION OF DESIGN AUTHORSHIP AND ENTREPRENEURSHIP

Steven McCarthy

Design authorship is several things. It is the confluence of designing, writing, image-making, editing, and self-publishing. It is the paradigm shift from neutral professional service provision to engaged involvement with message content. It is the proactive initiation of content, of messages, of slogans, of products, of services, and of experiences. It is the expansion of design from a trade to a discipline with social, cultural, political, and economic importance.

The notion of designers as authors, producers, and entrepreneurs has roots in technological advances over the past few decades, but at the heart of the concept is a philosophical sea-change. Designers, through their creativity, imaginations, problem-solving abilities, tools of empathy, facility with materials, and so on, desire a more influential role in life. They want to move beyond being the "hired hands" of business to having more freedom and impact.

When A. J. Liebling said in the *New Yorker* in 1960 that "freedom of the press is guaranteed only to those who own one," presses were large, heavy, relatively expensive machines requiring specialized expertise to operate (most commercial offset presses still are). Freedom of speech was tethered to notions of ownership, access, distribution, and influence.

In the new millennium, "press"—and by extension "publishing"—might be defined as a decentralized, ubiquitous, limitless activity that happens globally, instantly, effortlessly, and relatively inexpensively. Computers and desktop printers; mobile devices and Instagram, Twitter, and Facebook; Vandercook letterpresses, metal and wood type, and paper; screen printing on fabric and other substrates; Lulu, Blurb, Moo, and other digital, on-demand services; photocopiers and the Risograph; manual and electric typewriters; cameras and projection devices—the list of enabling technologies goes on and on.

Students of graphic design and visual communication own, or have access to, many of these tools of production. Besides the daunting choices about which medium might be the most appropriate, the most efficient, the most cost-effective, the most novel, the quickest, the most environmentally sustainable, reach the most people, the deeper issue is this: *What will the content of the message be?* because content + form = message, which has meaning to viewers, readers, consumers, or users.

Sometimes the message will be "Things go better with Coke" or "Yes we can" or "Think different." As eventual professional designers, students will have ample opportunity to give visual form to the advertising, branding, and packaging rhetoric of various companies, organizations, and institutions. Done well, done ethically, this can be honorable work.

But an education in design should not merely be a dress rehearsal for the status quo. Sure, students should develop competencies that make them employable, but they should also model intellectual and creative terrains that anticipate the future's vast unknown. It is incumbent upon design faculty to pose open-ended challenges of social, cultural, and political import (and not just *business* as usual), giving students latitude to develop their own voices.

There are a number of ways that this can happen. Writing and research—on many topics, not just design—can be rendered typographically or visually and then printed. Criticism and commentary—besides being written—can be visual, curatorial, or object-oriented. Entrepreneurial ventures offer students a chance to trade on their ideas and labor. Interdisciplinary collaborative interactions combine design with other knowledge domains. Faculty can create "safe places" for students to explore issues of identity, therapy, and self-expression as valid vehicles for personal communication.

Many of these qualities show up in *The Electric Information Age Book.* In it, Adam Michaels asserts that "intertwined content and form can be activated through widespread distribution as a means of creating profound connections with readers." Although he was referring to the seminal books created by Marshall McLuhan, Jerome Agel, and Quentin Fiore, this sentiment expresses how designers (as authors, as producers, as editors, as entrepreneurs) can harness media—both digital and analog—to get their messages published.

Unlike the privilege of press ownership referred to in the *New Yorker* quote, contemporary media can be borrowed, shared, traded, sourced, networked, hacked, reinvented, recycled, and jury-rigged. Today's emerging designers will as likely *make* a press (meaning both a machine for printing and a publishing house) as own one.

Freedom—of the press, speech, and other expressions—is contextualized, is not naturally guaranteed, and does not exist in a vacuum. Freedom to communicate comes with responsibility, which casts the designer as having an ethical obligation. Authorship willingly assumes this role, as designers' subjective involvement with content makes it harder to distance "what it says" and "to whom" from "how it looks." The attribution inherent in design authorship means that designers are shorn of anonymity—good works are applauded, dirty deeds attract blame.

Design authorship takes on many forms in today's networked media landscape. It can be individual or collaborative, synchronous or asynchronous, limited or public, philanthropic or entrepreneurial, activist or centrist—designers are free to determine how to use their voices.

Steven McCarthy (MFA, Stanford University) is a professor of graphic design at the University of Minnesota. His long-standing interest in theories of design authorship—as both scholar and practitioner— has led to lectures, exhibits, publications, and grant-funded research in a dozen countries. His book on the topic of design authorship, The Designer As ... Author, Producer, Activist, Entrepreneur, Curator and Collaborator: New Models for Communicating *was published in 2013 by BIS Publishers, Amsterdam, NL.*

"

It is incumbent upon design faculty to pose open-ended challenges of social, cultural, and political import (and not just business as usual), giving students latitude to develop their own voices."

———

FIVE QUESTIONS TO
JUHAN SONIN

1. Who or what influences informed you as you prepared for a career in design?

I was indoctrinated from birth. My mother was a Julliard/Manhattan School of Music-trained musician and my father was a PhD in Math and Aero Engineering and 40-year graduate department head at MIT. From grade school through university, I chewed on wildly different disciplines like architectural drawing; playing the violin; designing, building, flying, and crashing hundreds of model airplanes; and the fundamentals of mechanical engineering and film. Diversity was normal; it was an orgy of art and science. It continues through my life with classically trained mentors and colleagues with PhDs ranging from Biology to Signal Processing and yet who are hypersensitive to aesthetics and design.

2. Designers have a social and ethical responsibility to create and transmit meaningful forms of communication that benefit society and culture. Do you agree or disagree with this statement? Why?

Hell yes, I agree with it! Every citizen has an ethical responsibility to do good. In fact, the responsibility of citizenry should go farther, seeing that as United Statesians, we're only obligated to pay rather low taxes and rarely fulfill jury duty. There should be mandatory social service for the young. And every decade thereafter, for life, we give a year of public service. This is about everyone, not just designers. We have a Code of Ethics at our studio [Involution Studios] that captures this service-based ethos. Our studio citizens should expect a lot, but they should also be prepared to give a lot. From this comes a healthy, productive culture. Designers hold a special power because we are often the communication gateway for people and the world: we are shaping the things people see, use, read, and live with.

3. Health Axioms, a deck of cards to change people's health habits, is a project of your Involution Studios. Can you talk about your motivation to create the Health Axioms Card Deck and why it is important to do this type of work?

Our studio is driven by a mission to create better lives and a better world. We're part of a global movement to shift the healthcare system to one of non-invasive personal diagnostics, with highly specialized clinicians that work closely with patients and their families, encouraging self-monitoring, and self-empowered patients. Getting there is equal parts good technology, healthcare reform, and good design. We're here to help with the last part of that equation while evangelizing for the evolution of the entire system to better serve patients.

1.86 Health Axiom cards were created by Juhan Sonin and Harry Sleeper, illustrated by Sarah Kaiser, and edited by Jane Kokernak. *Photo: Juhan Sonin.*

1.87 Card front, "Vaccinate Your Child."

1.88 Card front, "Move More."

The Health Axioms help us get in touch with our bodies and have a better grasp of how we work. Most of us are in denial about our health. And as long as we're feeling okay, we think we're okay. Then health happens, usually when we least want or expect it. By broaching healthier habits, like eating more green food, moving more, and understanding that food is medicine, we stand a chance of fighting disease before we feel a hint of the condition. Designing a real service for nurses, doctors, and patients, used in a real clinical setting, is a potent vector in understanding and having impact on the healthcare system.

4. New roles are emerging for design professionals as their function is increasingly changing from that of generators to facilitators of ideas. Can you comment on this?
We still believe in the old school, that of idea generation. And, as generators, it is about being more multidisciplinary, about better synthesizing of art, science, and engineering. We see the trend to facilitation, but we don't think it is what will create the great systems, products, and services of the future. The Design Axioms (www.designaxioms.com) is our maker philosophy in a box, where we insist that designers know the fundamentals of engineering, write code, and prototype like crazy. Great creation, in this world of complex emerging technologies, requires not facilitation but strong vision underpinned by a remarkable breadth and depth of knowledge and understanding.

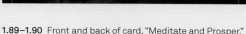

1.89–1.90 Front and back of card, "Meditate and Prosper."

5. What advice would you give a student studying visual communication today to help them prepare for contemporary professional practice?

Don't stop with communication theory. That's just a beginning. There are new insights in psychology, and in neuroscience, that get right to the heart of what visual communication is supposed to be doing. If you really want to be a spectacular visual communicator you must complement your training and knowledge in traditional art and design with science. It is the direction in which design is headed and, if you want to keep up and stay viable, it's where you need to go. Take pride in your artist vibe and be confident enough in yourself to put the science arrows in your quiver. You will kill it today, and be steps ahead for tomorrow.

Juhan Sonin is the Creative Director of Involution Studios (www.goinvo.com) and has produced work recognized by the New York Times, Newsweek, *BBC International,* Billboard *magazine, and National Public Radio (NPR). He has spent time at Apple, the National Center for Supercomputing Applications (NCSA), and MITRE. Juhan lectures on design and engineering at the Massachusetts Institute of Technology (MIT).*

FOOD FOR GOOD:
SELF-INITIATED PROJECT

Siân Cook, Year 3 Coordinator, Graphic & Media
Design BA (Hons), Faculty of Design, London
College of Communication, London, UK

CLIENT
Homeless charities like
the Salvation Army, the
American Church, etc.

PROJECT TITLE
Food for Good:
Self-initiated project.

DURATION
Preparatory research carried
out during the previous year.
Main focus on the project was
in 2012 for 12 weeks. The
project continues to evolve
and is ongoing.

BUDGET
£2,000 grant from UnLtd (an
organization that supports
social entrepreneurs in the UK)
to fund the pilot scheme. A further
£5,000 grant from the University
of Arts London SEED Fund
was awarded to develop the
project post-degree.

TEAM
Tutors: **Siân Cook, Monica
Biagioli,** and **Sarah Temple,**
Faculty of Design, London
College of Communication.
Student team: **Chiara
Astuti, Anna Cennamo,**
and **Martina Giulianelli.**
Key collaborators: Carluccio's
restaurants, Planet Organic,
"Feeding the 5000".

1.91 Screen-printed tote bag. *Photo: Anna Cennamo, Food for Good.*

DESCRIPTION We live in a world where the demand for a high standard of food generates a large volume of surplus and waste. At the same time, an increasing number of people in our society are experiencing food poverty. Food for Good aims to eradicate food waste and make a positive impact on the environment, simply by turning waste into value.

The project began through personal experience—witnessing how much surplus food was thrown away at the end of every day at just one bakery. In order to try to tackle the twin issues of food wastage and food poverty with a "real world" applied outcome, three students negotiated working collaboratively as part of their final year degree studies. Collectively, they looked at the core problem of how to redistribute unwanted food from restaurants and shops to people who could make good use of it.

While working on their Graphic and Media Design BA, students are encouraged to use their own observations and experiences as a starting point for identifying design problems to solve. The course also has a strong ethical philosophy that is reflected in the ways that students often choose to approach self-initiated work. When relevant, students whose projects have potential are supported in applying for funding and external support. This helps them develop entrepreneurial skills, fosters a sense of ambition for the work, and encourages the application of visual communication skills to the presentation of ideas in a professional context.

RESEARCH Initial research was conducted into the reasons behind food surplus and the impact this has on the environment, as well as the societal need for resource redistribution. Statistics and evidence were gathered to help make a strong case for a social entrepreneurial project to tackle these issues. The student team attended the Internazionale Festival in Ferrara (Italy) where they met food waste expert Tristram Stuart—prize-winning author of *Waste: Uncovering the Global Food Scandal* and founder of "Feeding the 5000"—who encouraged their endeavors and has remained a supporter of the project.

First ideas included looking at developing a web platform to facilitate food redistribution. This led to making contact with Plan Zheroes, an organization that had a similar online scheme. Connecting businesses and charities was already possible via their website, but there was a need to find ways to actually transport waste food between donors and recipients. Transport therefore became the focus of the project pilot scheme.

A number of experts and organizations were consulted at various stages throughout the project, helping to shape and guide the students' ideas as they evolved (the diagram on page 117 shows the extent of this network). Key case studies and interviewees were Fare Share, the People's Supermarket, Love Food Hate Waste, the Sustainable Restaurant Association, Pret a Manger (sandwich redistribution scheme), and Thames Reach (a homeless charity).

An important aspect of the research was attending and participating in conferences and events. Through networking and meeting with relevant organizations and activists, the team was inspired but also alerted to potential problems, which helped to build a more credible project plan. Food for Good attended a conference hosted by the World Food Programme, where they participated in workshops looking at global food issues. They were then invited by "This Is Rubbish" (a community interest company) to present at the "Forum & Feast Conference" at the Centre for Alternative Technology, Wales, where they talked about food wastage solutions. Throughout the research process, the students were constantly presenting, refining, and re-presenting their concept.

1.92 Range of products and promotional items.
Photo: Anna Cennamo, Food for Good.

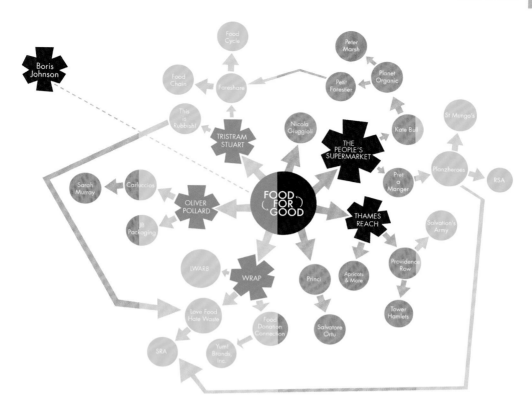

1.93 Map of project research and contact network. *Design: Food for Good team.*

CHALLENGES The biggest challenge for the pilot project was learning how to organize the logistics of food redistribution. The team had to consider timing (transportation had to occur at night after close of business), food storage, compliance with hygiene and food safety guidelines, and creating liaisons between businesses and charities.

While the 2-week pilot was successful, it also demonstrated that it would be a massive undertaking to continue on a long-term basis or to scale up the operation without a large number of regular volunteers and funding support. They would also have to consider different types of food in relation to charities' needs, alternative storage methods, and a more sustainable means of transportation.

As the project developed, the team benefited from the free legal advice that came with their successful funding bids. This helped them write service agreements and learn about intellectual property. Because of all these challenges, the creators of Food for Good realized that their role as social entrepreneurs could allow for projects to change, and that a more flexible overarching ethos encompassing a number of different strands might be a model for the future.

1.94 The Food for Good team: Chiara Astuti, Anna Cennamo, and Martina Giulianelli.

STRATEGY The first stage was putting together a definitive proposal and presentation in order to apply for project funding. Once this was successful, it was possible to devise a pilot scheme, in collaboration with the Salvation Army, to test how to redistribute food from restaurants and small supermarkets effectively. A refrigerated van was hired for 2 weeks and used to collect and transport surplus food overnight from two Carluccio's restaurants and two Planet Organic shops to Booth House and the American Church, where the food could be incorporated into the next day's lunch menu, serving homeless people in Whitechapel and central London.

At the same time, the students were keen to keep raising awareness about the wider issues and generate additional funding for the continuation of the project. The brand "Food for Good" was adopted and applied across a number of designed formats including flyers, a website, and badges. Posters and tote bags were screen-printed in the college workshops and sold at every opportunity.

To involve audiences further in the debate and challenge preconceptions about "recycled" food, ingredients donated by Plant Organic were used to create meals served to students during the college "Green Week" 2012. This method was also employed as a contribution to the "Feeding the 5000" lunch event in Trafalgar Square, part of a global campaign aiming to empower others and inspire positive solutions to the issue of food waste.

Since graduating, the students have continued to collaborate as Food for Good and search for further innovative and sustainable solutions to minimize food waste. This includes setting up a bespoke ethical catering service for which a range of serving accessories, made from off-cuts and recycled materials, were designed and made. The college hired this catering service for "Green Week" 2014, to serve 1,000 canapés and drinks to exhibition attendees. The catering aspect has been developed as an ongoing collaboration with chef Arthur Potts-Dawson, founder of the People's Supermarket and the Water House, the first sustainable restaurant in London. This was a useful contact because of his involvement in the area of food waste and interest in exchanging his cooking competence for the team's design and communication skills.

EFFECTIVENESS In an average night of the pilot scheme, 40 kg of food was saved and distributed. During the 2 weeks, 500 kg of food was repurposed in total. To celebrate the project's success and thank collaborators for their support and raise further funds, Food for Good hosted an evening at the college described as "A New Dining Experience." In collaboration with catering professionals, a dinner for 100 people was created from surplus food. Tristram Stuart attended and made a speech in which he expressed his support and admiration for the project team.

The project was shortlisted for the Student Enterprise and Employability Creative Enterprise Awards, selected to present at Pulse London, a showcase event for new products, trends, and insights, and has continued to attract media interest.

1.95 Screen-printed posters. *Photo: Anna Cennamo, Food for Good.*

"

Since graduating, the students have continued to collaborate as Food for Good and search for further innovative and sustainable solutions to minimize food waste."

———

ASSESSMENT This case study is unusual in that it quickly developed from a theoretical proposal into a practical service design that required a wide range of skills. What the students achieved was to independently source expertise, involve others with their infectious enthusiasm, and provide a good example of how to realize an ambitious undertaking. It illustrates positive reasons for students to work collaboratively, both with each other and externally. The college provided a "safe" environment for trialing the project while supporting the transition into outside work. Elements could "fail" because the reflective learning experience was always a priority above the project impact.

PACKAGED PETS

Maria Mordvintseva

CLIENT
Animal shelters in
Moscow, Russia.

PROJECT TITLE
Game-changing idea for
any social cause in Russia.
When I submitted my concept
for the School of Thoughts
program, I titled it *Packaged
Animals*, but afterwards I
changed the name to
Packaged Pets.

DURATION
3 weeks in 2012 (presentation
board for the concept) while
studying at School of Thoughts,
and 2 months in 2013 (more
detailed packaging design,
comps and visuals).

BUDGET
None.

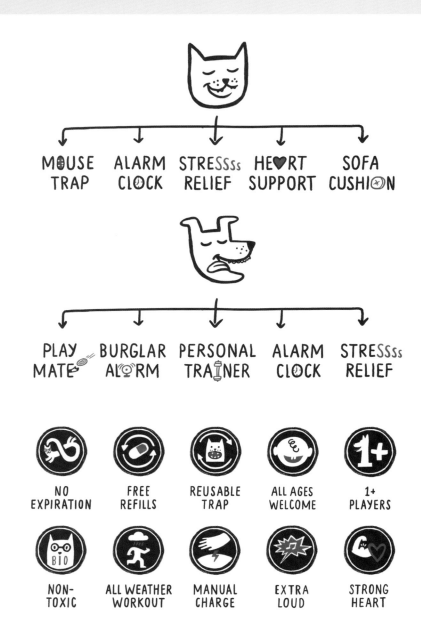

1.96 Icons developed to be used through the conceptual package design series. *Design: Maria Mordvintseva.*

DESCRIPTION The objective of the brief was to come up with a completely new idea to solve a social issue relevant in Russia. I decided to address the problem of overpopulated animal shelters to find a solution that would encourage more people to adopt pets instead of buying them from pet stores.

RESEARCH My research was based primarily on Russian animal shelter web pages and Facebook groups that search for people to adopt abandoned and stray pets. While shelters here have many feral animals that require special training before they can be adopted, they also house animals that were either lost or abandoned by their owners—around 30 percent of animals at the shelters are purebred animals given up by their owners. Not all the shelters are decent. Some are so dirty and overcrowded that the animals become aggressive and antisocial. Some animal lovers will foster animals from the worst shelters, and keep them at their own apartments until they are adopted. Unfortunately, most people in Russia have a very biased image of shelters due to the lack of information on the subject. The widely held belief is that the animals in shelters are wild, antisocial, and sick. People are therefore more likely buy a pet from a breeder than to adopt one from a shelter.

CHALLENGES Given that most Russian people have such a biased opinion of animal shelters, the main challenge was to create a solution to change that perspective by introducing potential adopters to individual pets housed in shelters. I also wanted my solution to inspire people who had never thought of owning a pet to seriously consider adopting one.

People will often ignore the issue of animal overpopulation in shelters because it is such a depressing subject, and because most advertising addressing the issue highlights the negative aspects. Therefore, one of the challenges was to also come up with an idea that could be funny and inspiring.

STRATEGY I discovered many fascinating facts about cats and dogs as pets while reviewing numerous articles about the advantages of ownership. Some facts are obvious, but others that I came across would be surprising to most people. Thus, the idea that pets can have alternative "functions" became the focus of my concept.

1.97 Cat "Mouse trap" package design showing all surfaces of the package proposal. *Design: Maria Mordvintseva.*

For example, cats can easily replace a mousetrap or an alarm clock. While it's common knowledge that hungry pets will almost never let you sleep in, there is scientific proof that cats are a great way to get rid of pests and vermin. Specific proteins found in cat saliva and urine can act as a mouse repellant. Cats are natural born hunters and will prey on small animals and insects. Dogs are great playmates and can substitute for a burglar alarm. According to research, people who own dogs tend to be more physically active and less obese than people who don't. There is therefore no need for a personal trainer if a dog can do the same job free of charge and in a fun way. Most people are also completely unaware of the many health benefits of having pets. Stroking a cat or a dog is known to bring down stress levels, as well as heart rate and blood pressure in many cases. A study conducted at the University of Minnesota found that cat owners could reduce their risk of heart attacks and strokes by more than a third.

One of my major challenges in this project was to develop a way of introducing people to individual animals by proving that many shelter animals are worthy of adoption. My idea was to give each shelter pet their individual package featuring their portrait, character, and physical features like weight and age. The package would also present information in support of the pet's "function" and other little known facts about animals. The presentation of this information would be non-scientific and humorous, which would enable the concept to stand out from the usually depressing advertising on the same subject. The packaging would be placed in corresponding sections of department stores, drug stores, etc., where people would least expect it to see it. If someone decides to adopt a pet, they would buy the package and collect the pet at the specified shelter. All of the profits would be invested into helping more animals to be rescued from the streets.

One of my goals for this project was to create a design that was adaptable for virtually any cat and dog. A limited color palette and a white background were a natural choice to keep the package simple to feature the individual animal. The clean, uncluttered design also makes the package stand out on the shelf.

EFFECTIVENESS Unfortunately, for now, the project only exists as a concept, and so there is no way to assess its effectiveness. If I had an opportunity to return to the initial design stage, I would think of a way to make the package production even cheaper. For example, the portraits of the pets and information that is individualized for each pet could be printed on stickers and later attached to packaging that is printed in bulk.

ASSESSMENT Before I began working on this brief I had always thought that doing work for social causes would be incredibly difficult and challenging. Most socially driven advertising tends to either scare or shock people and rarely is it creative, especially in Russia. This project demonstrated to me that this work could also be fun while being appropriate. I also learned the valuable lesson that doing a thorough job of researching can provide designers with useful insights in which they can develop a very solid and original idea.

1.98 Close-up of Cat "Mouse trap" package design back that introduces the individual cat to be adopted. *Design: Maria Mordvintseva.*

SEX SENSE

David Smith, Senior Lecturer in Graphic Design & Typography,
Dún Laoghaire Institute of Art, Design and Technology (IADT),
Dún Laoghaire, Ireland

CLIENT
A self-published undergraduate project submitted in support of candidacy for BA (Hons) in Visual Communication Design.

PROJECT TITLE
Sex Sense.

DURATION
18 weeks, spring 2014.

BUDGET
€500–750 for original print and exhibition materials.

TEAM
Project leader and primary supervisor: **David Smith**.
Co-supervisor: **Hilary Kenna**.
Student: **Ruby Henderson**.
The student worked independently with tutorial direction, peer support, and IADT support faculty.

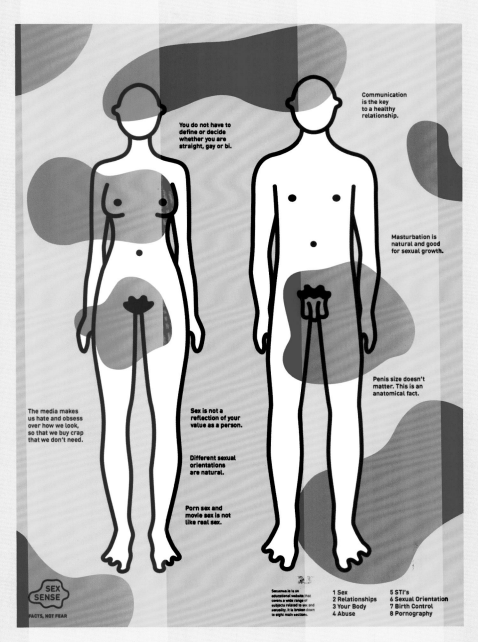

1.99 Sexuality poster promoting the Sex Sense website and online resource for teenagers. *Design: Ruby Henderson.*

DESCRIPTION Despite improvements in Ireland's secular credentials and an increasing separation of church and state, the influence of the Roman Catholic Church still permeates many aspects of Irish society. Today in Ireland, religious orders remain in the majority as the trustees of our schools, and advocacy for abstinence and chastity is promoted alongside more liberal and "objective" programs on sexual health and awareness. Yet despite the matter-of-fact nature of these more "objective" parallel programs, for many Irish teens their sense of sex and their own sexuality has been both shaped and distorted by religious moral thinking. It is this and other peculiarly Irish contradictions that were cited as motivations for Ruby when she explained:

I chose to do this subject as sex education in Ireland clearly needs to be modernized. It is too traditional and unwilling to include vital aspects of sex education. This is mainly due to the unfounded concern that if you tell teens too much it encourages them to be promiscuous. Due to this belief, teens will turn to their friends, pornography, the Internet and the media. These are unreliable sources, which inevitably leads to anxiety when the reality of sex and one's sexuality is explored.

The need for a coherent, holistic and reliable resource during teenage formative years was also clearly important to her when she said, "it is essential that Sex Sense is a reliable source that is genuinely appealing to the age group, while still treating the subject of sex and our sexuality with the necessary sensitivity and insight. Its main objective is to build confidence around sexual identity."

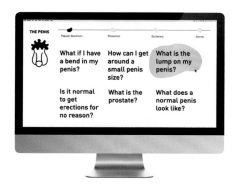

1.100 Web page contextualized on Mac. Illustrated using "Questions on Penis." *Design: Ruby Henderson.*

RESEARCH Concept development In the IADT Visual Communications program we place significant emphasis on authorship, and there is an expectation that all final projects are produced using a substantial proportion of primary text and visual sources. To achieve this, students are encouraged not only to engage with themes that they are interested in, but also to choose subjects about which they have a reasonable depth of prior knowledge. For some students one of the best resources available to them is their major dissertation. By developing a major studio project around aspects of their dissertation research, the discovery phase of the project is expedited and the initial research and concept development is greatly condensed, allowing the student to move quickly and confidently to the design and visual development phase.

In response to how she found a subject to inspire, engage, and sustain her for the three-month project, Ruby explained the value of "leaning on" the substantial body of research generated for the written component of her degree. The leap from addressing the prevalence of overtly sexualized and "pornographic" images in contemporary advertising to the sex education of teens may not be an obvious one. Yet it is clear from her research that Ruby recognized it was a perceived lack of credibility and currency in their formal "sex education" programs that contributed to teens "learning" about sex through the distorted prism of online pornography. This presented her with a unique opportunity to realize a major project that would address the gap in knowledge in a credible and unpatronizing way.

Content and visual resources Having effectively integrated illustration and image making into her practice, Ruby was committed to using contemporary illustration to resolve the visual identity and communications for her project. Former Airside designer and illustrator Malika Favre's *Sexy Alphabet* and her subsequent cover designs for the *Kama Sutra* were notable influences in both their graphic style and the way they illustrated sexually explicit activity in a non-provocative way. In her earlier studies the figurative elements initially had too obvious an association with "tribal art" and the lightness of the line work was not ideal for the range of applications and media under consideration. Subsequent development work, having referenced the graphic

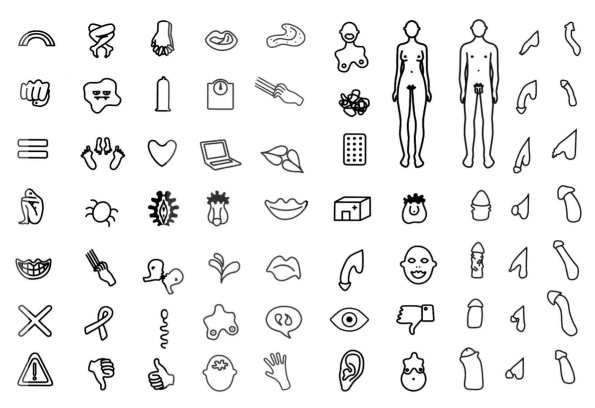

1.101 Full icon-set and principal illustrations for print and screen applications. *Design: Ruby Henderson.*

styles of designer Felix Pfaeffi and illustrator Sara Andreasson, greatly enhanced and improved the overall quality and distinction of her final illustrations.

CHALLENGES AND STRATEGY Ruby initially intended to make Sex Sense a portable "pop-up" exhibition that could be taken to schools around the country as apart of a broader educational and wellness program. She also considered making a film or a series of video stings for broadcast, but finally settled on a website/online resource as it is the most cost-effective platform, has the broadest reach, is always there when needed, and can be easily updated in accordance to current events and attitudes.

Ensuring that the editorial tone was appropriate and not patronizing was a major challenge and required multiple iterations and adjustments. Consistently mindful of the visual impact of her illustrations, Ruby recognized that their appeal alone would not be sufficient to genuinely engage

an audience of teenagers, so additionally the veracity and authenticity of the textual content was critical to the success of the project.

Due to the sensitivities of the subject and the difficulties in gaining the confidence of her audience, Ruby initially depended on her desk research to shape and inform the editorial content and gauge the attitude of the user group to existing forums and models for sex education. She explained:

I analyzed a lot of other sex education websites to see the kind of tone of voice they use and what kind of information they foreground. Nearly all of the sex education information provided by state agencies such as the Department of Health or child welfare agencies is fact based, so I didn't need to edit the content too much, except for integrating a friendly and credible tone of voice.

1.102 Final user interface and navigation illustrated using main landing page for "Questions on Sex." *Design: Ruby Henderson.*

However, she went further, and following consultation with the Institute's Ethics Committee she developed a survey to engage directly with a class of teens from her alma mater. These additional insights not only provided another layer of authentic and "real world" views on the subject from the core user group but also great insight into what was regarded as successful or acceptable quality of visual communications and tone of voice.

EFFECTIVENESS AND ASSESSMENT It was the additional challenge of tailoring the content to suit the audience which Ruby herself cited as being most demanding:

Based on feedback, comment and responses to my final designs I think the visual language is more than effective and suitable for this audience. However, I found breaking down the content quite difficult as there is such a wide range of subjects within sex education. Presenting this in an accessible and non-patronizing way was as demanding a task as creating the visual content. I also learnt a huge amount about editorial standards and the complexity of navigation systems and the importance of user experience.

Yet, despite her success, she recognizes that her motivation to fully realize the project faces additional challenges beyond the necessary financial and technical resources required:

I think the biggest obstacle I will face [in fully implementing this idea] will be gaining the support of teachers and parents. Their support is vital as it gives the project legitimacy. One voice is not enough; teens need to see their parents and their teachers acknowledge the significance and importance of sex education ... Ireland is finally becoming more liberal and this current generation of teenagers are not as bogged down by Catholic guilt. They are confident and sexually aware. Plus the LGBT community is gaining more and more support and recognition. The education system and parental supports need to ... acknowledge that there are new and better ways to educate and promote sexual health to teens today.

FORNIFY

about/contact

HOME
RELATIONSHIPS
SEX
ABUSE
LGBTQ
YOUR **BODY**
PORN
PREG**NANCY**
BIRTH CONTROL
STI'S
RESOURCES

Fornify is an organization that is
concerned with sex and sexuality
education. With the advent of the
Internet, young people can now find
out as much as they want on the
topic of sex. However, as wonderful
as the Internet is it is not always
the best teacher if you don't know
what you're looking for. Fornify is
a platform that gathers the best
bits of what's out there while also
correcting some of the distorted
truths. A lot of young boys, and
some girls, are turning to such
thins as pornography to educate
them about sex. Porn is great in
the sense that it is upfront and
personal about sex but it is not
always a true reflection of what
real sex is like. Sex Education in
schools is the opposite of porn in
a way, as it leaves out the gorey
details but highlights the risks
and dangers that surround sex.

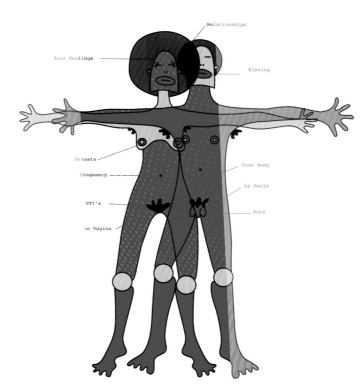

1.103 An example of initial designs exploring basic user interface, typographic treatment, and possible name for the online resource. The overtly tribal illustrations were discounted following additional visual research. *Design: Ruby Henderson.*

As with all student work, there are flaws and opportunities to improve and refine the final outcomes, yet it is a fine exemplar of our program's overall objectives. It is a project that is concerned with authorship and embraces the simple concept of "being a good designer" that uses his or her skills and knowledge for the betterment of others. In her commitment to be "good," Ruby's project marks a moment where the emerging designer becomes a citizen designer: "I now see how my design studies have empowered me to a greater degree as it has taught me how I can communicate a message powerfully and provocatively. It has also shown me the wide range of media that can be utilized to convey a message to the broadest possible audience."

In this project, Ruby Henderson has discovered an alternative way to effect appropriate and meaningful change for an audience seeking authentic and verifiable information on a complex subject. Such honesty of intent is commendable and has resulted in work that is contemporary and exciting. It is without doubt "good" work. More importantly, it is work that does good.

CULTURALLY APPROPRIATE GRAPHICS

Audrey Bennett, Associate Professor of Graphics, Department of Communication and Media, Rensselaer Polytechnic Institute, Troy, New York

DESCRIPTION Culturally Appropriate Graphics (CAG) aims to serve society by educating future professional design practitioners about the role cultural difference plays in the visual communication process. Its underlying premise is that people who consume designed images are culturally heterogeneous and require culturally appropriate aesthetics. A designed image is an image created using formal design principles in order to relay information that leads to positive cognitive and/or behavioral change in the target audience.

I assign this project in the Cross-Cultural Media (CCM) course that I teach at Rensselaer Polytechnic Institute annually in the fall semester. The course enrolls up to five Master's or doctoral students and 15 undergraduate students (who are typically citizens of the United States, Caucasian, female, and range in age from around 20 to 40 years old).

CAG is a term-long project that asks students to respond verbally and visually to the question: What role does culture play in the interpretation of designed images? Students grapple with this question as they read theoretical, critical, and evidence-based perspectives from interdisciplinary literature on what constitutes culture and its impact on meaning. They also use semiotics to interpret existing designed images from print and digital media and analyze how each image appropriately reflects (or not) cultural values.

The goal of the project is the development of the students' cognizance of the target audience's culture-based needs in order to design culturally appropriate images—that is, images that are free of culturally offensive or irrelevant language that could impede clear reception during the communication process.

1.104 Front cover for *"The Women's Position in Different Cultures."* *Written, designed, and handbound: Tong Pei, Cheong.*

CLIENT
No client; academic course.

PROJECT TITLE
Culturally Appropriate Graphics (CAG).

DURATION
15 weeks, fall semester.

BUDGET
N/A.

TEAM
Students work independently on this project.

Graduate students write a proposal to conduct fieldwork and successfully complete CITI (Collaborative Institutional Training Initiative) training; and undergraduate students write, design, and produce a book that defines the term "culture," explaining one or more of its paradigms of difference (e.g., gender, race/ethnicity, language, religion, sexual orientation, class, age, etc.). Upon completion of the project, graduate students are able to form a hypothesis about the role of culture in the development of culturally appropriate images, write a fieldwork proposal to test the hypothesis with human subjects, and demonstrate knowledge of ethical protocol for conducting human subjects research. Undergraduate students are able to manage an authorship and editorial design project from conception to production within a limited timeframe.

RESEARCH Graduate students engage in the preliminary stage of a human subjects research process in which they prepare to conduct fieldwork. They propose an empirical research project in which they will observe and interact with members of a target user group to study the cross-cultural effectiveness typical of existing designed images. They may propose to observe user interactions with the images; or, they may propose to solicit user feedback (through individual interviews or focus groups) regarding the images. In addition to drafting an IRB (Institutional Review Board) proposal, all graduate students must show evidence of successful completion of CITI training, a test that is required before a researcher goes into the field in order to prevent injury to human subjects. Researchers who pass CITI training are certified to conduct human subjects research for a given number of years.

The research process is different for undergraduate students working on this project. They engage in the final stage of a design-thinking process in which they analyze the effectiveness of images for cross-cultural communication. This project provides undergraduate students with an opportunity to learn from other professional designers' design decisions and outcomes. Thus, the work this project entails occurs in the final stage of the design-thinking process referred to in the discipline's literature as: *implementation*, *solicit user feedback*, *evolution*,

Students inform their analyses of the design outcomes by reading about culture from different paradigms, including gender, race/ethnicity, language, religion, sexual orientation, class, and age."

———

what works?, *learn*, and *test*. At this stage in the process, students use semiotics to analyze and interpret the design outcomes of professional designers of their choosing. That is, they research existing designed images that aim to communicate to or about a specific cultural group. They may choose images from print or digital media. Students inform their analyses of the design outcomes by reading about culture from different paradigms, including gender, race/ethnicity, language, religion, sexual orientation, class, and age.

CHALLENGES The course in which this project is assigned is cross-listed as a graduate course for doctoral and Master's students and an upper-level undergraduate course for graphic design majors. However, it also enrolls undergraduate students from other majors with little to no prior experience or training in applied design. This wide range of applied design knowledge and ability presents a pedagogical challenge for students completing this project. Students, particularly those who lack sufficient prior experience and training in applied design (including the industry-standard software), are challenged by the rigor of a term-long project that requires a synergy of reading, writing, and application skills, culminating in the production of a physical book. Thus, this project has proven to be quite challenging even for those with prior experience or training in design practice. In anticipation of this challenge I provide hands-on bookbinding training for students and a structured course schedule that guides them through the steps of completing their project.

STRATEGY All students spend the first half of the term reading and reflecting verbally and orally on knowledge gleaned from scholarly journal articles, newspaper articles, and books. Outside of class, students read and analyze theoretical, critical, and evidence-based perspectives from interdisciplinary literature about what constitutes culture and its impact on meaning. During class they discuss the assigned readings and semiotically analyze existing exemplars of culturally appropriate/inappropriate, relevant/irrelevant images from print and digital media that aim to inform a culturally specific lay audience and evoke behavioral or cognitive change. During the second half of the term, graduate students complete CITI Training and draft the IRB proposal to conduct human subjects research, whereas undergraduate students write, design, and produce the print or digital book.

EFFECTIVENESS This project requires undergraduate students to read and write more than they do typically in other design courses. It also requires a relatively shorter time for the production of a large-scale design project for which they must author their own content. While students enjoy reading the required course texts, they gripe about the large amount of writing required weekly, and struggle with the bookbinding component of the project. One way that I help students to meet these challenges is with a structured methodology with very specific guidelines and restrictions. An advantage of such an approach is that the evaluation process is easier because all of the students' books take the same specific form. One drawback to this approach, however, is that it can stunt the range of each student's creative voice and the development of his or her personal style.

ASSESSMENT The following messages from former students show the positive impact of this project on their current professional careers and confirm the emerging need for more cultural paradigms for the course and project curricula—for instance, "design geographies" might study graphic design styles in different parts of the world.

I am beginning to design several materials for NYU's Abu Dhabi and Shanghai campuses. I have already caught some pretty big cultural errors that were put in place before I arrived, and am thankful to say that many topics we covered in class are serving me well. I'd like to enrich my knowledge on the subject; are there any good reads you would recommend based on Chinese or Middle Eastern graphic design?
—*A. Rarig*, personal communication, August 7, 2013

I'm working on a project for work that involves developing diversity plans in NYC, particularly African-American and Latino cultures. I was wondering if you could send me the two readings we had in cross-cultural media last fall that focused on African-American culture as well as Latino culture. I believe one of them had a huge focus on the idea of machismo in the Latino culture.
—*N. Monti*, personal communication, August 1, 2013

I'm making Chinese banquet invitations for my brother and it has to fit both American and Chinese styles (as well as making something not bad luck in Chinese culture). I thought of you and your cross-cultural media class immediately!
—*J. Wong*, personal communication, July 16, 2014.

ÉNTOMO:
A NEW FOOD PERSPECTIVE

David **Smith**, Senior Lecturer in Graphic Design
& Typography, Dún Laoghaire Institute of Art, Design
and Technology (IADT), Dún Laoghaire, Ireland

1.105 Responsive screen design with new icon set and navigation for tablet devices. *Design: Lara Hanlon.*

CLIENT
A self-published undergraduate project submitted in support of candidacy for BA (Hons) in Visual Communication Design.

PROJECT TITLE
From Pupa to Plate: Feeding the Metropolis.

DURATION
18 weeks, spring 2013.

BUDGET
€500–750 for print and exhibition materials.

TEAM
Project leader and primary supervisor: David Smith
Student: Lara Hanlon.
The student worked independently with tutorial direction, peer support, and IADT support faculty.

DESCRIPTION In my experience it is not unusual for an undergraduate project to pique the interest of a knowing and often local audience—many of my students excel in presenting speculative solutions to "Irish problems," yet few if any succeed in conceiving solutions to "global problems." This entomologically inspired project does—it has been cited and awarded as an exemplar for how design practice and thinking can contribute to social innovation and how it can be effectively used to enhance and promote sustainability. *éntomo: A new food perspective* not only piqued international interest but provoked debate in China, Hungary, Turkey, Spain, Canada, and the United States on the global benefits of entomophagy (the practice of eating insects) and the opportunities that exist within this seemingly unpalatable cuisine.

RESEARCH

Concept development In an increasingly global market, food production is recognized as a significant "wicked problem." For Western urban-centric societies, to sustain environmentally and economically viable models of food production we require the smartest of answers. Such complex challenges understandably occupy academics, policy makers, and economists, but designer Lara Hanlon's graduation project sought to tackle the problem by using design to communicate the environmental, health, and economic benefits of making a basic change to our diets.

Presented with the demanding opportunity of authoring and directing her final degree project, Lara sought inspiration from a subject that greatly appeals to her. In response to questions on her primary motivations for the project, she answered that there were a number of reasons, both personal and objective. She said:

1.106 Evolution of éntomo logotype, motifs, and graphic elements. *Design: Lara Hanlon.*

Firstly, I would consider myself a food enthusiast who loves to experiment with new flavors and textures. I've always enjoyed the process of mealtime—the preparation, cooking, presentation and dining experience is really creative and exciting. Choosing a subject matter that I'm passionate about was key to sustaining my interest for the duration of the project. One of my personal goals that I set at the beginning of the project was to investigate current social and urban problems, and to understand how visual communications can be used to increase our overall standard of living. After researching food sustainability and discovering the term "entomophagy," I realized that there was an opportunity to not only enhance existing communications in this field, but also to propose and provide new information to a new audience.

She also cited the influence and inspiration of a new wave of contemporary chefs—such as Rene Redzepi (Danish chef and co-owner of Noma) and Alex Atala (Brazilia chef of D.O.M.)—who, through their commitment to experimental cuisine, food diversity, and sustainability, have become advocates for entomophagy in their respective Copenhagen and São Paulo restaurants.

Content and resources Key to the validity and integrity of her project outcomes was having current data and resources to support and illustrate her arguments. Much of the textual matter that informed her argument and provided the basis for her editorial content and direction was sourced from a key report published by the UN Food and Agriculture Organization titled *Edible Insects—Future Prospects for Food and Feed Security.* Auspiciously, the report examined in some detail the role of insects, the history of entomophagy, environmental and nutritional opportunities, economics, production, and preservation of insects as food.

CHALLENGES AND STRATEGY One of the obvious challenges was how best to demonstrate her talent and abilities as a designer (in support of her assessment) but also, hypothetically, to effect change in the perception of her audience/consumers in a convincing manner. The quality and extent of her research was central to enabling Lara to assume an expert position on the subject and demonstrate a deep understanding of the challenges in promoting cogent arguments for the benefits of entomophagy.

1.107a–1.107b Final user interface and navigation illustrated using sample recipe pages contextualized on iMac. *Design: Lara Hanlon.*

This was best illustrated in the particularly well-structured design and editorial strategy for the project. By employing different design vocabularies and considered media choices, Lara used her project to effectively illustrate and answer many questions posed by her peers and my colleagues.

Accessibility to information was of primary importance to her, and the decision to create a "digital hub" as an informational and educational resource was central to the success of the project. She explained:

éntomo's core objective is to provide information about entomophagy and to demystify the cultural taboos that are often associated with eating bugs. I wanted people to learn about insects as food in an engaging and easy manner, so I decided that the core output of the project would be an online resource. A website or digital hub can be easily and frequently maintained, updated and accessed by various users at any time, on any device. The site illustrates the benefits of insects as food through education, recipes, research studies, event information, external resources, and an online store—there are multiple levels of information that the user can interact with, download or simply explore.

The project's visual identity draws upon the simple conceit on the etymology of *entomo*—derived from Greek *entomon* for insect—literally: a creature cut into sections. This extends to the custom logotype and a palette of complementary graphic motifs and illustrations that are used throughout the project in a flexible way to provide visual coherency.

Through information design and the visual interpretation of data sets, Lara clearly and objectively presented the facts in support of entomophagy. Through consumer videos she provided engaging and humorous examples of consumers' first and surprising taste of insects (freeze dried and imported from Thailand) for a genuine and authentic response. Food was meticulously styled and art-directed before shooting all of the original photographs that richly illustrated the appetizing possibilities of "adding bugs to your diet." Finally, product packaging presents the food product in a contemporary and appealing style as a healthy and alternative snack for young urban professionals.

EFFECTIVENESS AND ASSESSMENT Receiving both awards and critical recognition, éntomo has clearly demonstrated its effectiveness both as a proposition and as a design project. Such early success could affect a young designer's opinion of her work. However, Lara said:

Looking back at the project now it's easy for me to unpick it and identify what worked and what was not so successful. There is a lot that I would change if I could get my hands on it right now, but that's only natural, particularly after a year of professional design experience … I think éntomo was not only successful in achieving the overall objectives set at the beginning of the project, but it also presented new possibilities for further ideation and development that unfortunately was not achievable within the given timeframe. This was not a bad thing—I've had many opportunities to continue my research post graduation, which was really gratifying, and realizing that it had more potential than I initially thought is still reassuring even one year on.

As an educator and supervisor of the project I agree with her modest assessment that there are minor design craft issues yet obvious potential to extend and develop the project. First and foremost, the success of Lara's project has to be based upon its quality and effectiveness as a communication design project. However, it is also without question an exemplar of our program objectives. Lara has demonstrated her ability to synthesize complex ideas and diverse design practices in a coherent multidisciplinary outcome. This is a demanding task for many and it is something she recognizes herself:

I think the greatest challenge and reward working independently on such a comprehensive project was the number and various types of design outcomes produced. All content was self-authored including the brand identity, web design and build, motion graphics and film, food photography and styling, copywriting, and editing.

1.108 Proposed packaging designs illustrated using original food photography and graphic motifs. *Design: Lara Hanlon.*

In his recent book *The Frugal Innovator*, Charles Leadbeater argues that technology is not always necessary for innovation and that massive change can be effected by simple and lean methods. He writes:

Frugal innovation is designed for and is a response to its times: to make the most of the limited resources we have in order to create better, more successful and sustainable ways to live.

With her project, Lara Hanlon has successfully embraced the principles of frugal innovation by suggesting that one of the most challenging of Western society's "wicked problems" could be resolved through smart design, clear information, a shift in cultural perception, and a change in diet and attitudes toward a sustainable and environmentally sound food source.

ADDITIONAL INFORMATION In March 2014, éntomo represented Ireland at the Shenzhen Design Awards for Young Talents in China, in association with UNESCO Creative Cities Network, where it received the New Star Award. This international competition welcomed over 150 entries from 16 cities across the world and rewarded those whose projects were successful in utilizing design to enhance sustainability and increase the standard of living in urban environments.

PART 2

DESIGN METHODOLOGY

"

What we do as educators, what we design as a curriculum, and the experience that we share with our students will necessarily shape the minds that then forge beyond us. We can use assignments as the premise to provide opportunities for students to engage, research and concern themselves with world issues. Exposing students to even a single social, environmental, or political issue will instill an understanding that this is the domain of the designer. To educate is not only to ignite an idea but to also foster the courage to pursue that idea beyond the classroom."

Cinthia Wen, Designer, Educator, Just Design

———

"

As design educators, we cast projects almost as a scientist designs a laboratory experiment. The formula and the variables conspire to slant the results in one direction or another. The project assignment and the project critique are powerful tools that teach far more than explicit goals, and carry strong implicit messages about design and designers' roles."

Kathy McCoy, Good Citizenship: Design as a Social and Political Force

———

"

Increasingly, designers are subordinating their own frame of reference to that of the user and are investigating methods and resources to infuse design with new value, beyond aesthetics and functionality. Talent and quality are as important as compassion, as design is becoming more socially engaged."

Anne van der Zwaag, Looks Good Feels Good Is Good: How Social Design Changes Our World

———

SECTION 1

COLLABORATIVE LEARNING

COLLABORATIVE LEARNING:
THE SOCIAL IN SOCIAL DESIGN

Teal Triggs

When was the last time you sat around a table with a group of 70-year-olds and had a chat with them about their life stories? And, when was the last time you learned about the cultural significance of food through the process of making a loaf of bread?

Over the last decade we have witnessed the rise of a "social design" movement; that is, a movement which centers on "enabling individuals, institutions and communities to build better lives and futures" (IDEO, *Human Centered Design Toolkit*, 2014). At the same time we have seen the primary motivation of the communication designer move beyond predominantly commercial objectives to those that focus on public sector bodies, non-profit and commercial service providers. This shift is aligned with a renewed sense of advocacy among the design community but also has emerged in response to a context of austerity politics and government policies focusing on, for example, healthcare and international development (Armstrong et al., *Social Design Futures: HEI Research and the AHRC*, 2014, p. 15). Recognizing that any move toward how design can help effect change requires innovative approaches and relevant tools and methods. For social design, these foundations firmly reside in an approach that builds upon the concept of shared participation. Specifically, this has meant drawing upon an established pedagogical practice termed "collaborative learning."

But what is collaborative learning? Elizabeth F. Barkley, K. Patricia Cross, and Claire Howell Major define this term in their book, *Collaborative Learning Techniques: A Handbook for College Faculty*, as "learning activities expressly designed for and carried out through pairs of small interactive groups" (2005, p. 4). Collaborative learning has its epistemological home in the theory of social constructivism, which positions learners as jointly involved in the construction of meaning. This type of peer-group learning proposes that knowledge is "socially constructed" through the process of students and teachers *actively* working together. Developing consensus, reaching an agreement, enriches learning. The process of collaborative learning encourages autonomous learners and by doing so, enables an articulation of well-considered judgments.

Social designers are drawing upon similar models of collaboration; clients and users are now seen as partners working toward social change. Whereas designers were at one time mediators of messages *for* an audience, now they are partners *with* their clients and their users/audiences in the creation of those messages. As for the "social" in social design, over the last decade the designer's relationship with the audience has become increasingly participatory in nature. In other words, the designer is no longer restricted to the role of mediator but rather joins as an active participant in the facilitation of shared decision-making processes. Thus, there are methodological implications. As the designer is embedded within the collaboration, this raises questions around maintaining objectivity but also about what role critical reflection might play within this process. At the same time, the application of collaborative learning provides a catalyst for additional insights into how empathy can be better understood through participatory design experiences.

To take one example from my own teaching experience: the role bread making played in bringing together local residents of a South London housing estate—the Aylesbury—during the process of regeneration, with MA Design Writing Criticism students at London College of Communication (Triggs et al., *Telling Your Story: People and the Aylesbury Estate*, 2011). Funded by the UK government's Department for Business Innovation & Skills, the Aylesbury Estate Kaleidoscope Project (2009) was a collaboration between InSpire, Creation Trust, Media Citizens, and the Research Unit for Information Environments, London College of Communication, with the intent to increase the number of adult learners who could access learning through local facilities and progress further along the route to employment.

Each participant brought to the table (literally) the ingredients for bread recipes that had been part of their own cultural traditions. Taking a basic white bread recipe, the aim was for students to engage actively in the making of bread, sharing ingredients while also sharing stories of lived and cross-cultural experiences; in particular, stories drawing on the social histories of the residents and students alike. The kitchen at the Estate's community center provided a neutral space for this activity and was where the bread was baked and distributed to the participants to take home with them. Such dynamic, social conversations resulted in a greater understanding of the residents' position in the history of the Estate, but also served as an empathetic trigger for what students had gleaned from the community as a sense of place and transformation.

Design is a social act, and it is through the process of designing that societal relationships are enacted. However, it is also worth noting that while this model proposes an equal set of relations among its participants, ethical questions remain as to what the designer's "accountability" is more broadly within this. Ann Light and Yoko Akama (2014) explore the subtleties of this collaborative dynamic in their essay "Structuring Future Social Relations: The Politics of Care in Participatory Practice." They look at a series of case studies around the theme of "care" and explore the "participatory structuring of social relations" (p. 3). They conclude that there is a role for participatory practitioners as "custodians of care" to create "spaces for others to reflect, make mistakes, learn and debate" and, where "collaborative future-making can be expected to have impact, possibly at many levels" (p. 9).

> " *Whereas designers were at one time mediators of messages for an audience, now they are partners with their clients and their users/ audiences in the creation of those messages."*

There is much talk of the citizen in other spheres of creativity, such as citizen journalists, citizen filmmakers, citizen cartoonists, etc. Design has a long tradition of this kind of work but only now is it being recognized as something that can inform our way of thinking about the core principles of the discipline. Design is forever in a state of flux in terms of its definition. But there is no doubt that this recent shift from designing *for* users to designing *with* users presents a model that is breaking down boundaries and establishing a new form of citizen designer.

Teal Triggs is Professor of Graphic Design and Associate Dean, School of Communication, Royal College of Art, London. Her writings on design education, history, and feminism have appeared in books and journals internationally. She is author of Fanzines *(Thames & Hudson, 2010) and, more recently, co-editor with Adrian Shaughnessy and Anna Gerber of* GraphicsRCA: Fifty Years and Beyond *(RCA, 2014). She is the co-editor with Leslie Atzmon of* The Graphic Design Reader *(Bloomsbury, 2016) and is editor-in-chief of the* Journal of Communication Design *(Taylor and Francis).*

FIVE QUESTIONS TO
JACQUES LANGE

1. What were the most important influences that shaped you as a designer?

My passion for design started with my family's set of *Encyclopaedia Britannica*. These beautiful objects were the treasure in my young universe. I loved engaging with these as containers of knowledge, wisdom, and aesthetic inspiration—in these voluminous pages, I saw great artists at work. I mimicked what I saw, although this sometimes got me into trouble. When I was 5 years old, I saw photographs of Picasso's *Guernica*. I was so inspired that I drew my own version on the side wall of our family's garage. I don't recall what my rendition looked like, but I do remember being in serious trouble for defacing a pristine white wall.

I continued to be creatively engaged and have learned many skills from books borrowed from libraries. Books, great teachers, and supportive mentors fueled my school and university years.

2. Do you agree or disagree with this statement: Designers have a social and ethical responsibility to create and transmit meaningful forms of communication that benefit society and culture? Why?

I read Victor Papanek's *Design for the Real World* as an impressionable student. The first two lines of his preface made an enduring impression: "There are professions more harmful than industrial design … possibly only one profession is phonier. Advertising design [persuades] people to buy things they don't need, with money they don't have, in order to impress others who don't care." This statement has haunted me throughout my career—I asked myself if I am one of these "phonies"? My answer has always been the same: "I need to do more to break this cycle." Yes, it is my belief that social and ethical responsibilities should be at the center of what designers do.

A plethora of great thinkers have shaped some "first world dimensions" of my thinking. It is, however, South Africa that has taught me most about "why" and "how" it is critical for designers to take ownership of societal responsibilities. The country is often described as one of the most diverse and complex societies in the world.

I grew up as a beneficiary of "privilege" under apartheid, experienced the most radical sociopolitical transformations in recent history, and saw how design played a role in shaping various iterations of "imagined new societies" where social and ethical responsibilities were essential as a tool of social engineering. The legacy of extreme socioeconomic disparities, the ways in which design manifests symbolically and materially, to harbor the ideological needs of institutions to manipulate class, gender, and race, ultimately to serve the needs of agency, all became issues that the empathetic and engaged designer could not ignore.

3. You were one of a group of designers from South Africa who conceived the idea to celebrate Nelson Mandela's life by collecting 95 posters from around the world, honoring Madiba's lifelong contribution to humanity. Can you talk about your involvement with the Mandela Poster Project and explain why it is important for you to stay involved and to do this type of work?

In May 2013, a group of like-minded thinkers came up with an idea to collect 95 posters in 60 days via social media to celebrate Madiba's 95th birthday, under the title "Mandela Poster Project." It was a humble concept: we aimed to build a collection of posters contributed by designers from around the world that represent the value system that Madiba brought to the world.

2.1 Installation view of the 95 Mandela Poster Project traveling exhibition at the Athenaeum Theatre, Port Elizabeth, South Africa. *Photography: Basil Brady.*

Days after we published the brief the project went viral and reached a vast community. The team was known as the Mandela Poster Project Collective (MPPC), and they committed their time and expertise to make the exceptional happen. In 60 days the MPPC tapped into its networks to collect more than 700 submissions from more than 70 countries.

The "magic" of this project lies in the makeup of the MPPC team. We are a group of people from radically diverse backgrounds, but, more importantly, we have a common goal and a shared value system. We therefore approached the Nelson Mandela Children's Hospital Trust (NMCHT) to offer our project as a fundraising initiative to help establish Africa's fourth dedicated pediatric hospital in Johannesburg—Madiba's final legacy wish. The global design community supported this alliance and contributed way beyond the original project's expectations.

The MPPC curated the more than 700 submissions, and 95 posters from 37 countries were selected based on their narrative relevance to form part of the *Mandela Poster Project 95 Collection*, representing 95 years of Madiba's life. The collection first went on public display on UN Mandela Day in 2013 and received a great deal of media attention from around the world. By December 2014, the *95 Collection* will have been exhibited at more than 25 venues.

Why is it important for me to do this type of work? Firstly, as a designer, I hope to see that communal efforts result in positive societal impact and that it contributes to positive changes in the quality of life for as many people as possible. Secondly, I am committed to collaborate with designers who are dedicated to positive social change.

4. New roles are emerging for design professionals as their function is increasingly changing from that of generators to facilitators of ideas. Can you comment on this?
Facilitating social change needs to be the primary priority for all designers, young or old.

5. What advice would you give students studying visual communication today to help them prepare for contemporary professional practice?
I posed this question to my students and they responded: "Teach us what we do not know instead of teaching us what we know better than our teachers." My additional advice is to is to read as much as possible and to travel broadly.

Jacques Lange is partner and creative director at Bluprint Design in Pretoria, South Africa, a design educator at the University of Pretoria, and advisor to various corporate institutions and NGOs. He has published widely on topics related to design practice, profession management, research, design promotion, policy advocacy, and contemporary design from lesser known regions. He is a former president of the International Council of Communication Design (Icograda).

PROTECT BALTIMORE:
HIV TESTING ACTION KIT

Ryan Clifford, Associate Director, MICA Center for Design Practice, Maryland Institute College of Art, Baltimore, Maryland

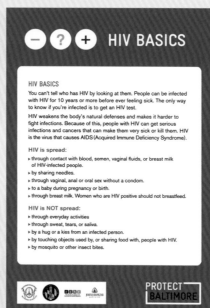

2.2a Protect Baltimore patient guide front and back cover. *Design: Center for Design Practice team. Final design: Heejin Suh.*

2.2b Protect Baltimore identity.
Design: Center for Design Practice team.

CLIENT
Johns Hopkins Center for Child and Community Health Research (CCHR), Baltimore City Health Department
Community:
The Baltimore-Towson Metropolitan Statistical Area. Primary audience: primary care providers in high HIV transmission areas. Secondary audience: patients in high HIV transmission areas.

PROJECT TITLE
HIV testing action kit.

DURATION
Spring semester, 2013.

BUDGET
The development of Protect Baltimore and the HIV Testing Action Kit was made possible by generous funding from the Centers for Disease Control and Prevention Category C Demonstration Project (PS12-1201).

TEAM
MICA team: **Mike Weikert**, Director, and **Ryan Clifford**, Associate Director, MICA Center for Design Practice & MA in Social Design; **Daniel Calderwood**, Undergraduate Graphic Design; **Anne Marie Jasinowski**, Post Baccalaureate Graphic Design; **Jackie Littman**, MFA Graphic Design; **Karen Shea**, Undergraduate Graphic Design; **Heejin Suh**, MA in Social Design.
Project partners: **Jacky M. Jennings**, PhD, MPH, Associate Professor of Pediatrics & Epidemiology, Associate Director, General Pediatrics & Adolescent Medicine, Director, Center for Child & Community Health Research (CCHR), Department of Pediatrics, Johns Hopkins University School of Medicine, Co-Director, NIAID Sexually Transmitted Infection (T32) Pre-doctoral Training— Grant, Joint Appointment, Bloomberg School of Public Health; **Amelia Greiner Safi**, PhD MS, Research Faculty, Department of Pediatrics, Co-Director, Biostatistics, Epidemiology and Data Management (BEAD) Core Center for Child and Community Health Research; **Christina Schumacher**, PhD, Research Associate, Department of Pediatrics, Johns Hopkins University School of Medicine.

DESCRIPTION Baltimore City has one of the most severe HIV epidemics in the United States. In Baltimore, HIV/AIDS is concentrated in poor neighborhoods, among high-risk groups, and especially among African Americans, who represent approximately 89 percent of all HIV/AIDS cases. High-risk groups include men who have sex with men (MSM), injection drug users (IDU), and high-risk heterosexuals.

While the Baltimore City Health Department has implemented extensive outreach testing services via mobile vans and through needle exchange programs, the extent of the HIV burden and changing epidemiology underscore the need for targeted HIV testing strategies.

Protect Baltimore is an educational toolkit for healthcare professionals to promote and practice HIV testing in high transmission areas of Baltimore City. This project is a collaboration between the Johns Hopkins Center for Child and Community Health Research (CCHR) and a multidisciplinary team of students from the Center for Design Practice (a studio practice within the Center for Social Design beginning September 2014) at the Maryland Institute College of Art (MICA).

Since 2008, the Center for Design Practice at MICA has engaged interdisciplinary groups of students and outside partners in projects that address entrenched social problems. MICA believes in a human-centered approach to problem solving, using collaborative, project-based learning that focuses on translating ideas into tangible outcomes. The ultimate goal is to change behaviors and to make a positive impact on society.

This project had three main phases: Research and Immersion, Ideation, and Pitch. Each of these project phases culminated in a formal presentation to our partners in order to share outcomes and conclusions. At the end of the semester, the CCHR received two complete HIV Testing Action Kit design concepts, and they were able to pick the final project direction through a comprehensive focus group process.

RESEARCH During the intensive research and immersion phase, the MICA students were given contextual and visual research assignments to better understand the culture and context surrounding HIV testing and prevention in Baltimore City. During the first 4–5 weeks of the project, much of their time was spent outside the classroom, developing and conducting interviews with primary care providers, visiting local HIV testing clinics and mobile testing centers, surveying HIV testing attitudes and compliance with a questionnaire they designed, and consulting with project partners from CCHR and the Baltimore City Health Department.

Contextual research To better understand the context for the issues around HIV prevention in Baltimore City, the student team was given access to current research, academic papers, and public health studies regarding HIV infection, transmission, and prevention. They were expected to synthesize and distill the information, and apply their findings directly to their problem solving and ideation. To achieve this, they read hundreds of pages of dense medical literature.

Infographics and data visualization To help the students understand and share what they had discovered, each team member proposed, researched, and designed an infographic or data visualization that was based upon information learned from individual research. These visualizations helped the students synthesize, distill, and clearly communicate complex epidemiological data sets and concepts, as well as open lines of communication with our partners at the CCHR. Infographics addressed HIV/AIDS statistics in Baltimore, HIV infection by zip code, Baltimore City demographics, HIV testing methods, community viral load, audience personas, and public health detailing methodology. Once completed, the infographics were given to the partners to explain and effectively position complex health and epidemiological concepts to a wide audience beyond healthcare professionals, including project stakeholders, the affected community, and potential funders.

Due to the complex, technical, and acronym-heavy nature of the language surrounding HIV testing and prevention, a glossary of pertinent terminology was also developed and integrated into the supporting research materials.

HIV BY CSA:
OLDTOWN, MIDDLE EAST

TOTAL POPULATION
10,021

AVERAGE ANNUAL
All-CAUSE MORTALITY
RATE*† 2007-2011
85.7

AVERAGE ANNUAL
HIV MORTALITY RATE*†
2007-2011
2.2

AVERAGE ANNUAL
HIV DIAGNOSIS
RATE*† 2009-2011
10.3

* PER 10,000 POPULATION
† EXCLUDES CENSUS TRACTS
  WITH MISSING MORTALITY DATA

HIV BY CSA:
ORANGEVILLE, EAST HIGHLAND TOWN

TOTAL POPULATION
9,131

AVERAGE ANNUAL
All-CAUSE MORTALITY
RATE*† 2007-2011
118.0

AVERAGE ANNUAL
HIV MORTALITY RATE*†
2007-2011
4.8

AVERAGE ANNUAL
HIV DIAGNOSIS RATE*†
2009-2011
2.9

* PER 10,000 POPULATION

HIV BY CSA:
PATTERSON PARK NORTH AND EAST

TOTAL POPULATION
14,549

AVERAGE ANNUAL
All-CAUSE MORTALITY
RATE* 2007-2011
103.9

AVERAGE ANNUAL
HIV MORTALITY RATE*
2007-2011
3.2

AVERAGE ANNUAL
HIV DIAGNOSIS RATE*
2009-2011
6.6

* PER 10,000 POPULATION

HIV BY CSA:
PENN NORTH, RESERVOIR HILL ⚠

TOTAL POPULATION
9,668

AVERAGE ANNUAL
All-CAUSE MORTALITY
RATE* 2007-2011
71.4

AVERAGE ANNUAL
HIV MORTALITY RATE*
2007-2011
1.0

AVERAGE ANNUAL
HIV DIAGNOSIS RATE*
2009-2011
17.9

* PER 10,000 POPULATION

Protect Baltimore | 20

2.3a–2.3b Protect Baltimore Provider Resource Guide HIV by CSA.
Design: Center for Design Practice team. Final design: Heejin Suh.

HIV BY CSA:
PIMLICIO, ARLINGTON, HILLTOP

* PER 10,000 POPULATION

TOTAL POPULATION

11,816

AVERAGE ANNUAL
All-CAUSE MORTALITY
RATE* 2007-2011

129.3

AVERAGE ANNUAL
HIV MORTALITY RATE*
2007-2011

3.3

AVERAGE ANNUAL
HIV DIAGNOSIS RATE*
2009-2011

7.6

HIV BY CSA:
POPPLETON, THE TERRACES, HOLLINS MARKET

* PER 10,000 POPULATION

TOTAL POPULATION

5,086

AVERAGE ANNUAL
All-CAUSE MORTALITY
RATE* 2007-2011

87.8

AVERAGE ANNUAL
HIV MORTALITY RATE*
2007-2011

0.0

AVERAGE ANNUAL
HIV DIAGNOSIS RATE*
2009-2011

11.1

HIV BY CSA:
SANDTOWN-WINCHESTER, HARLEM PARK

* PER 10,000 POPULATION

TOTAL POPULATION

14,896

AVERAGE ANNUAL
All-CAUSE MORTALITY
RATE* 2007-2011

121.1

AVERAGE ANNUAL
HIV MORTALITY RATE*
2007-2011

6.7

AVERAGE ANNUAL
HIV DIAGNOSIS RATE*
2009-2011

15.7

HIV BY CSA:
SOUTH BALTIMORE

* PER 10,000 POPULATION

TOTAL POPULATION

6,406

AVERAGE ANNUAL
All-CAUSE MORTALITY
RATE* 2007-2011

153.9

AVERAGE ANNUAL
HIV MORTALITY RATE*
2007-2011

4.0

AVERAGE ANNUAL
HIV DIAGNOSIS RATE*
2009-2011

1.0

21 | Protect Baltimore

Visual research The team also undertook detailed visual research, which included identifying existing local, national, and international HIV prevention campaigns, and acquiring and visually auditing existing HIV testing kits in use in other cities.

When analyzing existing prevention materials and campaigns, the students developed categories that described the voice and strategic approach of the campaigns that they were auditing. These categories included: celebrity endorsement, clinical/statistical, de-stigmatizing, fear-based, humorous, inspirational, and shocking.

CHALLENGES A priority focus of this project was identifying and lowering the barriers to HIV testing, both on the provider and the patient side. One challenge was gaining access to—and building trust with—primary care providers who were providing HIV testing and linkage to care in high transmission areas. These providers were the primary audience for the HIV Testing Action Kit.

Additionally, research showed that some private medical providers are uncomfortable discussing sexual health and recommending HIV testing for patients who do not have obvious risk factors for HIV infection. For example, patients over 65 who are sexually active are at high risk of sexually transmitted infections, including HIV and syphilis.

To be successful, the HIV Testing Action Kit must make it easy and desirable for the physician to offer testing, counseling, and linkage to care, and also help to de-stigmatize HIV testing for the patient. During the research and interview process, the MICA team developed a questionnaire for primary care providers to better understand the providers' current HIV testing knowledge, and to assess whether they offered testing. This data was critical to the development of the testing kit because it helped root the final design within pragmatic, real-world contexts.

Based on their research, site visits, interviews with healthcare providers, and primary care physicians, as well as background information provided by the partners at CCHR and the Baltimore City Health Department, the team developed a list of specific challenges to successful implementation of the HIV Testing Action Kit, which included the fact that HIV testing in Maryland is not compulsory.

STRATEGY When the team entered the ideation, design, and pitch phases, it was clear that the HIV Testing Action Kit required thoughtful and relevant branding that was Baltimore-centric, and that it must serve as a persuasive call to action for private health medical providers to prioritize HIV testing and linkage to care.

To successfully engage with the intended audience, the team and partners determined that it was critical that the HIV Action Testing Kit design proposals must reinforce these key messages:

1. Making regular HIV testing routine (every 6 months) de-stigmatizes testing.
2. Testing is for everyone: HIV doesn't discriminate.
3. Testing is simple.
4. Sexual health is part of total health.
5. HIV testing affects individuals and communities.
6. Open communication reduces fear of HIV and testing.

Instead of pitching one design concept at the end of the semester, the MICA team developed and proposed two distinct branding approaches and naming strategies for the HIV Action Kit, "Protect Baltimore" and "Reality Check." Both concepts spoke in a distinct voice that encouraged the user to take direct and immediate action, and both proposals provided the necessary tools and resources to make testing and counseling easy and desirable for providers and patients.

Approach 1: Protect Baltimore The Protect Baltimore mark is authoritative, yet friendly. It speaks clearly and in an engaging way that encourages the viewer to protect their city, their communities, and themselves.

Approach 2: Reality Check The Reality Check mark uses a check symbol in place of the word check, and utilizes wordplay to create an identity that resonates. It calls patients and providers to action in a direct, no-nonsense way.

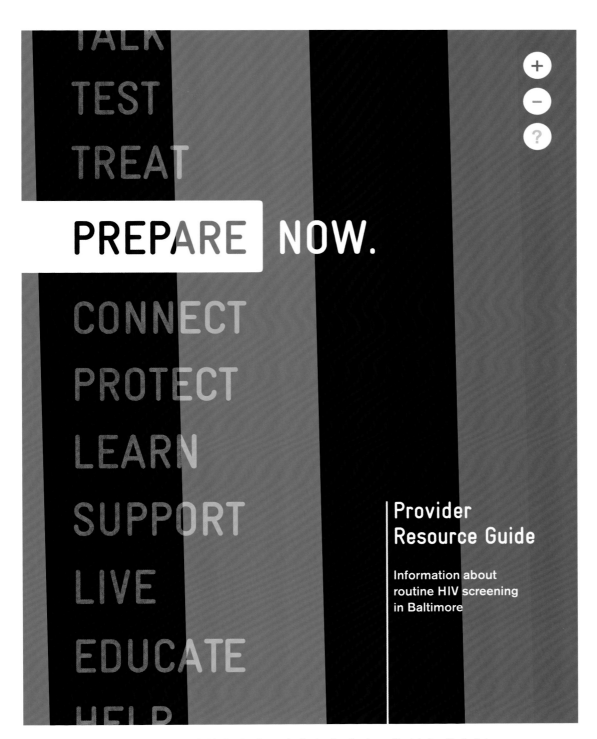

TALK
TEST
TREAT

PREPARE NOW.

CONNECT
PROTECT
LEARN
SUPPORT
LIVE
EDUCATE
HELP

**Provider
Resource Guide**

**Information about
routine HIV screening
in Baltimore**

2.4 Protect Baltimore Provider Resource *Guide. Design: Center for Design* Practice team. Final design: Heejin Suh.

Proposed Protect Baltimore and Reality
Check HIV Testing Action Kit components

Provider Resource Manual At the heart of the HIV
Action Testing Kit is a resource manual that includes:

- customizable, easy-to-update removable
  pages for up-to-date information about
  the HIV epidemic in the provider's local
  geographic area
- procedures for HIV testing
- data visualizations about HIV in Baltimore
- list of testing and treatment centers
  in Baltimore
- photocopy-ready forms for sexual
  health intake

Provider/patient conversation and counseling tool
This guide is for facilitating conversation between
doctors/nurses and patients:

- includes conversation starters
  and a testing script
- provides counseling resources about
  testing, treatment, and prevention
- addresses fears, stigmas, and
  misconceptions about HIV testing
- patient information cards.

A convenient takeaway flier with information about
HIV testing and treatment in Baltimore includes:

- information for patients who have
  received positive test results
- information about HIV testing
- information about preventative measures
  patients can take to protect themselves

HIV Testing Reminders Cards and text messages
to remind and encourage patients to get tested
regularly and to keep future appointments:

- takeaway appointment and testing
  reminder card with website link
- text message reminder system

Website and Mobile App The website and app
were designed to collect all resources for
providers and patients in one place.

Branded Giveaways The kit includes matchbook
condoms, buttons, and coffee mugs.

EFFECTIVENESS After the semester ended, the
project was funded for implementation and both
design concepts were taken through a comprehensive
focus group process to identify which campaign
should be produced and implemented in Baltimore
City. As a result of the focus groups, "Protect
Baltimore" was selected for implementation. CCHR
contracted with one of the student designers from
the MICA team to design the final Protect Baltimore
HIV Testing Action Kit and materials.

ASSESSMENT Protect Baltimore is currently
being implemented, and partners have
provided enthusiastic feedback about the
campaign's reception:

*The kits are professional and sleek—they are also
some of the most updated sources of information
providers have. They communicate an appropriate
degree of seriousness and sophistication—which
is important for an outreach campaign geared to
the medical community ... We have been repeatedly
complimented on the look and content of our
materials. We have had requests for copies from
around the country.* —**Amelia Greiner Safi,** PhD MS,
The Center for Child and Community Health Research

This project has become a model for a successful
partnership between MICA and CCHR and is the start
of long-term, ongoing collaboration. Primarily due to
this high level of engagement and direct collaboration
with CCHR, the project was able to address this
complex communications challenge, resulting in a
campaign that has been enthusiastically received
by primary care providers and their patients.

2.5 Protect Baltimore condom packaging proposal. *Design: Center for Design Practice team.*

RESOURCES/ADDITIONAL INFORMATION

Baltimore City HIV/AIDS Epidemiological Profile, Fourth Quarter 2011, Data reported through December 31, 2011, Center for HIV Surveillance, Epidemiology and Evaluation Prevention and Health Promotion Administration, Maryland Department of Health and Mental Hygiene. http://phpa.dhmh.maryland.gov/OIDEOR/CHSE/Shared%20Documents/Baltimore%20City%20HIV%20AIDS%20Epidemiological%20Profile%2012-2011.pdf.

"Public Health Detailing of Primary Care Providers: New York City's Experience, 2003–2010," Michelle G. Dresser, MPH, Leslie Short, MPH, Laura Wedemeyer, BA, Victoria Lowerson Bredow, MPH, Rachel Sacks, MPH, Kelly Larson, MPH, Joslyn Levy, MPH, BSN, Lynn D. Silver, MD, MPH. http://ajph.aphapublications.org/doi/full/10.2105/AJPH.2011.300622.

DESIGNING FOR DEMOCRACY

Christopher Hethrington, Professor of Communication Design,
Faculty of Design & Dynamic Media, Emily Carr University
of Art and Design, Vancouver, Canada

CLIENT
ElectionsBC.

PROJECT TITLE
Designing for Democracy.

DURATION
14 weeks, fall 2012.

BUDGET
$10,000. ElectionsBC
provided funding for the
project that fully supported
all the costs associated
with offering the course
as well as supporting
material expenses.

TEAM
Instructors: **Christopher
Hethrington**, Professor of
Communication Design,
and **Susan Stewart**, Dean of
the Faculty of Culture and
Community, Emily Carr
University of Art + Design.
Chief Electoral Officer: **Keith
Archer**, PhD, ElectionsBC,
Communications Manager: **Don
Main**, ElectionsBC. *Director of
Client Services:* **Allan Black**,
Elevator Strategy. Nineteen
students.

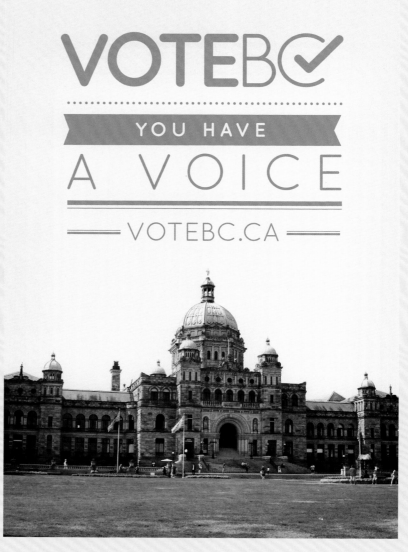

2.6 The "vote because" theme is expressed as multiple reasons for why one should vote.
Though the four parts of the campaign theme were—because it's easy, because it's important,
because you know, and because you can—this particular approach meant to convey
reasons beyond the limitations of the four. *Design: Megan White.*

DESCRIPTION In the lead-up to provincial elections in British Columbia, ElectionsBC, an organization that administers the Election Act and the provincial electoral process in British Columbia, recognized an opportunity to engage young adults in the process of improving youth participation in the electoral process. As with many electoral organizations, they had been challenged in the past by increasingly lower voter turnout, particularly from the demographic of 19- to 25-year-old youth. With provincial elections slated for the following spring, ElectionsBC needed to find a way to increase voter registration and actual voting participation by the target demographic. To do this, they reached out to Emily Carr University of Art & Design with funding and the desire to engage young creatives, but were completely open to what we might propose, providing a great deal of autonomy and support in both the conceptual development of the project and its ongoing operations. At an initial meeting it was determined that a special topics course would be created with the final outcome to take the form of a diverse media campaign that addressed the problem space. Broadly speaking, as most students themselves were representative of the target demographic, the campaign would largely take the form of *youth speaking to youth, in a youth voice.*

Though housed within the Faculty of Design, the course was promoted as open to all students at Emily Carr regardless of their area of study. This resulted in a diversity of student disciplines within the classroom including those from visual arts, critical and cultural studies, communication design, and industrial design. The multidisciplinary nature of the cohort created a real opportunity to explore collaboration in a context that was, for the most part, unlike any the participants had experienced in the past.

"Democracy" was in the title of the course and at the very core of the project itself, and so an opportunity presented itself to invest the methods and process of designing with those same notions of autonomy and responsibility. In some respects, the same choices faced when deciding to participate in voting were embedded in the core of how the class functioned—students had to decide how they would contribute and to what degree.

RESEARCH Students worked to their strengths to provide extensive secondary research in areas such as behavior change, key communication touch points, and social media ecology. They also did extensive precedent research into environmental and installation design, identity and branding, and existing campaign exemplars, both specific to the problem of young voter turnout and those successful in engaging youth generally.

A Critical + Cultural Practices major provided analysis of statistical research and survey interpretations that explored demographics, behavioral motivations and barriers, and communication channels. This research was specific to British Columbia and, as a result, was exceptionally relevant to the project and informed much of the conceptual ideation that followed. A student from the Interaction + Social Media program thoroughly assessed the impact and relationship of various social media touch points and how they might support or, alternatively, work to the detriment of the campaign. This was particularly important in developing a social media framework that would also insulate ElectionsBC from criticism in an environment where the kinds of explicit expression associated with the youth voice could run counter to the comparatively conservative and neutral voice of the client.

This up-front secondary research was supported by the precedent research that was generated by industrial and communication designers over the course of the conceptual development and ideation stages and through the final stages of development in a more reflective and iterative way consistent with their design process.

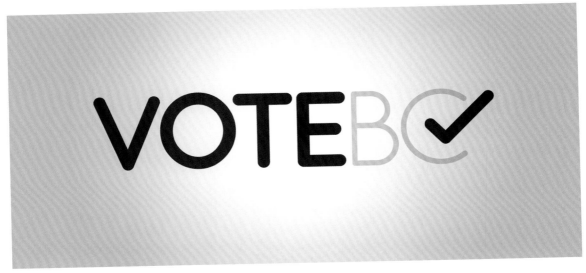

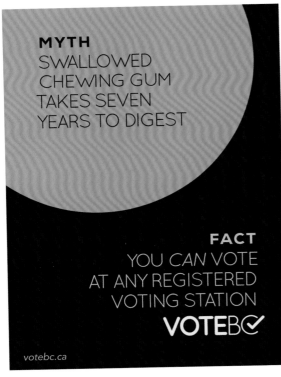

2.7a The three components of the VoteBC wordmark include the word "vote" as a call to action, the checkmark as an affirmation and a metonymy relating to the act of voting, and BC representing British Columbia and the text messaging short form of "because". "Vote because" was a four-part thematic anchor for the campaign. *Design: Kieran Wallace.*

2.7b–2.7c As part of the "because you can" theme, these large transit shelter posters sought to engage audiences with bold contrasting color and a mildly whimsical message that would draw attention and build curiosity. The Myths and Facts poster series focused on a key client concern regarding the misconceptions about district-specific voting locations. *Design: Kieran Wallace.*

CHALLENGES One of the focal points in the teaching method of this class proved to challenge the success of the project throughout the course of the semester. Embedding notions of autonomy and responsibility was particularly difficult given the relatively large numbers in the class, and self-organization across the disciplines compounded the problem. Diverse disciplines and personal responsibility effectively supported the research and ideation stages, but breakdowns occurred in the transition to the formal production development stage. Students began to see the project as a communication design problem rather than as a larger service design opportunity with a variety of touch points. In facilitating this project, I struggled to find the balance between encouraging autonomy and instructing or directing, and I found it quite challenging to bring forward the unique disciplinary strengths of some individuals who felt they needed to perform outside their field of practice in order to be of value.

STRATEGY From the outset, the strategy for implementing this project involved four objectives. The first was to create a working studio environment that would encourage students from diverse backgrounds, who often worked alone and independently, to instead work collaboratively and confidently toward problem solving, ideation, and implementation. As the client came to us with the specific intention of engaging youth in the communication problem, the second objective was to give students the authority and autonomy to organize and decide on strategic direction. This autonomy informed another objective, which was to ensure that their perceptions and intuitions, informed by research, took primacy over that of the instructor or even the client. This was a necessary strategy if we were going to truly embrace the notion of *youth speaking to youth, in a youth voice*. Finally, the diversity of the cohort offered the strategic opportunity to create a service design approach that offered multiple touch points from print and web to environment and performance.

2.8a–2.8b These poster examples were explorations in both the visual and textual vernacular of the target audience by using photographic treatments from social media, identifying a regional cultural icon that resonates with youth audiences, and adopting a self-aware exaggeration of youth slang co-opted from popular culture. *Design: Megan White.*

EFFECTIVENESS The project was very successful in determining a communications vernacular that would engage and persuade the target audience to act by effectively addressing areas that were otherwise a challenge for affecting behavior change. Students presented the final campaign proposal to the Chief Electoral Officer of ElectionsBC, the Communications Officer, and a representative of the ministry's advertising agency. The results of the research and ideation that led to the broader conceptualization of a targeted youth campaign were very well received by the client, and aspects of the project were implemented in the final media campaign that was launched the following spring.

The strategy of leveraging the multidisciplinary classroom, though successful in terms of research and ideation, proved less effective at the development stage. The project became progressively constrained to print and online touch points, and the opportunity to create a diverse and fully resolved campaign was largely missed.

In the lead-up to the elections in the spring of 2013, Emily Carr received a significant amount of local and national media attention. Many students were interviewed for print publications and television broadcasts, providing them with an opportunity to reach a wide audience and discuss their beliefs about democratic processes, and how design can contribute in this challenging problem space.

ASSESSMENT There were many positive outcomes from this partnered project with ElectionsBC, not least of which was the extensive media coverage that benefited all stakeholders. The opportunity to teach and learn in a multidisciplinary environment allowed the exploration of a kind of collaborative practice that is often encouraged in design teaching but seldom realized to such a degree. The challenges experienced, rather than being a deterrent, actually encourage greater engagement in these types of design methods and give insight into improving approaches in a reflective and iterative teaching practice that mirrors design processes themselves.

> "
> *Many students were interviewed for print publications and television broadcasts, providing them with an opportunity to reach a wide audience and discuss their beliefs about democratic processes and how design can contribute in this challenging problem space.*"

Continued community and government partnerships will support and inform new ways of working collaboratively across new and diverse disciplines, and evolve and improve our design practice as well as our methods of teaching. Finally, and particularly in emerging areas such as service design, these partnerships offer the opportunity to show how design can make a difference when addressing complex and challenging social service problems. As Martin Temple of the UK Design Council says, it will allow us "to show how design offers practical solutions which deliver real results on the ground" (http://www.designcouncil.org.uk/about-us/what-we-stand).

COMMUNITY PARTNERSHIP WITH ST. JAMES SCHOOL

Kelly Holohan, Program Head, MFA Graphic & Interactive Design, Tyler School of Art, Temple University, Philadelphia, Pennsylvania

CLIENT
St. James School, a Philadelphia middle school in the Allegheny West neighborhood, committed to educating traditionally under-resourced students in a nurturing environment.

PROJECT TITLE
Community Partnership with St. James School.

DURATION
16 weeks, spring semester 2014.

BUDGET
As this was the inaugural year of the project, the MFA students began without a set budget. They reached out to community partners for donations, including art supplies, printing costs, paper, catering, volunteering, and exhibition supplies. The project would not have been possible without generous support from Artist & Craftsman Supply, Di Bruno Brothers, Fireball Printing, photographer Sam Fritch, Masthead Print Studio, Tyler Printmaking, and Tyler Graphic and Interactive Design.

TEAM
Instructor: **Professor Kelly Holohan.**
MFA students: **Zan Barnett, Nikki Eastman, Joshua Schott, Stephanie Werning.**
St. James School seventh-grade class: **Zahkiyyah Crawford, Marquis Fabii, Diamond Gibbs, Ainyae Holmes, Tyrena Husbands, Ezekiel McLeod, Jonathan Newlin, Jamaal Oliver, Cordell Patterson, Sydnee Reddy, Kanyana Reese, Lashay Smith, John Taylor, Kwymaje Thompson, Jalieka Woodard.**
St. James School administration: **David Kasievich,** Head of School; **Laura Hoffman-Dimery,** Principal; **Deena Ball,** Art Teacher.

2.9a Ezekiel and Zahkiyyah work on ideas for their team's poster design. *Photo: Joshua Schott.*

2.9b Grad mentor Stephanie Werning's group proudly display their inspiring poster design. *Photo: Kelly Holohan.*

DESCRIPTION As part of their graduate thesis course at Tyler School of Art, first-year MFA students were prompted to choose a group project that would center around a collaboration with the St. James School, a middle school in the Allegheny West neighborhood of Philadelphia. After meeting with the St. James administration and learning about their mission, culture, and immediate needs, the MFA students were inspired by the importance placed on the arts in the St. James curriculum, and chose to create a project that could showcase the school's passion for art education.

The MFA Design class conceptualized a collaborative silkscreen poster project to take place over the spring semester 2014. They worked with the seventh-grade class at St. James School to create a large-scale poster exhibition in which the young students learned about design, the creative process, and exhibiting work. The graduate students worked closely with small groups of St. James students, acting as design mentors and creating posters with positive themes inspired by the St. James student pledge.

The pledge, which all St. James students learn to recite, highlights the core values of the school community. The MFA class wanted to incorporate these principles into the project, and asked students to pick their favorite themes from the pledge. The final themes were *knowledge*, *envisioning the future*, and *positive change.* The entire St. James pledge can be read here: http://stjamesphila.org/about-us/students/

Each graduate design mentor worked closely with groups of three to four students to conceptualize and design a silkscreen poster. Over the course of the semester, the MFA students were able to develop close relationships with the St. James students through repeated visits between the two schools. These visits involved creating their ideas, experimenting with design, taking field trips with the students, screen printing their posters, and celebrating with them at the climatic exhibition.

The exhibition took place at Tyler School of Art in a highly visible gallery space open to the public. The MFA students curated and installed the show, which included diptychs of the St. James student posters

2.10 St. James students and grad mentor Zan Barnett select colors for their silkscreen poster. *Photo: Kelly Holohan.*

and the MFA student posters hung side by side. Additionally, the exhibition included project photos, videos, posters displaying the St. James pledge, and process artwork made by the students. Sale runs of each poster were available for purchase along with promotional souvenirs. St. James students also helped to run a printing station, so exhibition guests could print their own postcard to commemorate the show.

RESEARCH Prior to meeting with St. James, the MFA class was assigned to read Andrew Shea's book *Designing for Social Change: Strategies for Community-Based Graphic Design* to prepare for the challenges of a community partnership. They visited St. James School several times to listen and learn about the school mission, culture, and needs. This dialogue was critical in defining a project that would serve the needs of both communities.

Once the basis of the project was formed, the MFA class began to research the history and process of silkscreen printing. They imparted this information to the St. James students through slide presentations of silkscreen artwork and an instructional video on the silkscreen process that the MFA class scripted, filmed, and edited. This video was shown to prepare the students for printing their own posters.

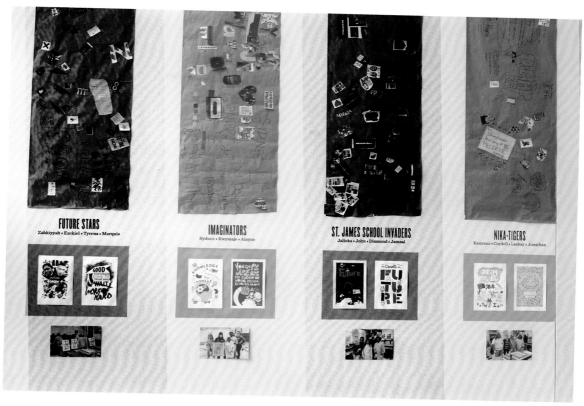

2.11 "Dreams on Screens" exhibition installation at Tyler School of Art. Posters were displayed as diptychs and hung with each team's idea comps and a group photo. *Photo: Sam Fritch.*

CHALLENGES The challenges included funding, time management, scheduling between the two schools, and St. James student attendance outside of events at their school. Since the MFA students defined their own project working alongside St. James, they had to address funding as the project progressed. Reaching out to community partners for assistance largely solved this challenge, although the design department supported us by covering the costs of the exhibition. Another challenge was time management, both with the project schedule and coordinating with St. James for all the necessary meetings with students. Solving this challenge required flexibility in scheduling on the part of both schools, in addition to open communication. The most difficult challenge was encouraging attendance of the St. James students at the exhibition; the St. James administration noted that student attendance at extracurricular activities was usually difficult to achieve. Though only some of the students were able to attend the exhibition, the ones who did spoke highly about the event to their peers. Students in attendance were excited to be an integral part of the exhibition.

STRATEGY

Phase 1: Planning The MFA class visited St. James and engaged in a dialogue about the needs of the school. Then, they conceptualized the silkscreen poster project and developed a presentation to pitch to the St. James administration. After feedback from St. James, the MFA class adjusted the details of the project to meet the following goals:

1. Involve the students of St. James and get them excited about the design process.
2. Raise awareness within the Philadelphia community about the mission and work of St. James.
3. Highlight the importance of progressive art programs in schools.
4. Attract potential donors and partnerships for St. James School.

Phase 2: Creative Process The MFA class visited St. James six times over the course of the semester. Visits included observing their art class, engaging in a silkscreen demo, creating mind maps based on the St. James pledge themes, designing posters, and screen printing their final posters. Additionally, the St. James students were able to explore the graphic and interactive design spaces on a field trip at Tyler School of Art. The seventh graders were given the opportunity to participate in a critique of their graduate mentors' posters. The search for funding started in this phase after the project became more solidified. Finally, the St. James and Tyler communities came together for the poster exhibition in phase 3.

Phase 3: Exhibition In preparation for the exhibition, the MFA students created the branding and identity for the collaborative project, "Dreams on Screens," and developed promotional materials. The MFA class and St. James administration shared the exhibition promotion with various media outlets. Then, the MFA class curated and installed the exhibit at Tyler School of Art.

> **"**
>
> *The graduate students worked closely with small groups of St. James students, acting as design mentors and creating posters with positive themes inspired by the St. James student pledge."*

———

EFFECTIVENESS We determined the effectiveness of our project in light of our original goals, and felt we were successful in getting the St. James students excited about design. We raised awareness for St. James School through publicity for the project, and the exhibit was well attended by the St. James community as well as the Tyler School of Art and Temple University communities. While it is difficult to measure the scope of the project in terms of potential donors, the artistic culture of St. James received much attention from the art community of Philadelphia.

ASSESSMENT Overall, the project met most of the goals that we set, but also had unexpected benefits. While the project didn't have a huge direct financial impact on St. James School, the strong relationship that was built between the two school communities will pave the road for successful future collaborations. Some things we will do to improve on future MFA class projects with St. James include the following: establishing a single contact with St. James to streamline communication between our schools; meeting with the St. James administration earlier and more often to allot more time for exploration in the planning phase; and securing funding for the project ahead of time. We hope that the exposure generated by this inaugural project will help gain financial support for future collaborations with St. James.

EUROPEAN STREET DESIGN CHALLENGE 2013

Sadhna Jain, Course Leader, MA Graphic Design Communications, Chelsea College of Art, London, UK

CLIENT

The Creative Co-operative, an agency for social and cultural creative practices, chose as its focus the Seine-Denis les Plaines area of Paris, which is made up of heavy industrial and multicultural areas and has large numbers of immigrant workers. Their project proposed, "How could social and cultural cohesion be encouraged through creative (re-) designs within the physical spaces or the digital/physical fabric of urban life?"

PROJECT TITLE

European Street Design Challenge (ESDC) 2013.

DURATION

Stage 1: Creative Co-operative spent 6 months identifying the brief, issues, and challenges, evaluating current practices with members of Saint Denis Council and the Bureau International des Expositions.
Stage 2: Student team received the brief and background information about the area in advance. This allowed time for the Teams to engage in further contextual research and build case studies of design practices.
Stage 3: Four days of site-specific development and designing.

BUDGET

Cap Digital and the Futur en Seine Festival provided financial support.

TEAM

Creative Co-operative, overall project directors: Andrew Bullen and Janine Huizenga.
Local expert advisor: Bernard Orantin—Aubervilliers (2012, 2013). *Project Manager:* Dr. Ouafae Benslimane, Research, Innovation General Council of Seine-Saint-Denis, Department of Planning and Development.
Chelsea student team: Prudence Djajadi and Haobo Chen, MA course in Graphic Communication Design; and Hiroshi Ito and Angelina Papaioannou, MA course in Interior Spatial Design.

2.12a Modular arrangement of floating platforms—daytime use.

2.12b Water Lily platform remote communications via social media and local connection with smartphones.

DESCRIPTION The Creative Co-operative proposed to critically explore models of World Expos to understand how visions of the future can create catalysts for sustainable urban regeneration and legacies for local communities. This was to encourage the making of engaging design proposals and prototypes that also served as a prompt to develop core values within public thinking.

Brief and aims of the design solution To design an exhibition installation, application, or pavilion with a dual role. The response must have a vision of digital technology and design used in the creation of a better urban life for the future; and present a practical and sustainable solution to the challenges of the Seine-Saint-Denis area, to remain as a legacy for the people of the area.

Achieving a sense of connectedness between the different communities of the Paris region, which would enrich a sense of belonging and diversity within the culture, was one of the two main priorities of the brief. The second of those priorities was to drive economic prosperity in ways that were sympathetic to cultural cohesion and at the same time inventive with the continuing uses of technologies and infrastructures.

ESDC was scheduled as a live research project within the Futur en Seine Festival, which annually showcases for the benefit of the public and industries the latest innovations in design, research, and entrepreneurship using digital technology. This festival has international standing, having up to 80,000 visitors, and is run by Cap Digital who are a non-profit organization clustering together SMEs, research labs, university departments, and corporations across France as experts for digital content and technological innovation. The Creative Co-operative were therefore keen to engage and test a systemic design approach to ESDC. For the student this meant experiencing first hand how to develop design practices that are directly embedded within locally organized actions, policies, and opportunities for the client.

RESEARCH For the Chelsea team, the research began several weeks before arriving in Paris. This included research about the region of Paris; identifying a variety of theoretical and practical methodologies that could be suitable for adaptive design and design interactions; debating the validity of design strategies that could complement ethnographic research. In Paris, primary research was made meaningful through the program of walking tours, lectures, and project critiques from different experts from the region of Saint Denis/Aubervilliers.

Observational studies also led on to two distinctive methodologies in preparation of the ideas stage of the project: (1) mental/emotional map, which involved remapping the sites visited, identifying the perceptions of working/living life and general emotional responses to the geography and architecture; and (2) value ladder, which required each team to identify values as designers, and then align this to the values of the brief requirements.

CHALLENGES The primary challenge for the Chelsea group was to introduce an idea of social cohesion for the community that could also grow within the plans for a developing city. The balance between "belonging" and "sharing" had to be met in order to create a sustainable design solution. A good opportunity arose at the site of the canal, as this location would encounter the solitude of the daily commuters and inhabitants, but could also become programmed within busy city-wide events when required.

STRATEGY Choosing a site Through historical research it was noted that Canal de l'Ourcq was once a lifeline of Paris, allowing for the transportation of goods and water sanitation. Also, many urban and rural communities worldwide continue to build cultural events around water to celebrate community identity in more symbolic ways. These two factors made concrete the decision of using the canal as the space for the design idea.

Identifying forms Inspiration from nature led the group to aquatic plants, quickly isolating the water lily as a form that could be exploited for its spectacular visual qualities but also its lesser known structural properties. With its lattice of hardened ribs and an upturned edge the largest of water lilies can support the weight of a human.

2.13 Canal de l'Ourcq disused space and Chelsea team site development.

Concept The idea of a floating platform on the canal in the guise of the water lily was proposed: units could be joined together to create a modular structure as medium-sized platforms or floated individually to help create a strong visual identity for the disused canal.

Problem solving As the canal is not currently in use but is highlighted as an area/facility for urban development, the student group felt they were contributing to the current strategies for city redevelopment and consequently felt their creative ideas would be supported. The modular nature of the design concept encouraged playful uses of the canal which would originate directly from the local community, and was also flexible enough to be physically maneuvered if and when water transport recommenced.

Function follows form Guided by human curiosity about balancing on water by standing on the water lilies, the group decided to make their forms platforms for people to physically use. If you could walk onto them then what else could you do?

Form follows function To facilitate a close relationship with the local neighborhood and to test their responses to the platforms, a variety of existing social media platforms were added to create a network of communications. Therefore, the Internet supported the platforms both locally and remotely. Remotely, users could ask questions, seek information about events, and suggest their own uses for the platforms. Locally, mobile technologies could interact with content and media effects, which could be embedded in the platforms.

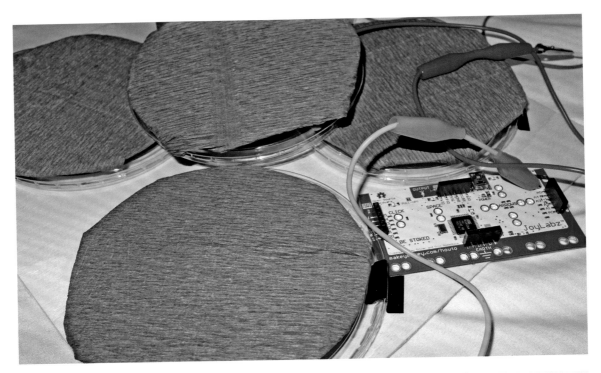

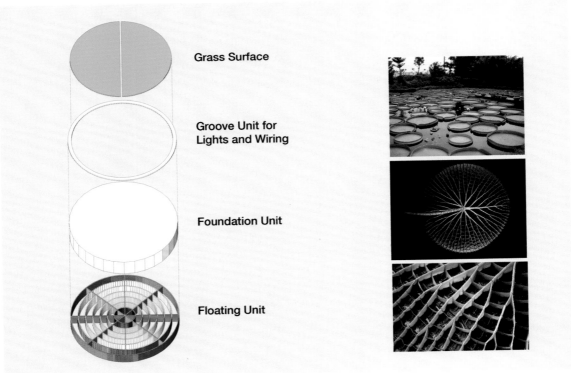

Grass Surface

Groove Unit for
Lights and Wiring

Foundation Unit

Floating Unit

2.14a Prototype testing interactive connectivity with MakeyMakey board.

2.14b Platform inspiration derived from nature and translated to material construction.

2.15 Students developing an interactive prototype.

"

The students as designers managed their social responsibilities quite well, which was evident in the way they afforded local residents practical ways to become stakeholders in the design."

———

The modular coupling of the platforms allowed multiple needs to be met simultaneously and a sense of solitude to be preserved for individuals or families. The platforms were designed to have different features depending on whether it is day or night, mimicking the variety of water lilies that change behaviors according to the environment. When less active, the water lilies with their curious forms would also help enhance the visual look of the neighborhood and its identity.

EFFECTIVENESS AND ASSESSMENT

I would probably focus more on the online features of the platform and start thinking about the interactive web features in order to attract Saint Denis to global viewers. —**Student**

We were struck by the poetry and aesthetic strength of the solution, combined with its flexibility and functional capacity. —**Creative Co-operative**

It is clear that the students listened carefully to the local experts and focused their decisions upon how to use the existing fabric of the environment and neighborhood. The students as designers managed their social responsibilities quite well, which was evident in the way they afforded local residents practical ways to become stakeholders in the design. Being more "savvy" by demonstrating exactly how economic revenue might be generated by the design solution, and asserting this as part of the answer to a systemic design approach, would show the project's overall design ingenuity to maximum effect.

THE WEST END WORKBOOK:
AN ILLUSTRATIVE CASE STUDY

Associate Professors Keith M. Owens and Michael R. Gibson,
The University of North Texas, College of Visual Arts and Design
(CVAD) Design Research Center (DRC), Denton, Texas

IN YOUR HANDS, YOU HOLD A SWISS ARMY KNIFE
FOR STRATEGIC URBAN PLANING. Less a rigid to-do
list based on a singular agenda, this Workbook is more
like the iconic red pocket toolbox—providing a handy
assortment of adaptable tools to assist you as you forge
a lively urban district out of neighborhood vitality and
economic vibrancy. >> Inside you'll discover useful insights and knowledge based on careful research; unique
strategies and ideas to activate and enliven place; and
usable methods for implementing ideas. Taken up now
and honed over time, these tools will help the West End
begin to answer some of the many challenges it now faces as it strives to honor its past, explore its present, and
invent its future.

CLIENT
The Dallas, Texas Historic
West End, on behalf of
Downtown Dallas, Inc.

PROJECT TITLE
The Historic West End:
Interdisciplinary Research,
Imaginative Revitalization.

DURATION
2010–12.

BUDGET
$4,500 research support
awarded by Downtown
Dallas, Inc. and The West
End Association, Inc.

TEAM
Faculty project co-leaders:
Associate Professors **Keith M.
Owens** and **Michael R. Gibson.**
Student investigators:
Nicole Hauch, MFA, Innovation
Studies, Design Research;
Sierra Mendez, MA, Innovation
Studies, Design Research;
and **Sam Williamson**, MA,
Innovation Studies,
Design Research.
Advisors, partners: Corgan
Associates, Inc., The West
End Association, Inc.

2.16 The *West End Workbook* was published to provide the
Historic West End with specific actionable and/or catalytic
solutions, and to provide for other Dallas downtown districts a
self-driven model for civic engagement and solution finding.
Student investigators: Nicole Hauch, Sierra Mendez, and
Sam Williamson. *Design: Keith Owen.*

DESCRIPTION The University of North Texas (UNT) College of Visual Arts and Design (CVAD) Design Research Center (DRC) worked in partnership with Downtown Dallas, Inc. to formulate and operate this participatory design research project. Downtown Dallas, Inc. is an organization focused on sustaining the vitality of the city's central core. This project was undertaken to accomplish three primary goals:

1. To first understand and then take action to address the unique civic revitalization needs of a designated historic district in Dallas, "The Historic West End." Located immediately west of Dallas's downtown business district, this area was struggling to recapture the positive allure of its past achievements while attempting to build a more sustainable future.

2. To invent, refine, and codify a design-driven model of urban research, engagement, and action that was flexible (i.e., generalizable) enough for use by other downtown Dallas districts.

3. To attempt to answer a simple but significant educational research question: *Could graduate students—both designers and non-designers— without backgrounds in urban planning collaboratively come to understand challenges inherent in a real civic problem, and then invent viable solutions to them?* As proponents of interdisciplinary, evidence-based design practice, my colleague Michael Gibson and I believed this question to be salient in light of the growing instances of designers working with diverse partners being challenged by complex projects occurring far outside of market-driven practice.

RESEARCH Research for the project preceded a multi-stage process composed of nine interdependent phases. The research focused on contextual, historical, and ethnographic discovery. The early investigations fueled later data collection that in turn informed analyses, conceptual framing, persona/scenario construction, and solution ideation. Students conducted a rigorous literature review of scholarly and popular information related to urban revitalization, community building, and socioeconomic and civic engagement.

Primary research, principally informed by ethnographic methodologies, employed *emic* approaches: survey instruments, individual and small group interviews, and "on-street" field interviews of convenience; as well as *etic* approaches: direct investigator observations correlated to time, district geography, and key stakeholders. Moreover, the students catalogued the district's physical makeup: businesses, buildings, parking, and wayfinding infrastructure. They also catalogued external perceptions of the district as expressed in 20+ years of articles appearing in the *Dallas Morning News* and postings found online. This multi-method approach yielded rich, sociocultural understandings of the district as a historic, civic, and communal entity, along with the evolving challenges it was facing.

Student investigators discovered that the district was laden with challenges that typically confront struggling neighborhoods: uneven use and living mix, high vacancy rates, and the costs associated with offering amenities tailored to diverse user groups (visitors, residents, workers, and college students). These combined with stakeholders invested in the district possessing no unified vision (or ways to invent one) regarding the district's possible future(s). This fragmented self-awareness retarded efforts to thoughtfully account for physical and human resources, confused public perception about the district, and dissipated any efforts to create an authentic and inclusive rallying point around which the district's stakeholders could unite.

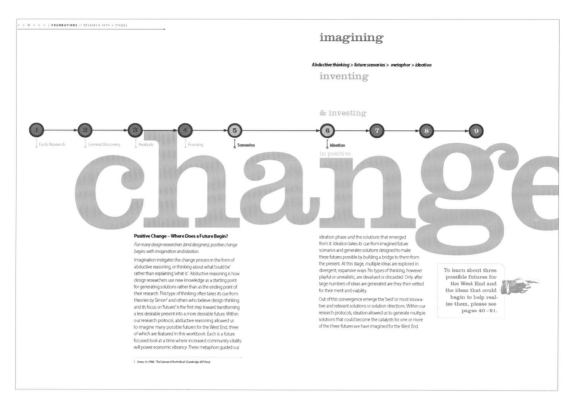

2.17 Page from the *West End Workbook* articulating scenario building and ideation along with the aspirational narrative, ideation organizational matrix, and solution descriptions. *Created by student investigator Sierra Mendez. Design: Keith Owens.*

CHALLENGES The project encountered research, educational, and implementation challenges. Research challenges included the difficulty of engaging with a significant number of research subjects representing key stakeholder groups. This hurdle was exacerbated by a fragmented decision-making and communication structure within the district. Student investigators also struggled with the complexities inherent to real-world (i.e., uncontrolled) investigations. Key educational challenges were twofold: the recurring difficulty in harmonizing educational outcomes with those associated with live field research and, despite careful documentation, a certain loss of institutional knowledge from one student research team to another over the two-year project span.

Moreover, the implementation of pilot projects to test research validity and solution utility was hampered by a lack of financial support by the district. When faced with these challenges, students thoughtfully recalibrated their approaches, adapted to less-than-ideal circumstances, and sought new ways to accomplish established goals. Fielding similar educational challenges on other DRC research initiatives, my colleague Michael and I continue to seek ways to seamlessly mesh the dynamics of applied field research with the expressed learning outcomes espoused by Communication Design's MFA/MA graduate program in Design Research.

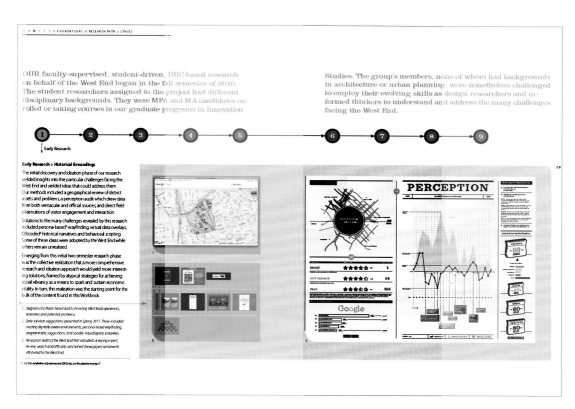

2.18 Pages from the *West End Workbook* detailing student research findings. *Student investigators: Nicole Hauch, Sierra Mendez, and Sam Williamson. Design: Keith Owens.*

STRATEGY The strategy guiding the West End project was twofold. As a *research and educational* endeavor, a multi-staged framework composed of nine distinct yet interdependent phases guided it. Inductive reasoning and ethnographic methods principally guided early discovery phases. Later framing, scenario-building, and ideation phases were guided by abductive, heuristic thinking. All phases were iterative: each step was progressively shaped by insights gained from the prior work and, in turn, informed future actions. This framework functioned as both a means to guide rational inquiry and innovation, and as educational scaffolding for students with little experience undertaking complex field research.

As a *solution-finding and innovation* exercise, the project allowed the students to consider new ways to address civic challenges without relying on traditional urban planning scenarios predicated solely on brute physicality—for example, infrastructure, economic footprint, and transportation. This prompt, supported by data gathered during the initial inquiry, guided an innovative strategy predicated on perceiving the West End as *an experience rather than a place*. The district was an ongoing, evolving "event" shaped by interactions between the totality of its built environment and the unique dispositions of the district's diverse user groups.

The fragmented self-image exhibited by district stakeholders also led the students to create three distinct, aspirational narratives that shaped their experiential approach *and* its corresponding solutions. Thus, the final solutions offered were not only tailored to address the district's current civic needs, but also sparked new thinking about the district's possible futures.

"

By augmenting controlled classroom experiences with the trials associated with indeterminate 'wicked' problems, students are challenged to adapt theory into practice in real time and in response to real concerns..."

———

EFFECTIVENESS AND ASSESSMENT In large part, the West End project yielded outcomes that met its stated goals. First, the district was presented with an extensive workbook that contained hundreds of ideas for pilot projects all logically derived from, and categorized by, the three aspirational narratives. These ideas could be implemented as presented or, as was suggested in the workbook, function as catalysts for the district stakeholders' own thinking and aspirations. Second, the *West End Workbook* also contained sections that extensively documented the research and innovation processes employed by student investigators. These sections explicated a meta-level, contextually transferable working model that other Dallas districts could easily adapt to their own, unique civic challenges. Third, the project gave strong credence to the idea that when designers and non-designers work collaboratively and are unfettered by strict disciplinary boundaries, refreshing new insights and innovative outcomes can result.

Educationally, Michael and I believe strongly in immersing graduate students in real-world, applied research problems. By augmenting controlled classroom experiences with the trials associated with indeterminate "wicked" problems, students are challenged to adapt theory into practice in real time and in response to real concerns—in this case, understanding and assisting a district comprised of diverse stakeholders confronting the difficult task of reinventing their collective future while honoring a distinctive past.

2.19 Examples of photographic documentation recording the West End built environment. Student investigators: Nicole Hauch, Sierra Mendez, and Sam Williamson. *Principal photography: Nicole Hauch.*

Ultimately, we concluded that all students involved in the project gained invaluable knowledge about evidence-based design practice, the challenges inherent to human field research (e.g., diverse factors, constituencies, temporalities, and agendas), the benefits of interdisciplinarity and collaboration, and the rigorous nature of demanding design research. The students also gained a more active, empathetic understanding of diverse stakeholders and their unique needs. This humanistic insight, often marginalized by other disciplines as they attempt to retain research objectivity, is nonetheless a vital component in evidence-based design practice.

ADDITIONAL INFORMATION A copy of the *West End Workbook* can be found at: http://designresearchcenter.unt.edu/projects.

ELISAVA 4 WALLS PROJECT

Raffaella Perrone, Head of Projects, ELISAVA
Barcelona School of Design and Engineering,
Barcelona, Spain

CLIENT
ELISAVA Barcelona School
of Design and Engineering,
Barcelona, Spain.

PROJECT TITLE
ELISAVA in 4 walls.

DURATION
December 2012–February 2013.

BUDGET
€2,400.

TEAM
In the first phase of the project,
22 third- and fourth-year
students from the Design
and Engineering programs
participated: **Carla Andreu,
Amelia Aponte, Luís Arenós,
Adriana Bertolín, Míriam Calleja,
Aleix Carricondo, Ester Córcoles,
Laia Corominas, Víctor García,
Gemma Guerrero, Ramon Mañas,
Xavier Mateo, Marc Miquel,
Núria Mora, Alexandre Pibernat,
Carolina Poch, Helena Puig,
Joaquim Rodríguez, Marta Seara,
Alma Topalovich, Júlia Torres,**
and **Aida Trujillo.**
In the second phase of the
project, two junior designers,
both ELISAVA alumni from the
Design program joined in: **Laia
Corominas, Carolina Poch**
and ELISAVA alumni: **Javier
Jabalera** and **Miguel Olivera.**
Advisor for both phases:
Ivan Bravo.
General coordination:
Raffaella Perrone, ELISAVA
Head of Projects.

2.20 Three levels installed. **From left to right: Miguel Olivera,** Javier Jabalera, Laia Corominas,
Ivan Bravo, Carolina Poch.

DESCRIPTION The goal of this project was to transform the School's interior through vinyl pieces that would modify space perception and interaction with users. The intervention consisted of large-scale illustrations structured along the four floors of the building. Each floor pictures students' experience during their four academic years. Four years portrayed in four floors: emblematic academic exercises, anecdotes, inquisitiveness, fears, tension, order, disorder, dreams, efforts, and a lot of coffee, an element that, surprisingly enough, is present in every floor.

The first floor/year depicts the beginning of a journey where we discover there is much to do. The second floor/year is a labyrinth-forest where we feel lost before the multiple options to choose from. The third floor/year is the time to specialize and travel abroad to study. The fourth floor/year is the moment to focus on the final degree project and launch our professional future. Lastly, each mural is a page from a diary where students can see themselves projected in the future, reflected in the present, and remembered in the past. To enhance the relationship between floors, we have included details that conceptually and physically connect the floors bottom-up, guiding the reading in a way that mirrors the concept of growth and evolution to be expected from a university career.

The students have reflected on what each course has meant to them, and, some months after the Creative Marathon, the work carried out by the students was displayed in the School's corridors thanks to the manufacturing and installation of a vinyl made by MACtac, a company which specializes in the manufacturing and sale of self-adhesive substrate intended for graphic and industrial decoration.

RESEARCH The students carried out two types of research: first, field research through photographic safari, ethnographic use interviews, and architectural and spatial observation; second, visual research on graphics applied in spaces and illustration styles, visual cataloging of iconic elements of the "ELISAVA collective imagination," and color research.

CHALLENGES The main challenge was to propose a creative collaboration to students from the Design and Engineering programs, in order to create a single illustration. Since 1997, ELISAVA has offered a blend of different yet complementary programs and professional training, including specializations in graphic design, industrial design, interior design, and design engineering programs. They all benefit from sharing faculty, classrooms, and students.

Proposing a joint project in the field of illustration seemed an interesting challenge to develop the creativity and imagination of our students, regardless of their field of study, by encouraging divergent thinking. For the ELISAVA community, the most important contribution was that students took over the space and decided to freely tell "their own story." The initial briefing was very open. From the school side, we just wanted to give free expression to their creativity, and we had asked them to "tell a story" on these four walls, maintaining the autonomy of each illustration/floor and, at the same time, the continuity between floors. It could have been the story of a growing tree or animals climbing the walls. The second challenge was the timing of the first phase—4 days—and the size of the surface to be covered—18 square meters per floor approximately for a total of 80 square meters.

What was most important was to find an advisor who had worked on graphic projects applied to large-scale space before, and who could lead the ideas of 22 students with the skill of an orchestra conductor. Ivan Bravo, a young professional illustrator and a former student of the school, proved to be an ideal choice.

Another important decision during the second phase of the project development (January–February, 2013) was to reduce the number of students who would carry out the final artwork, both as a matter of time management and to ensure an ensemble "style." All drawings had to be generated in detail, and it was better to reduce the number of hands in order to ensure uniformity. The decision to incorporate in the team two former students, junior designers, was based on their greater experience and availability outside the academic schedule, which allowed for intense workdays at the school itself, and sometimes even at Ivan Bravo's office.

2.21a Process sketches for ELISAVA in 4 Walls project.

2.21b Students working on sketches for ELISAVA in 4 Walls project.

2.22a Third level final artwork.

2.22b First and second level installed.

2.23 Fourth level final artwork.

"

The four walls quickly suggested the 4 years of coursework for both degrees, Design and Engineering."

———

STRATEGY The project was divided into three main stages:

1. Brainstorming and concept generation during the four workshop days in December 2012

On the first day of the workshop, after the initial briefing session with Ivan Bravo and myself, students were shown a number of graphical references applied as illustrations to a space, and were asked to find others that could interest them. Students then began working in a collective brainstorming session to decide "what story to tell." The four walls quickly suggested the 4 years of coursework for both degrees, Design and Engineering.

On the second day of the workshop, Ivan Bravo divided the 22 students into four groups, and he assigned an academic course and a floor to each one to study the uniqueness of each wall. Through observation of the context from the spatial-architectural point of view and user interviews, students "distilled" a number of important ideas to illustrate the floor and the course year that they had been assigned. The walls' spatial details (sockets and windows) were integrated as elements of the illustration.

During the third day of the workshop, the groups worked on the details of each mural and on integrating information into a single illustration. All groups worked in parallel in a classroom so that they were able to share ideas and ensure consistent and uniform results. Every 3 hours the groups met and commented on all the drawings. To enhance the spatial relationship between the floors and the transition from one academic year to the next, details that connect the walls were included, creating a steady narrative journey from the beginning (entrance to the building) to the fourth floor (top floor), where a large skylight lights up the entire space. This glass skylight ceiling primed the students to think about an analogy between heaven and finalization of studies with subsequent access to the professional world. This phase ended on the fourth day with the public presentation of general sketches of the four walls in pencil on A3 sheets.

2. Developing sketches and layout of the final art mural

In January 2013, the second phase of formalization and development of the initial sketches started, working intensively in the evenings for 2 weeks, and later spacing out the meetings with the advisor, Ivan Bravo, until late February 2013. Two junior designers drafted the details of each mural by hand using light tables, tracing paper, and pencil. Once the school management had approved the general layout, all drawings were digitalized and the color was applied. One of the students studied color specifically, and the overall palette was developed according to the school's space and the semantic value of the images.

This phase was completed with the digital files of the four walls in high resolution to send out to the company that had to produce the murals.

3. Vinyl production and placement

In March 2013, the files were sent for production to the company sponsoring the action, MACtac. The students assisted in the printing and production of the vinyl rolls and their subsequent placement in the space. The project was inaugurated with a lecture in which the entire process was explained.

EFFECTIVENESS Overall, we are very satisfied with the results, and the effort on the part of the advisor and students were rewarded as the project became a tangible reality. From the economic point of view, the budget was not appropriate for the time spent in coordinating and directing the project, but the students met the production budget, and this was a good learning experience for their future careers.

ASSESSMENT For the students, being able to see "their work of collective authorship" every day gives them great satisfaction. For first-year students, it is a "dream" to think of being able to do a similar project in the future.

As project coordinator, I could never have imagined such results. The project has greatly exceeded everyone's expectations, even the school management, who at first authorized use of the walls for only 6 months. A year later, it is still in place, and has become an iconic image of the school.

WELCOME HOME

Lisa Rosowsky, Professor, Graphic Design,
Massachusetts College of Art and Design,
Boston, Massachusetts

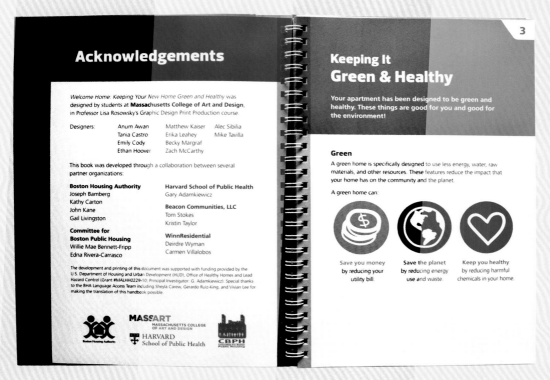

2.24 Inside cover of the book. *Photo: Lisa Rosowsky.*

CLIENT
Boston Housing Authority
and residents of two newly
renovated public housing
developments in Boston,
Old Colony and Washington
Beech Public Housing.

PROJECT TITLE
Welcome Home: Keeping Your
New Home Green and Healthy.

DURATION
12 weeks, fall 2011.

BUDGET
The cost of printing and binding
the book was $17,925 for 1,000
copies, and this was supported
with funding provided by the
US Department of Housing
and Urban Development (HUD),
Office of Healthy Homes and
Lead Hazard Control principal
investigator, G. Adamkiewicz.

TEAM
Instructor: Professor Lisa
Rosowsky. *Group of 10 graphic
design undergraduate students:*
Anum Awan, Tania Castro, **Emily
Cody, Ethan Hoover, Matthew
Kaiser, Erika Leahey, Becky
Margraf, Zach McCarthy, Alec
Sibilia, and Mike Tavilla.**

Advisors: **Dr. Gary Adamkiewicz,**
Harvard School of Public
Health; **John Kane,** Boston
Housing Authority; **Willie
Mae Bennett-Fripp** and Edna
Rivera-Carrasco, Committee for
Boston Public Housing; **Sheyla
Carew, Gerardo Ruiz-King,**
and **Vivian Lee,** translators
from Boston Housing Authority
Language Access Team.
Additional assistance from
Tom Stokes and **Kristin** Taylor,
Beacon Communities, LLC;
Deirdre Wyman and **Carmen
Villalobos,** WinnResidential;
Joseph Bamberg, Kathy Carton,
and **Gail Livingston,** Boston
Housing Authority.

177

DESCRIPTION The pedagogical aim of the Print Production course is twofold: to teach aspiring graphic designers what they need to know about getting their work commercially printed and produced, and to design and produce a collaborative print project for a community non-profit client. Most of our projects over the years have focused on public health/healthcare and education.

Our labor is provided at no cost, but the client is responsible for paying printing and production costs directly to the vendor(s). Because we work for free, we make an agreement with each client that what we produce collaboratively will not be sold. To provide my students with the best possible education about printing, we do not ask for vendor donations, but instead pay full market rates, allowing us to receive the same quality and range of services as any other design client. The cost of producing projects for this course have ranged from $10,000 at the low end up to $31,000 at the highest end.

Massachusetts College of Art and Design is located in the same neighborhood as Boston's famous Longwood Medical area, including Harvard's School of Public Health (HSPH). In 2011, I approached HSPH to ask if there were opportunities for collaboration, and Dr. Gary Adamkiewicz, a senior researcher in the Department of Environmental Health, expressed interest. He had been working with the Boston Housing Authority (BHA) on helping longtime public housing residents to transition into new "green" housing developments, and wanted our help to create an educational and instructional print piece for tenants who may never before have had access to thermostats, low-flow toilets, or dishwashers. We were supplied with a draft of the copy, which we were encouraged to edit and make "as visual as possible," with the aim of making this informational book accessible to residents with many literacy levels.

Based on their research, students designed a 48-page full-color wire-o bound book that opened from both sides: one way with text in English, and the other way with text in Spanish. A page of colorful vinyl decals was bound into the center for light switches and appliances, to remind residents to turn off lights, lower the thermostat, etc. The book had pockets on the inside of each cover, in which were cards in English and Spanish about how to use their appliances, as well as explaining the concept of the monthly utility bill (a novelty to residents who had never received one in prior public housing). Every resident received a book when moving into a new unit, and representatives from the building management company held follow-up meetings to go over the information (with interpreters) and answer questions.

RESEARCH This course always involves significant research both before and during each project. In this case, we began with a "facts and figures" talk about the history of public housing in Boston (the site of the nation's first public housing system) given by staff of the Boston Housing Authority; we also heard from the head of the Committee for Boston Public Housing, a grassroots tenant advocacy organization, who explained the challenges which longtime public housing residents face when occupying renovated "green" units. The following week, we were given tours of unimproved public housing and compared living conditions with renovated units elsewhere in the city; we took photos and video, and interviewed tenants. Students read and annotated documents supplied by both the BHA and the Harvard School of Public Health to learn about the range of health and safety hazards in the city's unimproved public housing developments, such as the effects of cigarette smoke, pesticides, and pests themselves.

CHALLENGES We faced several challenges during this project. One was editing the supplied draft to simplify the language for readers with limited literacy or limited English proficiency. Having worked on multiple healthcare projects during the history of this course, I have found that medical and research professionals can be blind to the presence of jargon, and benefit from having laypeople identify and "translate" it into commonspeak. Often, this requires a crash course on the topic at hand so that we have enough understanding to make the correct translation!

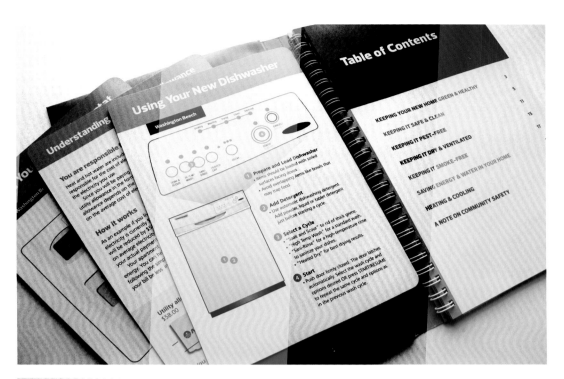

2.25a Pull-out cards in the front and back pockets explain topics such as how to use a dishwasher and thermostat, in both English and Spanish. *Photo: Lisa Rosowsky.*

2.25b A page of colorful vinyl decals was bound into the center of the book for light switches and appliances, to remind residents to turn off lights, lower the thermostat, etc. *Photo: Lisa Rosowsky.*

Another challenge was the bilingual nature of the book; while we had two students in the class who spoke some Spanish, neither was qualified to take on the task of translation. We were therefore extremely fortunate that the BHA supplied us with three translators, whom we brought on-site for the final 2 weeks of the class to assist us. This turned out to be essential when last-minute edits were being made and we needed to copy-fit in two languages.

"

Producing a project of this scope is incredibly challenging within a 12-week timeframe; we are up against the hard deadline of the end of the semester, when the students disperse for the winter holiday."

STRATEGY Producing a project of this scope is incredibly challenging within a 12-week timeframe; we are up against the hard deadline of the end of the semester, when the students disperse for the winter holiday. My strategy is to get as much as I can in place before the start of the semester, so that we can take off running from the very first class meeting. Typically, I line up that year's client and project 6–8 months in advance. This gives the client time to gather funding, if necessary, and to complete a draft of whatever copy we will be working with. It also gives me time to identify and connect with any experts we will need to visit the class and teach us about our subject.

One rule I have found to be extremely helpful is to strictly limit the number of people with whom we interact on the client side to one or at most two. In addition, the client understands that he or she must be dedicated to this project during the entire semester, and will be "on call" to respond quickly to questions that come up in order to deliver the product on time.

On our side of the process, I will typically divide up the class into smaller subgroups, each devoted to a particular task which suits their style and ability—editorial, design prototyping, image research, etc. We quickly identify which students are good illustrators, as we almost always need technical and/or informational illustrations. Subgroups are responsible for coordinating their efforts outside of class time, and each group has weekly deadlines. These subgroups eventually merge as the project develops, but this process is organic and varies from project to project. We also maintain a class wiki, and use it (along with Google Docs) to share files and information with one another during the week.

Roughly two-thirds of the way through the semester, we will present a rough version to the client and get feedback, which is absorbed and implemented as necessary. At that point, it is a sprint to the finish, with our point person generally joining us on site for the final class meeting for any last-minute edits.

The press check is scheduled during the break, and any students who are around can attend and get the chance to sign off on press sheets. Each student receives a copy of the printed piece for his or her portfolio, and I receive 5–10 copies for the course archive. Finally, several months after the project is completed, I request written documentation from the client about how the piece is being received and used.

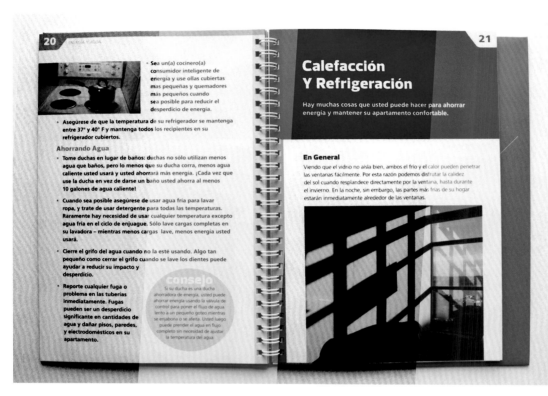

2.26 Interior spread from the Spanish-language side of the book. *Photo: Lisa Rosowsky.*

EFFECTIVENESS I learn something new with every project we work on for this course. With the *Welcome Home* project, an unusually large client-side team made it especially important to be sure that all parties were communicating with one another. Both the BHA team and our point person at HSPH were highly organized and ready to respond quickly with whatever information or access we needed.

ASSESSMENT Students who worked on this project learned "on the job" about the print production process from start to finish, and gained experience working with a client, a budget, and a tight schedule. And, in a program curriculum that emphasizes individual design work, a group project is always valuable.

For the BHA, and Dr. Adamkiewicz at HSPH, the *Welcome Home* book has been an unqualified success—tenants at the two newly green public housing developments have been enjoying the books since 2011, and, as an example of tenant environmental education, the book and our collaboration have been referenced at both national (HUD) and local levels.

THE BRIGHTMOOR FARMWAY PROJECTS

Hannah Smotrich, Associate Professor, and **Charlie Michaels**, Coordinator, Detroit Connections Program, Penny W. Stamps School of Art, University of Michigan, Ann Arbor

CLIENT
Neighbors Building Brightmoor (NBB), Riet Schumack.

PROJECT TITLES
The studio course was titled "Detroit Connections: Design Collaboration." The resulting projects were: *The Brightmoor Farmway: A Collection of Stories & Recipes from Neighbors Building Brightmoor* and *Lamphere House*.

DURATION
6 months, winter semester, January–June 2012.

BUDGET
The Detroit Connections engagement classes sought and received outside foundation funding to support our work. $4,500 of this money went toward the Design Collaboration course: $3,000 was used for print production costs for the publication, and $1,500 was used for materials and fabrication lab time for the Lamphere House project.

TEAM
Instructors: **Hannah Smotrich** and **Charlie Michaels**
Group of 12 art and design students: **Maureen Bacon, Alessia Cappa, Colleen Dennison, Patrick Holloway, Alicia Kovalcheck, Megan Lacroix, Ali Prentice, Hannah Ryou, Caramia Sitompul, Alexis Stepanek, Ryan Thurmer,** and **Nadia Todoroff.**

2.27 Student Alicia Kovalcheck paints fruits and vegetables on the chalkboard facade.

2.28 The cover of the book *The Brightmoor Farmway*. *Radish illustration: Colleen Dennison.*

DESCRIPTION An opportunity for collaboration and reciprocal learning, this course allowed our students to use their creative skills to engage substantively with a community of people working to improve their struggling northwest Detroit neighborhood. The process of developing appropriate project briefs was embedded in the research we undertook as the semester began. We spent time walking in the neighborhood, having conversations with neighbors and other stakeholders, and realistically assessing what we could accomplish with our skill sets, resources, and timeframe.

Our client and key collaborators were members of Neighbors Building Brightmoor (NBB), a group "dedicated to mobilizing, equipping, and helping each other to create a beautiful, healthy and sustainable community for ourselves and our children." Beginning in 2006 with the Brightmoor Youth Garden, an initiative to engage teens, NBB has evolved into an extensive community revitalization effort that spans 14 city blocks.

The NBB target area now includes over 34,000 square feet of parks, community and market gardens connected by a "farmway" walking path, and art and music enrichment programs for children. Despite the many achievements of the group, effort is constantly required to fight blight (and the public safety issues that accompany it) and transform abandoned properties into green areas or opportunities for artwork.

Designing a community cookbook was one of the project ideas that surfaced early. In fall 2011, a University of Michigan colleague who teaches writing had assigned her seminar students to interview members of NBB, write short essays, and solicit favorite recipes. It was clear that our Art and Design students could take this project to the next phase. Given our class size and semester-long timeframe, we worked to identify an additional priority: dealing with a burnt-out house that was situated in the geographical center of the target area, on the corner of Chalfonte Avenue and Lamphere Street. Thus, our two projects evolved: *The Brightmoor Farmway*, a publication, and Lamphere House, a community center of sorts, created with surface graphics.

2.29 The opening spread in the book *The Brightmoor Farmway. Photo: Patrick Holloway*

RESEARCH Our research consisted primarily of extensive conversations, interviews, and interactions with as many of the neighbors in Brightmoor as we could reach. Our class met in Detroit every Friday, and we would usually spend at least a portion of our day in the neighborhood.

NBB holds monthly potluck dinner meetings that also allowed us opportunities to pose questions, present options, and gather input from a large gathering of community stakeholders at once. Students took turns attending these meetings and reported back to the class as a whole. These evenings were opportunities for us to get feedback on our many questions, but, more importantly, they provided students with an incredible vantage point, a view into the concerns and realities of living in a neighborhood with both potential and challenges. Our presentations were just one item on a long agenda, and students could see the relevance of our projects in the context of the whole.

The guiding philosophy of NBB is that a project can only happen if the direct stakeholders take the initiative to begin it and commit to being its ongoing caretakers. If someone dreams up a project—a garden in the vacant lot next to their house, a mural on the burnt-out building shell they can see from their kitchen—and commits to maintaining it, then the full resources of the neighborhood (and its supporters) will be harnessed to help make that dream happen. In the context of the house project, which was intended to become a community-wide landmark, we needed to balance our work between the NBB as a whole and the focused group of adjacent property owners. Students spent a good deal of time assessing the physical aspects of the site and current structure, and learning about the constraints of producing exterior artwork in an uncertain environment (for example, using valuable materials like metal will attract unwanted attention).

CHALLENGES AND STRATEGY For the publication, it became clear that the existing content was not sufficient—nor was it really appropriate for a cookbook. The original intent was to produce a book that would be sold as a fundraiser by the teens that worked at the Brightmoor Youth Garden. We needed to reshape the concept for the book and generate additional content, both written and visual. The narrative shifted—from a cookbook that showcased recipes for fresh produce to a book that celebrated the Brightmoor Farmway community. Students produced beautiful watercolor illustrations of vegetables and fruits, and added content to broaden the story. Some students took photographic portraits of neighbors and conducted additional interviews. Others sifted through photo archives to find imagery that showcased NBB's work. Ultimately, *The Brightmoor Farmway: A Collection of Stories & Recipes from Neighbors Building Brightmoor* became a wonderful document of the community.

In the case of Lamphere House, the design challenge was to eliminate (or substantially defuse) the negative presence of the current house and create a "center" for the neighborhood. NBB had been boarding up empty houses and covering the boards with artwork for several years and, as a result, there were many beautiful paintings throughout the neighborhood. As designers, we asked ourselves how we could develop Lamphere House into something not only beautiful, but functional. We defined the brief as the creation of a community center. After some initial ambitious brainstorming, and given health and safety concerns and the scale of the project in relation to our available time, we restricted ourselves to working only with the facade of the building. Students analyzed the site: Who passed by? From what direction? In what way (by car, foot, bike)? At what speed?

We considered the role of a community space: How can a central space bring a community together? What functions can it host, and what tools could it provide? After students conducted many observations and developed several iterations with adjacent neighbors, the community at the NBB potluck approved a four-sided plan, phase one of which would be addressing the two most exposed facades. The east side of Lamphere House, the view seen on entering the neighborhood, was designed to have a map of the Farmway, welcoming visitors and orienting them to the presence of the many gardens and the trail that connected them; the north side of Lamphere

House; the facade best situated for neighbors, was used as a communication board. Throughout the farmway, we had noticed small blackboards that were used for community announcements. Students dedicated the entire north facade to chalkboard, which created a single centralized site for communication. The remaining two facades had more limited visual access and were slated for murals (that were implemented the following summer).

We decided to sheath the building fully to help it stand apart from the artwork on surrounding houses: 4 x 8 foot sheets that we prepped at school (priming and transferring map lines via projection) were brought on site for installation and painting. To add dimension to the design, large-scale lettering and vegetables were hand drawn, then digitized and laser cut out of construction foam and applied to the walls.

EFFECTIVENESS The house has become a real centerpiece of the neighborhood and a place of pride for neighbors. We have gotten incredibly positive feedback. Riet Schumack (a key community organizer in the neighborhood) told us, "Everybody in the neighborhood loves the house. They call it *the* house. And *the* map ... it draws the community together ... It's not only artful, it's also a communication—and a unification—piece." Bill Hickey, who lives across the street, said that he sees high school students coming to take their senior pictures in front of *the* house.

In addition to creative work, students were reading about and discussing Detroit in general, and our ongoing connection with the neighborhood was critical to contextualizing this content."

———

2.30 The house has become a real focus point for the neighborhood.

Students, most of whom had not created work at that scale, were energized by the impact of the house's presence in the landscape and felt a tremendous sense of accomplishment.

Once the publication's intent was better aligned with its content, it was also successful. Neighbors celebrated the book at their annual summer picnic and it seemed to create a sense of validation for the community's work thus far and added momentum to their efforts going forward. Students learned about engaging substantively in the process of editorial shaping, developing appropriate imagery, and more general aspects of publication design. Although the books sold out quickly and presumably raised some money for the group, the high production cost was problematic. Our funding covered costs for the first edition, but the neighborhood cannot sustain the project. We suspect that the value of the book was ultimately more significant emotionally than financially.

ASSESSMENT The Brightmoor community was very positively impacted by both projects, and our students (and we faculty) learned a tremendous amount about how a well-organized community group works. In addition to creative work, students

were reading about and discussing Detroit in general, and our ongoing connection with the neighborhood was critical to contextualizing this content.

Our major challenge as teachers was the relationship of our workload to our available time! Class met only once a week in order to accommodate travel to Detroit. We did not have sufficient time to focus explicitly on methodologies for creative collaboration. As one student aptly reflected, "we would have benefited from middle management" (i.e., clear student leadership roles). And we did not have enough scheduled class time that overlapped with our community partners.

Even with these limitations, our students learned a great deal about what they can contribute. Throughout the semester, they were surprisingly timid about producing "real" work for others. While we appreciated their care and concern, we were pleased to see that their experiences over the course of the projects fostered significantly more confidence.

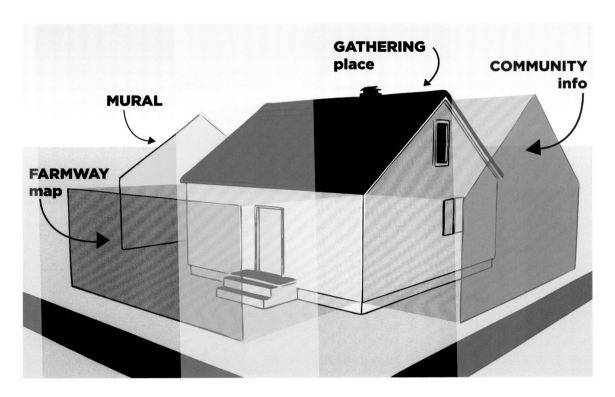

GATHERING place

COMMUNITY info

MURAL

FARMWAY map

2.31a Students studied the differences from each approach and designed content accordingly. *Schematic: Ryan Thurmer.*

2.31b Student Maureen Bacon presenting plans for the Lamphere House at a NBB potluck meeting.

SECTION 2

PARTICIPATORY DESIGN

SOCIAL INNOVATION THROUGH PARTICIPATORY DESIGN

Helen Armstrong

A larger participatory movement is sweeping through our culture. Citizens eagerly generate and share content, expressing themselves on a daily, sometimes hourly, basis. They upload images to Instagram, posts to Facebook, entries to blogs. They write product reviews, self-publish books, design T-shirts. Participatory graphic designers welcome these acts of amateur creation. Acting as community builders, such designers reach out, soliciting user-generated content. This engagement can happen early in the design process—during initial problem exploration, concept development, and testing—or later in the process—as the design deliverable takes form. Some designers utilize both approaches, integrating user content throughout. As this profusion of user voices infiltrates the traditional design process, the hierarchical structure of designer and user destabilizes, resulting, in the best instances, in unexpected social innovation.

PARTICIPATORY DESIGN EARLY IN THE DESIGN PROCESS Process-oriented participatory design emerged in Scandinavia in the 1970s. During this period, a participatory strategy involving workers, unions, academics, and political activists came on the scene: the Collective Resource Approach. Using this approach, workers could directly contribute to the integration of technology into their workplace. Experts worked with rather than simply for workers to design the most effective solutions. The Norwegian Iron and Metals Workers Union first sponsored a project that engaged with researchers in this new collaborative manner. The core democratic impulse behind participatory design thus surfaced: users and stakeholders have a right to express themselves through the design process, particularly marginalized voices that would not typically be heard. The designer, from this perspective, no longer works with a team of experts to deliver a finished artifact, service, or

environment to users. Instead, the experts and users take on the design problem together.

Recently, methods used in process-oriented participatory design emphasize hands-on activities, bringing together designers, users, and other stakeholders, often face to face. This represents a shift away from earlier forms of collaborative discussion and research toward one of collaborative making instead. Participatory theorist and designer Liz Sanders, in her essay "Perspectives on Design in Participation," categorizes such approaches as "Making Tangible Things," "Acting, Enacting and Playing" and "Talking, Telling and Explaining." The first strategy includes collages, prototypes, mock-ups, and models. The second is more performative: games, scenario making, improvisation, role-playing, and body storming. And the third uses verbal description: stories and storyboards, diaries, self-observation, documentaries, and experience timelines (2013, pp. 69–73). The playful nature of these activities encourages creative insights, while building community among the participants.

The challenge of activity-based process-oriented participatory design, as described above, lies in the facilitation or the design of these collaborative experiences. Activities should provide participants with enough freedom to creatively explore but, simultaneously, enough constraints that they are not overwhelmed by possibilities. In addition, including representative participants of all stakeholders is crucial. And the facilitator must be ever wary of shifting the power balance of the experience too far in favor of the experts present. Other forms of less direct process-oriented participation might also include user testing, polling, and forum-based commenting, each of which presents its own challenges.

Participatory design, over the last 40 years, has begun to infiltrate mainstream commerce and culture in the United States. Increasingly our always on, instant feedback society of users demands a voice in the products, services, and environments in which they engage. Many businesses recognize that without user-generated content they cannot respond quickly and accurately enough to satisfy user needs. In addition, many designers nourish the original democratic impulse of participation as a positive social force. Sanders (2013) correlates this growing interest with a countermovement to disrupt the unsustainable cycle of consumption that dominates our culture. Citizens, she maintains, are seeking strategies for social responsibility. Participatory design, through its emphasis on inclusive exploration, has emerged as just such a strategy (pp. 61–2).

PARTICIPATORY DESIGN AS DELIVERABLE

Process-oriented participatory designers build community through hands-on interactions with users at the start of the design process, often before the design problem is fully articulated. They work with users rather than for them, engaging in acts of co-creation. Outcome-oriented participatory designers engage users as well. Their engagement, however, takes place through the project deliverable. The design process results in an open-ended system that requires user content for completion. In other words, the designer develops a platform that empowers users, rather than clients, to express themselves. Outcome-oriented participatory designers can, and often do, engage with users early in the design process, as well.

We can trace outcome-oriented participatory design back to avant-garde artists and designers as they attempted to enact radical social reform. Dadaism and Soviet Constructivism, for example, experimented with social participation during the early twentieth century by urging viewers to join in collaborative public experiences and mass spectacles. Later, in the 1960s, postmodern values of open meaning, multiplicity, and disruption renewed interest in participatory art. Indeed, participatory movements popped up all over in the 1960s: Situationism and GRAV in France, Happenings in the United States, Neoconcretism in Brazil. These movements challenged existing power structures by disrupting the relationship between artist and audience, shifting the meaning of the piece away from authorial intent and into the hands of the participants.

Today, the participatory impulse has moved beyond the experimental arena. Flexible brands encourage users to visually inject their own meaning into logos, text message-based advertising campaigns provide venues for user expression, and large-scale collaborative designs take form only when multitudes of users contribute individual pieces of content. In such projects the designer foregoes predetermined client messaging in favor of user expression. They relinquish control, thus allowing the users to determine the nature of the final piece.

Designers typically structure such projects using modules or templates or a combination of both. Modules allow each user to construct new meaning by interacting with a set of pieces. Templates provide spaces in which users can insert their own content. These structures solicit participation—visual form, thematic messaging, physical movement or action— then translate that participatory act into something greater. Although the initial contributions are simple, easily carried out by the user—a photograph, a sketch, a doodle, a word, a movement, a vocalization, a touch—they flourish in unexpected ways when put into the context of a larger participatory project.

Process-oriented participatory design provides a hands-on structure through which users and designers co-design early in the process. Outcome-oriented participatory design transforms the end result of the design process into an open-ended structure that joins with users to generate meaning each time a contribution is made. Both strategies spring from a democratic spirit of enabling the expression of many voices as opposed to a select few. When users, designers, and other stakeholders come together in an act of co-creation, the potential for social innovation soars. We can see this for ourselves in the projects described in this section. Design becomes not just a single creative act but a continuing dialogue.

*Helen **Armstrong** is an Associate Professor of Graphic Design at North Carolina State University. In addition to teaching, she is the principal of her company, Strong Design. She has authored* Graphic Design Theory: Readings from the Field *(2009), co-authored* Participate: Designing with User-Generated Content *with Zvezdana Stojmirovic (2011), and authored* Digital Design Theory *(2016). To read more about her work, visit http:// helenarmstrongdesigner.com/.*

FIVE QUESTIONS TO
ASTRID STAVRO

1. Who or what influences informed you as you prepared for a career in design?
I'd say everything but graphic design. My dream was to become a writer/journalist. As a young girl, I can remember sending letters to the Pope protesting the fact that nuns are not allowed to marry—some Spanish Cardinal politely replied. I sent anti-war letters to the Spanish newspaper *El Pais*, and most of them were actually published. I sent letters to authors I deeply admired. I studied literature and philosophy. My best teachers have been the books I read: classics by authors such as Herman Hesse, Knut Hamsun, Thomas Mann, Borges, Julio Cortázar, Gabriel García Márquez, Sartre, Camus, Proust, Shakespeare, Baudelaire, Rimbaud, Chandler, Thoreau, Walt Whitman, William Faulkner, Hawthorne, Hemingway, Melville, Mark Twain, Kurt Vonnegut, Paul Auster, Orwell, James Joyce, Cesare Pavese, Italo Calvino, and Thomas Bernhard to John Berger, Susan Sontag, E. M. Cioran, Wittgenstein, Bertrand Russell, Roland Barthes, Adorno, Walter Benjamin, Georges Perec ... the list is too long.

However, there is one very special person who has inspired my future as a designer—my father, who is both a publisher and a printer. I spent my childhood in my father's printing office, surrounded by paper, printing machines, wood and metal letters. My playground was his office—and what an office it was! An impressive eighteenth-century building—an authentic printing warehouse with crackling, wooden floors and old linotype machines. The place smelled amazing, like the pages of a medieval book. I have blue blood: there's ink running through my veins.

2. Do you agree or disagree with this statement: Designers have a social and ethical responsibility to create and transmit meaningful forms of communication that benefit society and culture? Why?

I couldn't agree more. As a matter of fact, it stupefies me to see how uninvolved many designers are in this sense, considering the vast amount of designers on planet Earth. Imagine if every motivated designer with something to say decided to actually do something about it. It would be a revolution. Artists like Barbara Krueger and Jenny Holzer have been very inspirational in this sense. They are the first artists who helped me understand the power of words and images, the power of communication, and the seductive grammar of visual language.

3. EnsaimadArt is a project whose centerpiece is Majorca's most emblematic product, the ensaimada. Its aim is to raise awareness of Amadip Esment Foundations' work, to extend it by inspiring new social initiatives, as well as to raise Majorca's profile at an international level. Can you talk about your involvement with the EnsaimadArt Project and why it is important to do this type of work?
I have a son with a life-long disability. He was diagnosed at the age of three. This, of course, has made me sensitive to disabilities in general. There are some things in life that are impossible to understand unless you experience them personally. But this is only a partial reason. Like any human being, I am naturally affected by the world around us.

In the midst of the toughest economic collapse in Spain's history, we came up with an idea to help raise funds and awareness for the fiftieth anniversary of Amadip.esment, a non-profit organization specialized in creating opportunities for people with intellectual disabilities, and urgently in need of new funding options. We called the project EnsaimadArt, inviting creatives from around the world to create stickers to decorate a limited edition series of the iconic octagonal boxes containing Majorca's quintessential pastry, the ensaimada. The brief asked them to think about how design interacts with society. We encouraged action by raising a simple but provocative question: Can a sticker have a positive effect on society? In other words, can design enable ideas to change the world?

The production process was carried out by the workers of the organization—printing, die-cutting, and manual affixing of the stickers, using the organization's printing facilities and equipment—with all profits from the sales of the boxes contributing to raise funds for them. EnsaimadArt has had a deep impact on a local, national, and international level. It became one of those rare and heart-warming things: a small-scale charitable initiative that has ended up becoming a global phenomenon. As a catalyst for social change, the campaign has been an overwhelming success. None of us remained untouched by this project; it transformed our way of working and the reasons behind it.

4. New roles are emerging for design professionals as their function is increasingly changing from that of generators to facilitators of ideas. Can you comment on this?
The digital era has changed everything. The "reader" now has become a "user." The processes of production and manufacture are now within designers' immediate reach. What began as "desktop publishing" has blossomed into desktop fabrication. The ability to send designs from the computer directly to the manufacturer has made the once prohibitive cost of fabrication more economically viable.

As the design disciplines become more interrelated, newer generations are no longer hesitant about jumping into other fields. Design students, for example, are not only prepared to develop solid portfolios showing evidence of requisite skill sets, they are encouraged to produce ideas that have entrepreneurial resonance. They are urged to become "authors" of content in the academic sense, or entrepreneurs in terms of business. It is essential to reconsider the role of the designer in order to encourage more user participation in design, and to facilitate innovative collaboration and platforms for social inclusion within the design practice.

2.32 EnsaimadArt project boxes with stickers. Clockwise from left to right: Marion Deuchars, Zak Kyes, Fernando Gutiérrez, A Practice for Everyday Life, Sonya Dyakova, Coralie Bickford-Smith, OK-RM, James Goggin, Bianca Chang.

5. What advice would you give a student studying visual communication today to help them prepare for contemporary professional practice?
Never give up.

Film on the EnsaimadArt Project: www.youtube.com/watch?v=W8SsvwUaIX4#t=16.

Astrid Stavro graduated with distinction from both Central Saint Martins College of Art & Design and the Royal College of Art in London, before relocating to Barcelona where she founded and directed the award-winning Astrid Stavro Studio for 10 years. Stavro writes for various design journals and is currently art director and contributing editor of Elephant magazine. In 2013 she co-founded Atlas with Pablo Martín, an award-winning design consultancy based in Palma de Mallorca (www.designbyatlas.com). She is a member of Alliance Graphique Internationale (AGI).

COLORS FOR LIFE

Diego Giovanni Bermúdez Aguirre, Professor,
Pontificia Universidad Javeriana Cali, Columbia

2.33 One of the painted murals in a city school. *Photo: Diego Giovanni Bermúdez Aguirre.*

CLIENT
La Pedregosa School,
Fe y Alegría Foundation,
Cali, Colombia.

PROJECT TITLE
Colors for Life.

DURATION
8 weeks, ongoing project
since 2011.

BUDGET
Students cover the project
costs, with the exception of
transportation, which is
covered by the university.

TEAM
Instructors: Professors
**Fernando Arboleda, Tatiana
Rojasm** and **Diego Bermúdez**.
60 students: 40 design students
and 20 psychology students.
One schoolteacher and 30
schoolchildren.

DESCRIPTION Since 2011, students studying in both Visual Communication Design and Psychology from the Pontificia Universidad Javeriana Cali have worked on a participatory design experience called *Colors for Life*. This project was initially conceived to integrate student learning within visual communication design projects that address various needs in the city of Cali, Colombia. As a faculty, we endeavor to employ our academic knowledge in service to social change to achieve equality, solidarity, inclusion, and dignity.

2.34 Children interacting with one of the painted murals in their school. *Photo: Diego Giovanni Bermúdez Aguirre.*

The fundamental aim of this project is to create murals in a school environment that build on stories and drawings made by the schoolchildren in illustration workshops. Such murals improve the school environment, help to impart the values of the community, and generate a sense of belonging, respect, and teamwork. Additionally, visual communication design students illustrate children's books from the drawings and stories generated from the illustration workshops. These books reflect the hopes, dreams, and personal stories of the school children.

In 2013, the project evolved to include psychology students who help to design teaching materials according to the educational needs of the children. The Colors for Life project focuses on achieving individual and collective well-being in public schools and community centers in low-income areas within Cali such as Melendez, Marroquín, Aguablanca, Cascajal, and Polvorines. At times, children from public schools in the city feel alienated; this project seeks to integrate the children with future young designers through design and writing workshops to create personal and friendly primary school experiences.

RESEARCH Prior to meeting with the schoolchildren, the students define activities that meet their learning goals as articulated by their teachers. The student designers utilize the methodology of user-centered design and design thinking, and the student psychologists utilize the structure of cognitive task analysis. As a result, different characteristics, tastes, interests, and needs of the children are discovered, and tools are developed which respond to existing educational requirements.

CHALLENGES The Colors for Life project presents many challenges to its implementation as it involves working with people from other disciplines and immersing our students in a very different context. The school community welcomes us warmly, but it is necessary to establish a strong bond of trust, which is not always easy to do.

2.35 Student working with schoolchildren. *Photo: Diego Giovanni Bermúdez Aguirre.*

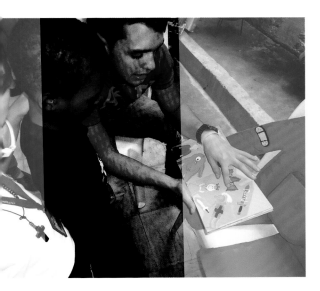

2.36 Design student interacting with schoolchildren.
Photo: Diego Giovanni Bermúdez Aguirre.

STRATEGY The Colors for Life project starts at the beginning of the semester with design and psychology teachers defining the objectives, goals, activities, and expected results of the project. Subsequently, the teachers visit the La Pedregosa school community to discuss the school's specific interests and current needs with the school principal and one of the teachers, Ofir Cuero; once we have all discussed and established the expectations and requirements of the project, we are ready to begin.

Week 1: The semester starts with a meeting with students in class during which work teams of student designers and student psychologists are formed, and each team studies the project brief and begins discussing and developing their plan of action.

Week 2: The student group makes a first visit to the school community in order to become familiar with the conditions of the project and to establish trust and a bond with the school community. The conditions and requirements of the context are analyzed to understand the thematic depth and scope of the intervention. Student psychologists and student designers begin to define the specific topics that have informed and inspired them during their visit.

Week 3: Informed by their visits to the community, the student psychologists on the team use cognitive task analysis to determine which learning requirements to address, while the student designers use design thinking (understanding, observation, research, and definition) to plan the intervention.

Weeks 4–5: First prototypes (sketches) are evaluated in class to determine if they meet the objectives of the exercise. The dynamics generated by each teaching tool designed are defined.

Weeks 6–7: Prototypes are built, taking into account conditions of form, material, color, and the potential dynamics of each material for teaching. It is essential that children's learning tools (games, books, toys, etc.) are designed to educate.

Week 8: The teams deliver their projects. Each project provides educational features and strives to meet the children's defined learning goals.

EFFECTIVENESS The Colors for Life project is effective because it encourages the sharing of ideas expressed by all participants in this community project. As a project designed and implemented by college students for the schoolchildren of our city, it not only enables the transfer of knowledge, but also encourages the development of a shared visual language among all the participants.

ASSESSMENT Design education involves contextualized learning; students not only acquire design knowledge but also learn about their own society. Learning by doing provides students with a new way of knowing the world, allowing them to feel like agents of social change in the community and empowering them to transform their lives and future. As a teacher, I can see the transformation in my students when they use design as an instrument to improve lives in our society—and we see it in the results of this project that provides quality learning for schoolchildren.

WHONOTWHAT:
A PHOTOVOICE EXPLORATION

Mark Biddle, Professor of Art,
Department of Visual Arts and Design,
Weber State University, Ogden, Utah

Laura Santurri, PhD, Assistant Professor, Department
of Health Promotion and Human Performance,
Weber State University, Ogden, Utah

CLIENT
LGBTQA community and
Weber State University.

PROJECT TITLE
Research, Design, and Culture.

DURATION
15 weeks, January–April 2014.

BUDGET
$3,935.00: $1,150 for Canon
camera equipment for participant
use; $1,503 for exhibition
promotions, exhibit materials,
and 50 catalogs; $1,282
for miscellaneous lunches,
incidentals.

TEAM
Principal investigators:
Mark Biddle, Laura Santurri.
Student researchers:
Cami Benedict, Kaitlyn Ott.
Student designer/researchers:
Jeff Smith, Nestor Robles,
Brett Ferrin.
11 student research participants
from the LGBTQA community.

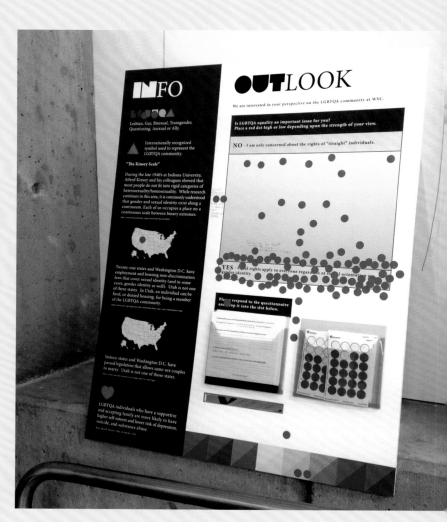

2.37 Kiosk interface showing an information strip on the left, a question and response field on the upper right, and a short survey with deposit slot below. *Design: Jeff Smith, Nestor Robles, Brett Ferrin.*

DESCRIPTION Members of the lesbian, gay, bisexual, and transgender community in the United States face significant health disparities, including increased risk for depression, suicide, substance abuse, and homelessness. Environmental and societal factors, such as discrimination and stigma, have been correlated with these disparities. Much of the Utah population is traditionally conservative and some LGBTQA students face considerable risks in coming out (participants preferred LGBTQA to LGBT where Q = queer and A = asexual). Weber State University (WSU), a state-supported, liberal arts institution with an enrollment of approximately 25,000, had recently scored below average on the national Campus Pride Index, which attempts to measure the "friendliness" of a university environment for LGBTQA students.

Since 2005, under the ongoing project title *Sticks + Stones*, the graphic design program at WSU has explored intercultural issues across institutional, disciplinary, and national boundaries (http://www.sticksandstonesproject.org). Of particular interest are the relationships between cultural diversity, xenophobia, and graphic communication—how various ethnicities, religions, and sexualities see themselves compared with the way they are stereotyped and represented. Our work in this context assumes that designers occupy positions of power in a global culture, and that they should assume proactive roles in support of community and society.

WhoNotWhat provided an opportunity for us to collaborate with colleagues in the health professions over shared interests. The project included both immediate and long-range goals: to raise awareness among the student body and administration of the issues and obstacles to success faced by the LGBTQA community; to initiate dialogue leading to new levels of acceptance and respect for the LGBTQA community; to contribute directly to evidence-based programming and policy at the university.

RESEARCH The project was built around a qualitative research plan, guided by Dr. Laura Santurri, to better understand the perceptions and experiences of LGBTQA students using Photovoice participatory methodology. Participants would be given cameras and asked to respond to the framing questions below, photographically:

1. What are your experiences as an "out" or "closeted" LGBTQA student at WSU?
2. In what ways do you feel supported as an LGBTQA student at WSU?
3. In what ways do you feel challenged as an LGBTQA student at WSU?
4. In what ways is it difficult to be an LGBTQA student at WSU?
5. How do you feel your experience at WSU might be different from a student who does not identify as LGBTQA?

In order to initiate public dialogue, data would also be collected from the university community at large.

CHALLENGES Results from the Photovoice phase would have to be exhibited in some form that also provided a way for the public to react. Feedback instruments should be haptically appealing, should communicate intuitively and draw out sincere responses. An exhibit venue in the center of campus was secured for presenting Photovoice imagery. This space receives a high volume of pedestrian traffic and was perfect for gathering public input. LGBTQA participants were enthusiastic about the project and what it might achieve, but some were fearful of being so exposed. All were reminded that their names and expressions would soon be featured in a public forum and were offered a final opportunity to reconsider participation. None withdrew. To address goal number three, the entire project would need formal documentation that was easily distributed.

STRATEGY The first step for the design team was to title and graphically brand the exhibit. *WhoNotWhat* derives from participant descriptions of their coming-out experiences. Members of the LGBTQA community are sometimes objectified in the limited terms of their gender identity or sexual orientation. The title suggests that we should understand one another in terms of "who" we are, and not "what" we are.

Photovoice results were analyzed for content, paired with reflective statements by participants, and formatted for overall consistency. Quotes from participant discussions were grouped onto separate panels. Scale, quantity, and sequencing questions were balanced by the need for installation efficiency. Just a few hours were available to install the exhibit and only inexperienced volunteers were available to assist.

The team decided to solicit input from exhibit patrons on questions regarding the importance of LGBTQA equality, whether their views of, and support for, LGBTQA individuals are positive or negative, and how their views may have changed over time. Graffiti boards, marker boards, Post-it notes, and other options for data collection were considered, including surveys. Graffiti-oriented forms were rejected because of their potential to invite hate speech and some options were deemed too vulnerable to erasure or theft. Finally, the team decided to build free-standing kiosks that would allow some responses to remain public throughout the exhibit and would include a small survey, which could be completed and placed into a secure enclosure. The stations were modeled with paper and constructed with foam core.

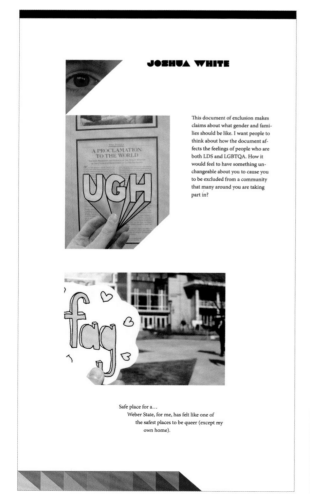

An exhibit catalog would be produced and distributed at research dissemination points and to the university administration. This will extend the project's influence and, hopefully, contribute to the direction of university movement as student life issues are considered.

EFFECTIVENESS Kiosks asked exhibit patrons for apply-the-dot responses to opening questions and, from there, encouraged respondents toward the survey. Each question received 200–300 dots, a few uninvited written comments and some errant dot placement, but there were no instances of hate speech. Sixty-three surveys were submitted. At least two-thirds were supportive of the LGBTQA community and many respondents indicated a trend toward greater acceptance as they became more informed:

They [my views] have gotten more positive the more I hear & understand about homosexuality. I am still trying to combat the societal prejudice I grew up with. —**Student**

I can't imagine the pain of being LGBTQA & being raised Mormon. I wish people would be more understanding of love. It's not "loving" to politely tell people they don't have the right to marriage. —**Student**

Almost a third of the comments were negative. Some indicated that LGBTQA people should just keep to themselves. Others expressed the view that sexual orientation reduces simply to a matter of choice and expressed disdain for homosexuality based on religious tenets. One leveled a curious charge of reverse discrimination.

People are not born this way, & they can change. —**Student**

...close friends growing up were gay, but it does not change the foundations of my faith ... —**Student**

What's up with the idea of tolerance, when obviously most of these boards [Photovoice panels] show little tolerance for religions who oppose them ... —**Student**

2.38a–2.38c Exhibit panels showing photos and comments by Chloe Jesse, Rosie Gerrish, and Joshua White. *Design: Jeff Smith, Nestor Robles, Brett Ferrin.*

2.39 Exhibit logotype and title panel motif including the eyes of 11 LGBTQA participants.
Design: Jeff Smith, Nestor Robles, Brett Ferrin.

2.40 Exhibit installation. *Design: Jeff Smith, Nestor Robles, Brett Ferrin.*

ASSESSMENT Informal feedback directed to the research team indicated that the project was timely, engaging, and informative. A dialog was indeed begun which, given the wide-ranging responses, is clearly in need of expansion. A subsequent iteration of the project should include an online blog, which would enable the discussion to continue to grow beyond the exhibit.

Members of the research team would have considered us LGBTQA "allies" from the outset but, with this project, gaining another measure of respect for the LGBTQA community became our problem. Students of this community report that they experience real prejudice on a daily basis. There are safe zones on campus and areas that still feel hostile to them. Educators everywhere should realize the importance of visibly marking the faculty office as a place where LGBTQA students can feel welcome.

This was a reality project for the design team with all the critical components of professional activity included: client interaction, intense teamwork, hard deadlines, and a public face. It focused attention on the importance of design beyond commerce and there was the very real sense that our work was effecting positive change—that design matters in contemporary culture.

INDEFYNABLE:
STAND TOGETHER, STRUGGLE TOGETHER

Audra Buck-Coleman, Associate Professor of Graphic Design, University of Maryland, College Park, Maryland

2.41 Giveaways at the event included coasters, T-shirts, and stickers.

CLIENT
Jude Paul Dizon, coordinator for Asian Pacific American Student Involvement & Advocacy, and the Multicultural Involvement and Cultural Advocacy (MICA) unit on the University of Maryland, College Park (UMD) campus.

PROJECT TITLE
Social Impact Design Research Assignment.

DURATION
September 2013–April 2014. Design research work was created during the fall 2013 semester. Students hosted the event during the spring 2014 semester.

BUDGET
$1,865. The project's budget was funded through three sources: a Rise Above grant from the UMD Office of Diversity and Inclusion; the UMD Department of Art Friedgen Family Fund; and the UMD MICA event budget. These monies were used for research and brainstorming supplies, focus group meals, event supplies, and event giveaways.

TEAM
Instructor: Audra Buck-Coleman.
Students: Senior design students enrolled in "Advanced Graphic Design Principles: Design in Society" course.
Creative director: Kelsey Marotta.
Co-creative directors: Laura Pavlo, Alyssa Pennington, and Melissa Silverbush.
Design team members: Taylor Callinan, Dominique Graham, Safira Klein, John Lee, Miles Ma, Michael Maharajh, Erin McNally, Leslie Osmont, Hea Park, Katherine Pepe, Sarah Persing, Jennifer Rothschild, Annie Snedegar, Lauren Sumner, and Valina Yen.

DESCRIPTION "Asian Pacific American" is a broad term that minimizes the numerous diverse groups collected under this one designation. Although the title can create a sense of community and bring populations together, it does not capture the population's heterogeneous demographics. In addition, as with other cultural identities, the population's members are often regarded in cliché stereotypes. This issue is of particular concern at the University of Maryland, which ranks in the top 25 percent of all US public universities for diversity. Approximately 12 percent of the student population is Asian Pacific American (APA).

Our design program includes a senior-level (fourth year) course on design research and social design. Learning goals include the ability to appreciate and articulate the value of social design; to conduct, comprehend, organize, and apply design research to address a social issue; to learn to problem solve when the problem and/or the "design solution" are

not explicitly defined; and to gain cultural competencies through design research and making. This issue, along with the numerous APA populations and cultural organizations on campus, made it an appropriate project for the course.

The enrolled UMD senior graphic design students were assigned to address the APA disaggregation issue through an appropriate design response. The end result was deliberately left unspecified so as to allow the design students full consideration of possible responses. The students conducted a series of research probes (see below) and completed secondary research and related reading assignments. Throughout the semester, they discussed and prioritized the research findings to direct their project.

After full consideration of the research, the design students created an event to raise awareness about and disaggregate the different APA groups on campus. "InDEFYnable: Stand Together, Struggle Together" aimed to promote APA students' coexisting

2.42 The University of Maryland design students created a rotating, three-tiered pillar to address the different identities associated with Asian Pacific Americans. Approximately 150 people span the pillar during the event.

cultural and individual identities. APAs are members of their cultural groups, but they also have other interests and activities as well. The event took place at an on-campus outdoor plaza in April 2014. The primary draw was a six-foot-tall rotating pillar that displayed portraits of six UMD APA students. The pillar was a fun, surprising way to talk about how APAs are both part of a group and individuals. Event visitors spun the pillar and tweeted "selfies" to win InDEFYnable T-shirts. To complement the pillar, there were informational banners about the six students featured on the pillar, and about the event itself and the Asian Pacific region.

The event also included participatory activities to encourage students to examine their own identities, whether or not they self-identified as APA. Provided with markers and a blank coaster, passersby were invited to contribute written and illustrative descriptions in response to a prompt of "I AM …" Visitors described themselves in a variety of ways including through their culture (e.g., "I AM 100% Latina" and "I AM British + Zimbabwean"), their emotions, opinions, and beliefs (e.g., "I AM standing up for myself" and "I AM inspired"), their professions (e.g., "I AM a writer" and "I AM a future soldier"), and their physical descriptions (e.g., "I AM left-handed" and "I AM hairy"). The coasters were displayed as they were completed, creating an evolving mural of identity. The range of responses exemplified the different ways we consider our identities. This also made the overall event more inclusive of other campus populations.

Lastly, the APA student involvement groups and the MICA office hosted tables at the event, which created awareness about cultural opportunities on campus. Also, the UMD APA Heritage Month planning committee used the InDEFYnable branding as the identity and theme for the events. This expanded the visibility and impact of the project. Collectively these activities and information encouraged the UMD community to view one another as individuals, not just as stereotypical members of a culture or ethnicity.

RESEARCH Throughout the fall 2013 semester, the graphic design students met with and researched the different APA student groups on campus. They also met with Jude Paul Dizon, coordinator for Asian Pacific American Student Involvement & Advocacy, who served as a bridge to the APA groups and provided knowledge and feedback about the project direction. In addition to secondary research, the design students employed four different research methods to collect this data: graffiti walls via rolling chalkboards, an online survey, the love letter/breakup letter approach (which asks respondents to write positive or negative comments as if they were reaffirming or ending relationships with the research subject), and a focus group. The students deemed these methods to be the most appropriate for the project at hand. The data gained from the first three methods informed the focus group discussion. Course meetings included regular examining of the research results, identifying trends in the findings, and prioritizing of the next prompt's content. Through the research methods, the APA students shared that they are proud of, but not obsessed with, their culture, and that they prefer to be regarded outside of cultural stereotypes. This became the foundation for the InDEFYnable design response.

In a post-project course survey, approximately 80 percent of the design students agreed or strongly agreed that the course expanded their understanding of the needs and concerns of different cultures, races, ethnicities, and/or religions."

2.43 Event visitors were invited to create a response to a prompt of "I AM ..." on blank coasters. The finished products were displayed at the event as an evolving mural of identity. More than 130 coasters were created by the event.

CHALLENGES The event worked best in an outdoor, high-traffic location. The students chose an outdoor plaza near the student union. The original event date was scheduled to be in December, at the conclusion of the fall semester. However, the weather forecast was not in our favor. This worked out in the end because we were able to reschedule the event during the following April, which is Asian Pacific American Heritage Month. Rather than functioning as a standalone event, the InDEFYnable Celebration was incorporated into the month-long series of APA events.

Another challenge was engaging the APA community through the research process. Although the design students hit the ground running when the semester started and engaged their social APA networks, it was difficult to garner participation in some of the research probes. Getting the APA students to meet with the design students—even when the invitation included free food—proved to be a bigger stumbling block than expected. However, the design students persevered and got the participation and data that they needed.

Results for **indefynable**

···   Remove

Top / All

Photos · View all

Katharine Friedgen @KFriedgen · 10h
A #latergram congratulations to @umdart's #graphicdesignconcentration project: @indefynable. #indefynable instagram.com/p/mjE5zxkKFH/

Expand   ← Reply   ⇄ Retweet   ★ Favorite   ··· More

[Jorelle] @YO_oitsMingMing · 14h
@indefynable thanks for the freebies! Great event! 😁

Expand   ← Reply   ⇄ Retweet   ★ Favorite   ··· More

cameron malagar @yerpiboicam · 14h
@INDEFYNABLE # indefynable #busta @tintinbaninnin Follow **Indefynable!**
pic.twitter.com/dl97n9OtQR

2.44 @InDEFYnable became the tag for the month-long series of Asian Pacific American Heritage Month events. People who tweeted selfies with the pillar during the InDEFYnable Celebration event received a free T-shirt.

STRATEGY The design students wanted to create an inviting, upbeat, and innovative design response to engage the campus population about APA stereotypes. However, they did not want this to feel overly "preachy" or heavy-handed, as they felt their peers would be turned off by this approach. The project also needed to have the right mix of lightheartedness and thoughtfulness to have a suitable impact. The design students also recognized that although the event was focused on dispelling myths about the APA community, they wanted to broaden the event and its message to be more encompassing of the disparate campus populations. The pillar, which served as the primary draw for the event, struck the right balance between playful and serious. The other activities made for a more inclusive event.

EFFECTIVENESS The event was a success in terms of engaging passersby and creating a fun, engaging way to address stereotypes and cultural clichés, and as a way for design students to engage their skills to address a complex issue. The coasters and other participatory items were effective in making the event more inclusive. We heard many complimentary comments how about innovative and effective the event was relative to our goals. Unfortunately, stereotypes and prejudice are ongoing issues. The event was a short-term success, but more consistent, long-term events such as these are needed to make a more permanent impact upon the campus climate.

ASSESSMENT An estimated 150 people span the pillar, and 102 tweets were posted about the event, including 62 selfies with the pillar. Those who tweeted @InDEFYnable selfies were given free campaign T-shirts. Approximately 200 coasters, 80 stickers, and 400 buttons were given away at the event.

The design students conducted immediate impact surveys via iPads during the event. Of the 71 students who completed the survey, 88 percent said they "agreed" or "strongly agreed" that the event helped them to think more critically about complex identities of APAs. Ninety-two percent of the respondents indicated they would attend this event again in the future. One question asked respondents to choose three different terms or words to describe the event and another asked them to do the same about their impressions of APAs. Responses to both questions were overwhelmingly positive. Survey respondents wrote words such as "all-inclusive," "fun," "interesting" to describe the event and wrote terms including "diverse," "awesome," and "smart" to describe APAs.

In a post-project course survey, approximately 80 percent of the design students agreed or strongly agreed that the course expanded their understanding of the needs and concerns of different cultures, races, ethnicities, and/or religions. Nearly 90 percent agreed or strongly agreed that the course made them think critically about the value of social design, that the course expanded their understanding of graphic design's potential role in society. All of the students either agreed or strongly agreed that the course helped them think critically about the value of design research.

ACKNOWLEDGMENTS InDEFYnable is an offshoot of Sticks + Stones, a collaborative project that investigates culture, stereotyping, and representation through design. http://www.sticksandstonesproject.org/indefynable/.

DESIGNING ALTERNATIVES

Emma Gieben-Gamal and **Dr. Sónia Matos**, Lecturers, Edinburgh College of Art, University of Edinburgh, Edinburgh, Scotland

2.45 Tower Bank Primary School logo design proposal, *Julia Beck*, May 2014.

CLIENT
Towerbank Primary School, Edinburgh, Scotland.

PROJECT TITLE
Designing Alternatives.

DURATION
8 weeks, 2013.

BUDGET
None.

TEAM
Course leaders: Emma Gieben-Gamal and Sónia Matos.
Selected student group: Julia Beck, Dimitri Hadjichristou, Ioanna Kyrtatou, and Emily Rowe.

DESCRIPTION "Designing Alternatives" is a third-year undergraduate course from the Contextual Studies component of an Honors degree in Design at Edinburgh College of Art. This course uses a teaching and learning framework based on participatory action research as a means to bring theory and practice together and to encourage more socially and critically engaged design in the students' own work. The course challenges students to work in groups on one of a selection of "live" grassroots projects. Following a short lecture series on socially engaged design, 35 students were asked to put core research methods into practice. This case study will focus on one group of three graphic design students and one product design student who worked with a primary (elementary) school to develop a new visual identity.

The course was first developed as a lecture series in 2011–12 in an effort to extend the learning opportunities for tackling social, economic, and environmental issues through design within Edinburgh College of Art's curriculum. While the lecture series was successful in meeting students' increasing interest in these issues, we realized that this interest was not always transferred into the studio and often remained disconnected from the students' own design practice. Following a successful trial of short community-based fieldwork projects, the course was modified in 2013–14 to address this imbalance. With the objective of overcoming the still-common divide between humanities courses and "studio" courses in design education in the UK, we aimed to create a course that employed an integrative and reflexive approach to learning, and teaching that blended critical theory and practice through action.

RESEARCH This active approach to learning was achieved through a combination of three elements of the course: a lecture series on the history, theory, and context of social design; a live brief provided by community groups, which the students were required to work on in small groups; and an emphasis, in the assessed element of the course, on students' critical reflection on the research process (and experience) and responses to the brief. Thus while the aim was to produce real outcomes for each of the community clients, students were assessed not on the quality of the outcomes but rather on the quality of their reflection upon the process.

Students were required first to conduct background research about the project they were engaged with—in this case, the development of a new visual identity for a primary school that had no budget or design expertise allocated to it. They were then expected to design a research and engagement plan, and put into practice the qualitative research skills introduced earlier in the course that form the basis of participatory and socially engaged design, such as informal conversations, interviews, direct observation, and participation with both adults and children.

CHALLENGES The challenge for students taking the course was to understand both the broad history and context of socially engaged design, as well as the specific context of their own design project, and the methodological complexities of working on a socially engaged project with a client who has no knowledge of design or experience of working with designers.

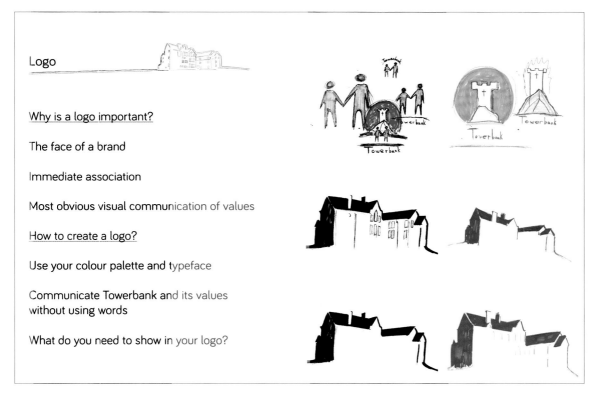

2.46 Page from the *Branding Booklet* for Towerbank Primary School.

Mrs J Gilmour

Head Teacher
Towerbank Primary School
Figgate Bank,
Edinburgh
EH15 1HX
Tel: 0131 657 3907
Email: admin@towerbank.edin.sch.uk

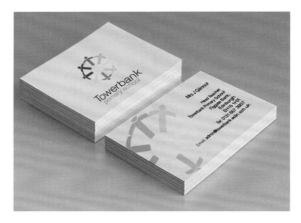

2.47a–2.47c Tower Bank Primary School logo
design proposal application, *Julia Beck*, May 2014.

STRATEGY Their first task was to grapple with the ill-defined initial design brief before going on to practice primary forms of research introduced in the lecture series. Through all this they were expected to develop the ability to engage with the process of research and design through active engagement with their client in a critical and reflexive way:

Your task is to write a 3,000-word report critically evaluating your design project and the ways in which design can be used to tackle the issues at stake. Within this you should consider the design strategies employed and how this shapes the nature of the project. You are expected to draw on your primary and secondary research to help set up and explore the issues raised. You might also consider using sources from our lecture series, other critically engaged texts and examples of relevant solutions or design-based projects to critique and think through your argument.
(Course Assessment Brief, 2013)

Having assessed the scope of the project, the students realized that there would be insufficient time to adequately research the values and ethos of the school and develop a new visual identity scheme as first requested by the school. Instead they revised the initial brief in collaboration with the school's senior management to focus on research and strategy—agreeing to deliver a set of workshops as part of the engagement process and design a booklet guiding the school through the branding process to enable them to continue the project. However, one of the students also took the project forward as part of a second semester studio submission. As well as continuing to work with this student, the school gained skills in identifying and articulating its needs as well as confidence in its ability to participate effectively in the design process. The students, for their part, gained practical experience in applying research methods and conducting workshops, and also recognized the role and value of design as a strategy for change, not just as an outcome.

EFFECTIVENESS The course provided a unique opportunity to develop work with a real community group outside the remit of the educational environment. Students were challenged by the "limitations" of the projects—the lack of time, the changing brief, etc. This caused some frustration but also provided an opportunity for reflection about the nature of live projects. As Emily Rowe, one of the students, noted: "The project challenged my thinking in that it changed my perception of clients; I had not anticipated how much hard work would go into meeting the client's needs, and this was what I found most difficult about the project as it took up a lot of time and consideration." Another of the students,

Dmitri Hadjichristou, was struck by how the "project massively challenged my thinking" and noted that the "best part of the process was by far the workshops; although they didn't go as planned, I think [they have] been one of the most valuable experiences during my time in ECA." Both students remarked on how much they learned from each other and the people they were working with (the staff, and children at the school).

The students' feedback, as well as our own assessment of their work, provided clear evidence that practical experience "on the ground" and working in collaboration with others can make learning more active and effective than that elicited by the teacher-centered format. The live projects also demonstrated that the research process can yield positive outcomes even where there are no design products at the end of the project, and that the impact for the students' learning is long-lasting.

ASSESSMENT One of the limitations of the course was that, in retrospect, the timeframe was too short to accommodate both a taught element and a live brief. Students required more support to critically reflect on their research process, and more time for discussion and reflection among the class to maximize the potential for peer learning. The longer-term impact is still being evaluated, but many students reported that the course stimulated an interest in socially engaged design and opened up new prospects for their own work.

Students also reported that the project provided a valuable opportunity to test out and develop core research skills, learn new research methods, and set these within a theoretical context. For the external community groups that participated, the experience also provided a valuable opportunity for reflection upon their own skills and resources and improved their understanding of the potential benefits of so doing. Nonetheless, while we felt that the relationships with the client were well managed, a greater focus could have been paid to post-project appraisal and evaluation, which we will endeavor to build into future iterations of the course.

2.48 Students Julia Beck, Dimitri Hadjichristou, Ioanna Kyrtatou and Emily Rowe showing a page from the *Branding Booklet* to children at Towerbank Primary School, November 2013.

That said, we would argue that the participatory action research approach was largely successful in managing the balance of needs of both the students and the community group, including the potential "failure" of students to provide viable design outcomes (which is one of the key challenges of running community-led projects as educational opportunities). Thus, by setting such projects within the framework of action research and critical pedagogy, the potential for "failure" can be transformed into a valuable learning experience, not just for the students but also for the community.

Moreover, the reflexivity that this approach engenders encourages deeper, more long-lasting, outcomes than those tied to a specific design brief. For many of the students this has resulted in a clearer sense of themselves as "active agents in society" and created in them a continued interest in participatory design and the desire to engage with social issues in their own work.

FAMILY VAN: WRAP REDESIGN

Elizabeth Resnick, Professor, Graphic Design,
Massachusetts College of Art and Design,
Boston, Massachusetts

2.49 The Family Van with new van wrap. *Design: Milly Houstova.*

CLIENT
The Family Van, a community-based mobile health initiative of Harvard Medical School that provides free preventive health services, education, and referrals to residents across Boston.

PROJECT TITLE
Advocacy Awareness Project.

DURATION
Fall 2012: 4 weeks of in-class concept development.

BUDGET
The initial van wrap concepts were developed as a classroom project at no cost. The Family Van received grants from the Massachusetts Medical Society and Alliance Charitable Foundation to fund this project.

TEAM
Instructor: **Elizabeth Resnick.** 14 graphic design students, Graphic Design 2 course, Massachusetts College of Art and Design, Boston. *Director of the Family Van:* **Jennifer Bennet**, and her staff. *Director of Center for Art and Community Partnerships (CACP):* **Cecilia Mendez.** *Director, The Sparc!:* **Ekua Holmes.** ArtMobile team, Massachusetts College of Art and Design, Boston.

DESCRIPTION The Family Van is a mobile health clinic, a program initiative of Harvard Medical School. It travels to underserved Boston neighborhoods each week providing free preventive health services, health education, and referrals for individuals. Jennifer Bennet, Family Van director, contacted the Center for Art and Community Partnerships (CACP)—whose mission is to match MassArt community with neighborhood organizations to create mutually beneficial, sustainable partnerships in art and design—for help with a design project, a new van wrap for the Family Van mobile health clinic.

For 4 weeks starting in early September through early October 2012, the challenge for 14 junior (third year) graphic design students was to reimagine the existing visual exterior of the Family Van that was considered "off-putting" to the very communities the van served. Director Bennet was present for each of the four consecutive weekly class meetings as an active participant in the design process. In the fourth week of the project, students presented the final results of their van wrap redesigns to Director Bennet and her staff. The 14 designs were then collected and taken back to the staff office to be shared with community stakeholders.

Five of the 14 van wrap designs were selected to undergo community testing. To accomplish this, Cecilia Mendez, Director of CACP, enlisted MassArt's Sparc! The ArtMobile, a mobile base for organizing innovative design programs and events in the local Boston community. The Sparc! team, led by Director Ekua Holmes, traveled with Family Van staff to Dudley Square, Codman Square, Madison Park High School, and East Boston neighborhoods to survey and assess community response to the five selected student designs. The ultimate goal was to have the local community residents and in particular, teens select the new van wrap.

"

Neighborhood residents— many of whom are immigrants from many different cultures —were too afraid to enter the van to ask for help."

———

RESEARCH On the first day of class, both Director Bennet, and her program coordinator, Lunecee Eligene, delivered two introductory visual presentations: the first was on the Family Van initiative and its mission to serve the underserved neighborhoods in the city of Boston; the second was on the diverse cultures who live and work in the neighborhoods the van serves. Director Bennet's presentation also identified two key concerns the students needed to address in their visual proposals: first, that the current van exterior projected a very "cold and clinical" medical environment. Neighborhood residents—many of whom are immigrants from many different cultures—were too afraid to enter the van to ask for help. Second, there was a deep concern to address the apparent lack of awareness of the services the van can provide among the high-risk youth in these areas.

The students were asked to reflect on the presentations and the needs articulated by the client. They were also given to read a packet of articles that addressed the specific challenges facing mobile health clinics in the United States, and the importance for designers of engaging in social impact design initiatives. Students were asked to visit the Family Van at one of its five locations—a different Boston neighborhood for each day of the week before beginning their visual research.

CHALLENGES Only one of the 14 students actually visited the Family Van on site. It was a shocking revelation when the students finally admitted to not fulfilling this very important aspect of their research. Their reasons were twofold: scheduling difficulties in making a visit to a particular outlying Boston neighborhood inaccessible from the college; and, when the van was in a neighborhood in the near vicinity of the college, students stated that their school class schedules did not permit a visit during the van's hours of operation. If I were to assign another project like this where a site visit was required, I would need to schedule a class field trip early in the process in order to accomplish this goal.

STRATEGY Students were placed into small groups to do a collective brainstorming session directly after the initial client presentations. In preparation for our second class meeting, and informed by this group exercise, students were asked to begin their individual process by making a list of keywords that described the project. They were to select a few of these keywords to develop into individual thought maps, and then into small sketches. From these sketches, students developed initial concept ideas that were put in the form of a projected visual proposal, and presented to our client the following week for her feedback.

Based on feedback students received from the client, their classmates, and their instructor, they developed first-round visual concepts that were presented at the third class meeting for another round of response and feedback. By the fourth class meeting, students had developed tight visual comprehensives using a van wrap template provided by the client in which to present their designs.

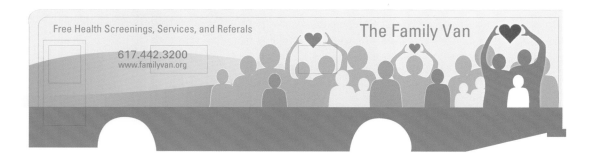

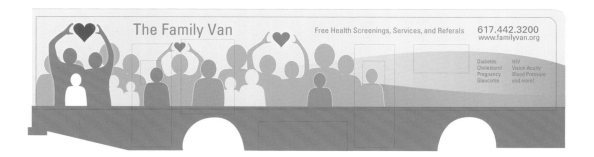

2.50a Van wrap concept proposal. *Design: Casey McGee.*

2.50b Van wrap concept proposal. *Design: Milly Houstova.*

2.**51** Students brainstorming in groups. *Photo: Elizabeth Resnick.*

EFFECTIVENESS When the results were tallied by the outreach and participatory design efforts of the Sparc! team and the Family Van staff, the top two proposals were from Casey McGee and Jarmilla (Milly) Houstova. Casey's visual proposal was favored by older community residents, while Milly's visual proposal, which incorporated vivid colors and imaginative imagery, was favored by the teens and was deemed the best representation of the Family Van's mission, to "increase access to health and improve healthy behaviors by providing culturally and linguistically appropriate health services" to the communities that it serves. It is interesting to note that Milly was the one student who actually visited the Family Van on site during the early research stage.

ASSESSMENT Milly Houstova agreed to have her van wrap design concept proposal put into production. CACP and the Family Van staff worked together with Milly, who was hired as a freelance designer, in the months that followed. Commenting on this experience, Milly remarked:

I was glad that the stakeholders didn't want me to change the concept, it was only a matter of adding a couple of things and also getting the correct translations in all of the languages. They wanted less clutter, which I completely agreed with. The most frustrating part for me was communicating between the stakeholders and the vendor. It seemed the stakeholders were just as new to the process of printing the final design wrap, as I was.

This is a good example of an undergraduate design project of "good intentions," that developed beyond the classroom into both a professional and meaningful experience for one particular student, although all the students benefited from the experience. The "new" van wrap was well received in Boston press outlets when the final design was unveiled in August 2013.

LLAGOSTERA YOUTH CENTER

Ariel Guersenzvaig, Lecturer, ELISAVA,
School of Design and Engineering,
Barcelona, Spain

2.52 The kitchen is a social and learning environment; the users can learn to cook and prepare meals for their friends.

CLIENT
Llagostera (Girona, Spain)
City Council and Autonomous
Government of Catalonia
(Spain).

PROJECT TITLE
Llagostera Youth Center
(Casal Jove Llagostera).

DURATION
4 months, September 2013–
December 2013.

BUDGET
€9,800.

TEAM
Faculty advisors: **Núria Coll,
Stefano Colli**, and **Ariel
Guersenzvaig**.
External advisor: **Mercè Graell.
Supervision: Albert Fuster.**
Students: **Banui Barragán,
Mar Ferrer, Laia Fusté,
Maria Massó, Christopher
Montserrat, Laura Oliver, Laia
Pascual, Albert Puig, Jordi Ros,
Berta Sagristà, Ariadna Veas.**

DESCRIPTION Llagostera (pop. 7,700) is a municipality
in the autonomous community of Catalonia, Spain.
It is located 20 km south of Girona (pop. 750,000) and
15 km west of the Mediterranean Sea. ELISAVA, a
design and engineering school located in Barcelona,
was commissioned by the client to develop an
innovative solution for the redesign of an existing
youth center located in Llagostera. The redesign
would include the interior and exterior of the center's
building as well as the center's service offerings.

The existing youth center is a public-funded space where young people aged 15–35 can meet and participate in activities. Its current user base is small, and the center does not connect with the needs of the people it serves.

This project was developed by recently graduated students from various design disciplines (interior, graphic, and product design). All students were familiar with people-centered design techniques, but for most of them this was the first real deep dive into a complex challenge involving real people.

RESEARCH The students performed three types of research: desk and field research, consisting of a photographic safari, architectural observation, benchmarking, and mystery shopping; user research, with ethnographic interviews and contextual observation; and participatory design using co-creation.

CHALLENGES The main challenge was to design a space and a set of offerings that would serve the needs of a broad group of users. Another important challenge was to step outside of a self-referential frame in order to create new solutions that work. In order to achieve that, the team needed to research and gain deep understanding of the people using the center: What were their needs? What were their dreams? What did they expect from the future? How did they behave? What would they do to get the future they wanted?

STRATEGY As in most projects with a "fuzzy" front-end, our project did not evolve in a linear manner but iteratively. Nonetheless, the project could be divided into four main stages:

1. **Discovery** After initial briefing sessions with the client, the students used online research to get a sense of what type of youth centers were available and what kind of services were offered. They visited several youth centers to gather brochures and leaflets and to learn about the physical spaces that housed these centers. They developed empathy with the services' users and got an understanding of the dynamics that took place in youth centers.

At this stage the students conducted ethnographic interviews and contextual observations of the end-users. Through these techniques, the students gained a deep understanding of the users needs, their attitudes toward the service providers, and especially the possible role the new youth center might have in their lives.

Several participatory design sessions were held. The toolkits created by the students specifically for these sessions were used to facilitate the sessions. The main co-creation techniques used were visual card sorting and storytelling and the creation of visual experience maps and mood boards to explore present issues (i.e., the user's daily chores, leisure activities, or states of mind) and future issues (i.e., what their ideal space for sharing time with friends or family would look like).

> "
>
> *All students were familiar with people-centered design techniques, but for most of them this was the first real deep dive into a complex challenge involving real people."*

2. **Interpretation** Interpretation was mainly carried out by means of clustering techniques such as affinity diagrams. Main themes were explored through rapid sketching techniques. In our view of design, interpretation of research and problem finding (an analytic task) is deeply linked to problem solving through the exploration of solutions (a synthetic task).

2.53a The club has an open meeting place where users can meet their friends, read a book or simply relax.

2.53b The club includes an open and modular co-working space where courses are offered and the city's future entrepreneurs can meet each other.

Four main themes emerged during this stage: *learning*, *identity*, *shared ownership*, and *place*. Each thematic cluster yielded several insights that were used to define opportunity areas, seen as open-ended questions to be answered in the next stage. The main opportunity areas that were defined were: how to get there, inside and outside the youth center, learning to learn, and connected community. While finishing this stage, the team framed a solution: The center was there to help local young people learn about and understand the present and future world around them.

3. Concept generation Through divergent design thinking, sketching, and rapid prototyping we aimed to rapidly generate many different conceptual solution ideas. These ideas were evaluated according to their fitness for purpose (how well they matched the insights and how well they fit the opportunity areas). Several (partial) conceptual solutions were chosen and incorporated into a comprehensive conceptual framework consisting of three pillars: open youth center, activate the neighborhood, and entrepreneurial learning.

4. Delivery In this stage the conceptual solutions (the *what* of the solutions) were further developed into technical designs (the *how* of the solutions). The technical designs had a service design element—the service for the youth center was defined, and then an element was designed that defined the spaces that would accommodate that service. The technical designs were the project's end results and will be used by the client moving forward to communicate with the architects, engineers, and contractors who will implement the design. Deliverables included customer journeys, service blueprints, floor plans, and architectural renderings.

EFFECTIVENESS If we were faced with a similar challenge in the future we would allow more time for participatory design during the concept generation stage. Overall, we are very satisfied with the results and so are the clients. They are currently planning its development and construction. The project will become a reality.

ASSESSMENT This project was an eye-opener for all of the students. They realized that working side by side with the people they are designing for increases the quality of the end solutions and their likelihood of success. The techniques and participatory tools we used pleasantly surprised the community's young people. They enjoyed the activities and could share their views with the design team and see how this process was translated into concrete solutions. The client experienced how our design methodology can provide new ways of reaching meaningful and innovative solutions. For me, as a teacher, it was a wonderful opportunity to see young designers at work and assist them in their first complex professional challenge.

2.54 Chris Montserrat, Jordi Ros, and Maria Massó (left to right) making sense of raw data obtained through user research and participatory design.

THE HUMAN STORY

Jackie Malcolm, Lecturer, Duncan of Jordanstone College of Art & Design, University of Dundee (DJCAD), Dundee, Scotland

2.55a–2.55b Frames from Addiction Kinetic Typography film produced for the ISAM Conference Dundee 2015. *Design: Danny McCormick and Teo Almonte.*

CLIENT
International Society of Addiction Medicine (ISAM) Dundee 2015.

PROJECT TITLE
The Human Story.

DURATION
12 weeks for each project: September–December 2013, January–March 2014.

BUDGET
£250 provided for each of the projects by the Dundee Alcohol and Drug Partnership.

TEAM
Level 2: In Communication Design (Graphic Design, Illustration, Animation), 75 students worked in teams of five to six, September–December 2013.
Level 3: In Graphic Design, 28 students worked in pairs, January–March 2014.

DESCRIPTION Duncan of Jordanstone College of Art & Design (DJCAD) was invited to facilitate an exhibition of artwork addressing the subject of substance misuse, to coincide with the ISAM (International Society of Addiction Medicine) Dundee 2015 Congress on addiction scheduled for October 2015 in Dundee, Scotland. DJCAD's role was to facilitate a connection between the scientific conference and the local community.

Two student projects were developed to engage local community organizations and individuals in DJCAD through the subject of addiction, providing a context for the project briefs. The level 2 project briefing included contextual talks by Steven Dalton of the Dundee Alcohol and Drug Partnership (ADP), who presented the social and behavioral perspective, and Dr. Alex Baldacchino, a psychiatrist from Ninewells Medical Hospital—responsible for bringing the conference to Dundee—who spoke about substance misuse viewed through a scientific lens. Students were asked to use their group interdisciplinary skills to develop a short animation communicating one aspect of substance misuse. The focus for this brief was in critically understanding what we mean by "good" design, examining the design intention of any communication giving consideration to the design's impact.

The level 3 project briefing delivered a very different contextual understanding of the subject by inviting three individuals, now in recovery from substance abuse, to share their experiences of drug addiction. The individuals came from very different social backgrounds to ensure there was no stigma attached to the social context for substance misuse. Their human stories were recorded and students worked with the transcriptions to develop a "typographic motion film," one minute in length. The focus for this project was the narrative and the real-life experiences of people suffering from drug addiction.

RESEARCH John Booth Davies, in his book *The Myth of Addiction* (1997), suggests, "The drug issue usually attracts our attention through media presentations which seek to reduce the issue to a single, instantly comprehensible message but in the process [give] an inaccurate and largely false impression." Social science research can present the designer with an understanding of social contexts, helping us to visualize community activity that is based on evidence and experience. Due to the subject matter and ethics, and for reasons of safety, we could not allow students to approach individuals suffering from drug or alcohol addiction, and it was therefore necessary to bring such life scenarios to the students.

Students too often understand "research" to mean a visit to the university library and an explore of the Internet. Sadly, this can result in the kind of "media presentations" Davies refers to above with which we are all too familiar. Embedding social research methods within projects facilitated a much deeper understanding of the human context.

2.56 Frames from Addiction Kinetic Typography film produced for the ISAM Conference Dundee 2015.
Design: Danny McCormick and Teo Almonte.

CHALLENGES Allowing students to engage with people who might be socially excluded from society adds a social science dimension to the process of design. Many professional projects require designers to develop communication for vulnerable groups, but without engaging with the people whose lives are truly affected—thus the resulting design work can be misguided. By embedding social science research methods within the design process, students were made fully aware of the consequences that their designs can have for individuals and the wider community.

To establish a design framework that addresses the learning process, linking critical reflection from one project to the next, the REASON: Research / Environmental Evaluation / Analysis / Solution / Outcome / Nexus design process model was used (Malcolm, 2010). It is crucial that students gain an insight into their learning journey, critically reflecting upon the design process to establish what knowledge and skills have been attained, acknowledging how it can influence the future of their design intention. To identify these attributes, students were asked to submit a learning map, identifying their own interpretation of the learning journey through their design process, and afterward they produced a 500-word critical reflection on their experience.

With 104 students working on this project, it was likely that some were affected personally by drug or alcohol addiction. It was therefore important for the educators to offer pastoral support, although some preferred not to discuss it openly. This is where the critical reflection process provided some interesting insights. Students were able to provide personal perspectives or experiences within a confidential written format. As the facilitator of the project, I was challenged to ensure that a level of care

> **"**
>
> *By embedding social science research methods within the design process, students were made fully aware of the consequences that their designs can have for individuals and the wider community."*
>
> ———

2.57 Frame from Addiction Kinetic Typography film produced for the ISAM Conference Dundee 2015. *Design: Stuart Lamont and Ruhua Liu.*

2.58 Frames from Addiction Kinetic Typography film produced for the ISAM Conference Dundee 2015. *Design: Stuart Lamont and Ruhua Liu.*

and responsibility was applied to all of the participants who generously offered to share their experiences. It became evident that the experience of sharing was emotional, and beneficial, not only for the students but also for the participants.

STRATEGY The strategy for "The Human Story" project is interconnected with the vision for the ISAM Dundee 2015 Congress. The international event is meant to effectively communicate new movements in clinical medicine associated with drug and alcohol addiction. What makes the Dundee Congress unique is its vision to include art and design as a facilitator for community engagement. The films produced by the students will be used by local community service organizations to help inform society of the issues surrounding substance misuse. Having an international audience means that the work will have a wider impact, driving a new vision for future ISAM conferences. Ultimately the hope is that the design projects may change lives by empowering people to move into recovery, or be used in schools to educate students and prevent future substance misuse.

EFFECTIVENESS We will not be able to fully realize the potential effectiveness of the films until they are released in October 2015—however, the response by Dundee Alcohol and Drug partnership (ADP) was highly positive. Vered Hopkins, the development officer for ADP, stated that "the students really grasped the messages we wanted to communicate and, most importantly, the ethos behind the messages." Vered identified "a very positive shift from traditional ways of communicating the risks associated with substances (which in the past often tried to scare people by using exaggerated and often not entirely accurate information). This, in my view, is very powerful."

The students' learning experience was enhanced through their deep engagement with the subject of substance misuse, and interactions with the people who gave their time to inspire and encourage the students to produce effective design communication around this issue.

If we as educators equip our graduates with the skills to consider an ethical and responsible graphic design solution, we can begin to see change happen. This requires the self-realization to act with conscience, and respond with compassion and empathy, recognizing the impact design can have within society.

ASSESSMENT Working in groups always brings complexities when assessing student performance, requiring an acknowledgment that there might be stronger students who can carry or drive weaker individuals. It is therefore important to have individual submissions so that we as educators can look beyond team dynamics to understand personal perspectives and learning experiences. The reflective submissions, sketchbooks, and learning maps are therefore individually assessed, whereas the final work is assessed as a group.

ADDITIONAL INFORMATION Links to the two short videos can be found at: https://vimeo.com/116104893 https://vimeo.com/116104892

DEMENTIA LAB (D-LAB) MASTER'S MODULE

Andrea Wilkinson, Senior Designer and Researcher, Interactions Research Group, Media, Arts and Design Faculty, (MAD-faculty), LUCA School of Arts, Campus Genk, Belgium

CLIENT

The Dementia Lab Master's Module is a class that stems from ongoing design research that works closely with local organizations/care facilities that specialize in the treatment of people with dementia.

PROJECT TITLE

Dementia Lab (D-lab) Master's Module.

DURATION

2 months, 9 class meetings. The course has been offered annually since 2011.

BUDGET

This project is carried out without any additional support or funding apart from the care and time provided by the facilities and organizations.

TEAM

Lecturers: **Andrea Wilkinson,** Senior Designer and Researcher, Interactions Research Group, and **Niels Hendriks,** Senior Researcher, Interactions Research Group.
Students: Master's students from the following disciplines: Graphic Design, Interactive Design (CMD), Photography, TV & Film, Game and Product Design.

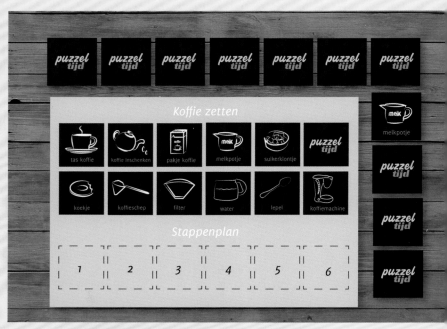

2.59a Initial prototype of card game to make coffee.
Design: Goele Peeters, Dementia Lab Module 2013.

2.59b Conversation starter photo cards.
Design: Blossom Aerts, Dementia Lab Module 2012.

DESCRIPTION Context The association most people have with the term "dementia" is that of forgetfulness, when in fact dementia is an umbrella term used to describe a variety of psychiatric and cognitive symptoms that affect daily life differently for each person. The American Psychiatric Association (2000) states that on a cognitive level, people with dementia almost always suffer from a deterioration of memory, difficulties in language and communication, the inability to perform purposeful movements and/or orientation in time and place. Additional behavioral and cognitive problems such as irritation/frustration, short attention span, restlessness, an inability to learn new routines or adapt to changing situations can also occur.

Expectations What is asked of students of the module is simple: their brief is to make the life of a person with dementia more *aangenaam*, a Dutch word which means nice, pleasant, and lovely. This confronts students with an open-ended design problem and offers them no prescribed end result such as "build an application," "design an interface," or "make a campaign for." Instead the student must familiarize her/himself with the environment and context, actively research a role that design can play within the context, test and retest their concepts together with the person with dementia, and deliver a working prototype that tells a story—which is to say that the thing created works as an artifact of the entire design process.

The educational purpose of the module is to place students in contact with a new experience in which they use their design skills in a new and perhaps "undesignerly" context. Students are encouraged to respond as designers instead of being limited by their own domain. In this way, photographers become object makers, graphic designers become game makers, digital students become product designers, and product designers sometimes become tour guides.

2.60 Geertrui Storms working on-site at the care facility, testing prototypes.

RESEARCH Because of the level of research required at every stage of the project, the module is run with little or no distinction between the act of designing and the act of researching. Central to this is the Dementia Lab Module vision concerning the importance of inclusion in the design process. In contrast to the common view that a person is a *user* within a greater *user group*, this project refers simply to individual people and their needs. The prototypes that are created are custom designs created on a one-to-one basis. Because the module focuses on *designing with* instead of merely *designing for*, it encourages the participation of the person with dementia through the entire design process.

In order to achieve this, students must search for ways to include people with dementia in their design processes by using principles of participatory design. The module tries to inspire students to think "outside of the box" and to look for ways to modify existing research methods or to generate new ones to make them inclusive. The goal is to allow people with dementia (and their professional or informal caregivers, family, and friends) to become peers within the design process, so much so that the artifact/design/prototype presented at the end of the module could not have been created without their involvement.

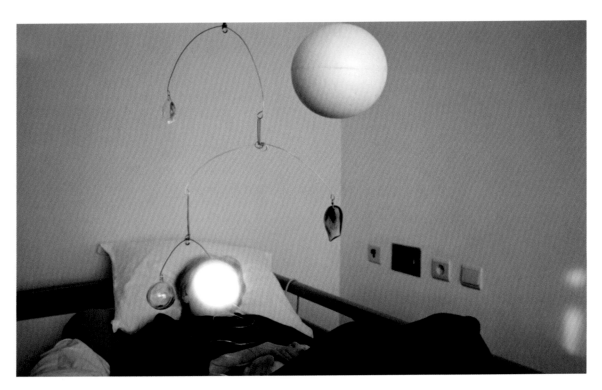

2.61 Mobile installed in a care home bedroom. *Ilse Raps.*

CHALLENGES This project is full of challenges: from building a good relationship with a care facility to winning over the minds of family members who are skeptical about the process. The project must also be open to failure; designs that are expected to work well sometimes don't work at all. Moreover, there is a stigma surrounding people of advanced age and what is deemed as "care at the end of life." Students and lecturers alike are anxious on the first day, and so a challenge each year is to manage this introduction so that this anxiety is minimized.

STRATEGY The Dementia Lab Module has two key pillars: a final prototype that responds to the experience of an individual with dementia, and the methodology of inclusion that the students create.

Gathering knowledge Specifically placing students outside of their comfort zone, this course requires students to rapidly learn about dementia and build not only a knowledge base, but also empathy. Students follow practical workshops in which they learn the basics of the condition and watch documentaries that portray views of dementia and aging as both poetic and harsh. In addition to these influences, the module takes place *in* a rest home and, when possible, includes a 36-hour sleepover. Instead of an idealized portrait of what a rest home should be, students are confronted with the actual care experience: its pace, the time spent waiting, how a day is filled, the food, smells, and arrangement of rooms, and the sounds in the night. Instead of designing for traits of dementia, the student is designing for how dementia manifests itself in a particular person.

One of the best additions to the module over the last year has been its being embedded within a care facility. This move changed the experience for all involved and brought aging as a social concern into the everyday."

———

Defining their inspiration The openness of the project brief requires students to seek either their own design problems or situations they want to address. After the first full day in the care facility, students are asked to reflect on their impressions and summarize their experience. These impressions are then used as triggers and touchstones that the students continue to reference in their design process. For example, Blossom chose to take the module specifically because her next-door neighbor had, a few years prior, been moved into a rest home. She had not visited her due to anxiety about what she would be able to talk about or what the home would be like. Blossom's initial research looked at this anxiety and found that it was very common among family members of people with dementia. Hoping to mediate this experience, she developed a series of conversation-starter cards that guided people in simple conversations.

Making the design process inclusive As previously stated, students are asked to open their design process and develop a way of working which allows them to explore subjects together with individuals with dementia. Students Jannelien and Roelie were interested in designing for the moments between meal times, when people with dementia living in a care facility busy themselves with waiting. They

wanted to create a project for a woman who was unable to communicate but still very active and mobile. Although they supplemented their knowledge about the woman by talking to nurses and family members, they also developed a method by which they took repeated walks with her over the course of several weeks, noting each time what path she chose to take and what she looked at and responded to when she paused to rest. The students then proposed a design that incorporated the content of these pauses within their design.

Generating prototypes Generating designed responses as a result of the research is an iterative undertaking. Students are encouraged to refine their designs through testing and retesting and to maintain an openness to unexpected directions which stem from these encounters. Another student, Ilse, was specifically triggered by the care given to a person who was bedridden with advanced stages of dementia who perpetually shifted between agitation and calmness. Based on her research and observations into sensory impulses (light, sound, and movement), she created a mobile that hung over the person's bed. Each successive prototype refined the textures, size, colors, sound, imagery, etc., and tested the context in which it had to exist, also taking into consideration the amount of time that a caregiver had to give care.

EFFECTIVENESS One of the best additions to the module over the last year has been its being embedded within a care facility. This move changed the experience for all involved and brought aging as a social concern into the everyday. Another strength of the project is the fact that the research mirrors the research interests of the lecturers who, in parallel projects, are carrying out similar activities to those of the students. In this way, the research expertize and experiences of students mutually reinforce each other; it's a win-win situation and a model that is ideal for education.

2.62a–2.62c The Colorful 1950s' coloring book being used in a care facility, 2013. *Design: Sara Nysten.*

ASSESSMENT This module is run with an idealistic view that this way of working will eventually trickle down into industry (both the design and the care industry). It is our hope that this project plants a seed in the minds of future designers that their domain need not be limited to media production, but instead can be applied in new and varied contexts. On a practical level, the benefit for care centers is immediate as a steady stream of young people interacting with a dementia ward is a very welcome sight. Particularly for students who work with family members or family friends, this project offers a chance to create something meaningful and valid; there are sometimes very new experiences for student designers.

For example, Sara's grandfather had dementia triggered by Parkinson's. As part of his daily exercises he was encouraged to color pages in coloring books. Although her grandfather really enjoyed this activity, the family found it embarrassing that their father/grandfather was coloring childish images. Sara wanted to create something that suited her grandfather's life experience and reduced the family's feeling of loss. She created a prototype of a coloring book for people with dementia, using the same simple line work and detail of children's coloring books but with imagery related to the 1950s.

This meaningful encounter is not only shared by the students, but also by those impacted by the thing designed. Goele's grandmother had been diagnosed with dementia 2 years previously but still lived at home. Her condition had progressed so that she was no longer able to carry out regular duties at home such as cooking, doing laundry, and so on, yet she became angry when her husband did these tasks poorly. Triggered by her grandparents' frustration, and utilizing her grandmother's love of playing cards, Goele developed a game which, when played with a support person, provided her grandmother enough support to carry out basic tasks such as making a cup of coffee. Her grandfather summed up the practical and meaningful impact of this prototype by saying, "It's the first cup of coffee my wife has made for me in 2 years."

2.63 Geertrui Storms working on-site at the care facility, testing prototypes.

Working in "real life" contexts instills a sense of urgency to the prototypes created. Instead of letting the developed prototypes collect dust, the lecturers actively seek funding to support students either to further realize their concepts or to continue with additional research into these concepts. The coloring book is a good example of this, as it has been further developed into a coloring book that is available in Belgium, the UK, and the United States.

2.3

SECTION 3
SERVICE DESIGN

DESIGNING FROM THE END TO THE BEGINNING AND BACK AGAIN:
INTRODUCING STUDENTS TO SERVICE DESIGN THINKING

Michael Gibson

A TACO-CENTRIC OVERVIEW OF SERVICE DESIGN

It is a relatively safe bet that most university-level design students studying in the US and select locations in the UK, Saudi Arabia, South Korea, India, Canada, Puerto Rico, and the Philippines know that a *Crunchy Taco™* can be purchased at a Taco Bell® restaurant near them for relatively little money. They can also be reasonably sure there will be almost no difference in the taste of a *Crunchy Taco™* purchased in Manila, London, Montreal, or Kansas City. Additionally, they can also be reasonably sure that all of the factors that combine to shape the experiences they have from the moment they enter a Taco Bell® until the moment they leave in these geographically diverse locales will be similar. In this context, the term "experiences" refers to the entire tangible and intangible array of what these students, and most other Taco Bell® customers, encounter and undergo during the span of time they are inside a particular Taco Bell®.

These experiences are affected by what they will observe, hear, smell, taste, and feel, with the latter referring both to physical, sense-of-touch (haptic) sensations and their immediate and eventual (remembered) emotional responses. The designers of the more than 6,500 Taco Bell® locations around the world have consciously designed the amalgam of experiences that contextualize, or *frame*, a visit to these environments. They have carefully considered how and what their customers will perceive, as well as how these perceptions will influence their thinking and, thus, their behavior during their visit and well beyond it. The designers' principal aim in doing this was and is to ensure that a particular set of needs and expectations can be met effectively and efficiently on behalf of those who use Taco Bell® to quickly procure relatively inexpensive, tasty-if-not-tasteful, "Tex-Mex" food products. Determining (a) why and how the needs and expectations of Taco Bell® customers have evolved as they have, and then (b) using this knowledge to design the totality of their experiences during each visit to an individual restaurant in ways that are *desirable*, *useful*, and *usable* to them, exemplifies one of the primary tenets of effective service design.

Most of the university-level design students described above probably understand that while the service experience at a Taco Bell® restaurant near them is conducive to quickly providing them with cheap tacos, it is *not* conducive to encouraging them to stay and enjoy the environmental ambience of the restaurant itself for any longer than it takes to actually consume their food. Would one of these students who wishes to make a favorable, romantic impression on a "special someone" accomplish this goal by taking him or her on a first date to Taco Bell®? Presumably not in most cases, unless they wish the first date to also be the last. Understanding why this is true can help students understand the issues that service design attempts to address.

The design of the services that comprise a visit to Taco Bell® are very different than those that comprise a visit to a food truck that sells tacos, or to a one-of-a-kind restaurant that sells "specialty" or "specific recipe" tacos, or to a restaurant that serves entrées that start at US$50 and that strictly enforce a dress code. Other large, multinational restaurant businesses have designed the services they facilitate differently than has Taco Bell®, as have smaller, more regionally focused restaurant chains. The tacos on offer in some of these environments do taste different than those on offer in others, but, when sampling the gamut of tacos served at the outlets of the larger chains, taste is not much of a differentiating factor.

Neither is price, and, more recently, neither is brand, especially to the student mentioned above who wishes to make a favorable impression on a first date.

If the outcome of this first date is to yield a second, choosing a dining venue that has carefully considered its service design will likely help tilt the odds in this direction. Just as the needs and expectations of the people involved in the first date scenario form its practical, emotional, and aspirational center from its beginning until its end, so do the needs and expectations of the people being affected by the delivery of a particular service or system of services. This essential idea aligns with the thinking of Andy Polaine, Lavrans Løvlie, and Ben Reason, authors of *Service Design: From Insight to Implementation* (2013): service design emphasizes planning, implementing, and effectively sustaining "interactions among people, technology and processes" over set spans of time.

THE ADVANTAGES OF DESIGNING BACKWARDS

When the thinking that informs service design has been effectively applied to affect how a given group experiences a specific situation or "scenario of use," the systems and processes that facilitate its operation improve in ways that deliver multiple benefits to these people. They come to feel emotionally and physically satisfied, are inspired to loyalty and find it easier to participate, contribute, perform, and use. Service design can positively affect the development, implementation, and sustenance of services across a broad spectrum of day-to-day situations including, but not limited to, transportation, retail, finance, food procurement, education, healthcare, and information acquisition. Yoko Akama (*Warts and All: The Real Practice of Service Design*, 2009), a researcher and communication design educator at RMIT University in Australia, describes the contexts for service design projects in complex and broad terms: "Because it reflects the myriad of value systems that operate and are evolving in the lived world, there is no single, unifying framework or schema that encompasses exactly what service design is or accomplishes."

This fuzzy, ill-defined aspect of service design provides students trying to understand the practices that inform it with a productive way to begin their inquiries. By trying to understand what factors frame and comprise a given service in ways that make it easy and pleasing to experience on behalf of a given population, students must begin working from what usually constitutes the end of the design process—an improved set of artifacts, situation, or system—back to its beginning. The "beginning" consists of "what" (the things in a given environment, how they are arranged, and the nature of the people involved) combined with "how" (how and why the elements that form the "what" function over time, and according to which working principles and premises). This beginning can only be determined once a set of parameters has been established that describes what a specific group of users or customers defines as desirable, useful, and usable, and essential understandings have been reached among the students about the belief systems that inform this group. In an article published about design thinking in *Design Studies* in 2011, industrial design engineer and researcher Kees Dorst described this process as *abduction*, a basic reasoning pattern for guiding productive thinking.

Service design can positively affect the development, implementation, and sustenance of services across a broad spectrum of day-to-day situations including, but not limited to, transportation, retail, finance, food procurement, education, healthcare, and information acquisition."

——

The design of the services facilitated in contemporary settings where goods and services may be purchased, consumed, or experienced often begins by addressing one or more aspects of the service design that are *failing*, or causing some form of dissatisfaction. Utilizing ethnographic methods to gain empathic understandings of why a particular population's sociocultural values and belief systems affect how they experience various phenomena has yielded practical and constructive knowledge to social scientists for many years, and has also proven beneficial to service designers. This is especially true when a designer is trying to gain understanding about why and how a specific aspect of a given service is perceived to be failing by a particular group. An ethnographic approach requires that the designer make an earnest attempt to observe the evolution of a select situation from the viewpoint, or from "behind the eyes," of the customers, or "users," whose needs and expectations she is trying to meet.

In this way, service design is a user-centered design endeavor, as those who will be affected by the decision-making processes that guide service design must be allowed to directly affect their evolution. Students need to be sensitized to the fact that a service design challenge transpires as a sequence of interconnected events, each of which affects the others. Finally, the entire array of people, technology, and processes that comprise the environment within which the service occurs must be comprehensively integrated as the service design process evolves. Students need to understand this as a holistic undertaking, one that is broadly rather than myopically informed, and that champions plurality over singularity.

Michael R. Gibson is an Associate Professor of Visual Communication Design at the University of North Texas College of Visual Arts and Design, Denton, Texas. He is the coordinator of two Master's level graduate programs that immerse designers in learning experiences informed by evidence-based approaches to design. As a design researcher, he has worked on several interdisciplinary projects that have addressed issues involving children's health and well-being, the development and implementation of technologies to facilitate diverse approaches to teaching and learning, urban revitalization and freshwater conservation, among others.

FIVE QUESTIONS TO
JAKE BARROW

1. Who or what influences informed you as you prepared for a career in design?
Growing up in the Australian outback, my exposure to design was limited, but art and artists influenced me. Eventually we moved to Melbourne, and it was my surroundings that had a great influence on me. Not a day passed that I wouldn't take time to study the ads in my environment. Even now, I stop and take in everything—bus shelters, train stations, and billboards—then ask myself what works and what doesn't.

2. Do you agree or disagree with this statement: Designers have a social and ethical responsibility to create and transmit meaningful forms of communication that benefit society and culture? Why?
All people have a social and ethical responsibility toward society. The difference with creative professionals is that we have know-how and the resources to influence society on a much broader scale. Being in this privileged position, I do think we bear some responsibility to contribute to a better society in some form, because if not you, then who?

3. The Human Walking Program is a pet adoption campaign you created for the Lost Dogs Home, Australia's biggest animal shelter. The idea is that dogs that were up for adoption let office workers take them for a lunchtime walk. Can you talk about your involvement with the Human Walking Program and why it is important for you to do this type of work?
The idea to have some kind of dog-walking service was conceived during a very heavy work period. I remembered a time when I would occasionally walk a friend's dog, and thinking of how therapeutic it felt. Working together with a group of talented people in the agency, we molded the concept into the "Human Walking Program." We approached the Lost Dogs Home with the idea, and they shared our enthusiasm from the start.

The campaign was a great success, for the sole reason that it was based on a very real human insight—that sometimes humans need just as much rescuing as shelter dogs. Good ideas can have a profound effect on the world, so for me it's important and really satisfying when I can use my ideas to do some greater good.

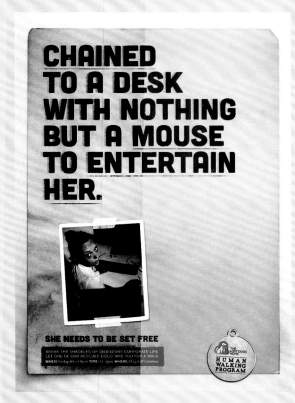

2.64 Human Walking Program advertising. *Design: Jake Barrow.*

4. New roles are emerging for design professionals as their function is increasingly changing from that of generators to facilitators of ideas. Can you comment on this?

Roles in the creative industry will always shift and titles will always change. But we'll always need clever ideas and good design—that should be the yardstick to measure any design professional by.

5. What advice would you give a student studying visual communication today to help them prepare for contemporary professional practice?

Creating something meaningful will ultimately have more impact on society and on you as a designer.

Jake Barrow is Senior Art Director at iconic Australian advertising agency George Patterson Y&R. He has a degree in design, placed 2nd in the prestigious Australian Writers and Art Directors School, and has since created breakthrough advertising campaigns for some of Australia's biggest brands. In 2012 he was ranked in the Top 10 Art Directors in the world by Cannes Lions, and in 2013 he was ranked in the Top 20 by the Directory Big Won report. Video of the Human Walking Program: http://vimeo.com/92823193

2.65 Human Walking Program advertising. *Design: Jake Barrow.*

2.66 Human Walking Program advertising. *Design: Jake Barrow.*

FLY-IN-FLY-OUT:
DESIGNING A BETTER FLY-IN-FLY-OUT LIFESTYLE IN WESTERN AUSTRALIA

Dr. Christopher Kueh and **Dr. Stuart Medley,** Senior Lecturers, School of Communication and Arts, Faculty of Education and Arts, Edith Cowan University, Perth, Western Australia, and **Jacinth Watson**, Chief Investigator, Child Health Promotion Research Centre, Edith Cowan University, Perth, Western Australia

CLIENT
Child Health Research Promotion Centre, Western Australian mining industry, and broader community.

PROJECT TITLE
Fly-In-Fly-Out.

DURATION
Two 12-week semesters, July 2013–July 2014.

BUDGET
Although there was no budget limiting students' proposals, students were asked to consider the practicality and economic rationale for their projects.

TEAM
Students: 12 postgraduate students with various disciplinary backgrounds, and undergraduate students in fashion design, advertising, spatial design, interaction design, and creative services. Individual students, in concert with in-class discussions and feedback sessions, implemented the projects. Fly-In-Fly-Out was a collaboration with Child Health Research Promotion Centre's research project Raising Adolescents: Strategies for Fly In/Fly Out Families, which was supported by the Western Australian Health Promotion Foundation (Healthway) through research grant no. 22913.

Researchers: Jacinth Watson and **Liz Wenden** were involved in the project by providing relevant direction, life experiences, anecdotal observations, and feedback to students. They also have experiences in being in FIFO families and acted as stakeholders in the project: **Jacinth Watson,** Chief Investigator, Child Health Promotion Research Centre, **Stacey Waters,** Associate Professor, Chief Investigator, Child Health Promotion Research Centre, and **Liz Wenden,** Chief Investigator, Child Health Promotion Research Centre, **Edith Cowan University,** Perth, Western Australia; **Leanne Lester,** Associate Professor, School of Sport Science, Exercise and Health; **Melanie Epstein,** Senior Research Fellow, Telethon Kids Institute, The University of Western Australia; **Dr. Barbara Spears,** Senior Lecturer, School of Education, University of South Australia.

2.67 Leandro Misseroni's proposed app provided the stay-at-home partner of a FIFO worker with assistance and motivations to accommodate to the lifestyle. The app could be customized to suit the needs of the stay-at-home partner throughout various stages of the lifestyle: beginning stage, those who are starting to get used to the lifestyle, and those who are well into the lifestyle. *Design: Leandro Misseroni.*

DESCRIPTION FIFO (fly-in-fly-out) refers to the lifestyle of workers who leave home to stay in a designated camp, mainly mine sites, for a period of time, and are back at home for a short period of time before repeating the process again. The increase in FIFO work patterns has exposed more Western Australian families to the repeated and cyclical absence of parents who adopt this mode of paid employment. FIFO families can experience loneliness, isolation, resentment, and difficulty readjusting to the frequent and repeated parting and reunions. Anecdotal evidence suggests the FIFO lifestyle causes relationship problems for couples, excessive alcohol use and drug use by workers, and increased risk of suicide.

This project focused on the development of effective communication pathways and platforms to assist families with FIFO parent(s)/partner to better manage the challenges associated with the FIFO lifestyle, and to help individuals or families that are planning to take up a FIFO lifestyle to understand and assess the potential situations. Addressing challenges facing FIFO communities, this project aimed to introduce a design-thinking process as a series of holistic strategies to define problems, develop and prototype ideas, and propose implementation pathways.

RESEARCH The project required students to engage in practice-based research through a rigorous design process. Students conducted their design development based on the following design thinking framework:

(Re)Define challenges One of the strongest skills a good designer has is the ability to approach a given problem from multiple directions. Students conducted in-depth literature reviews focused on FIFO lifestyle issues, and were given a summary of research outcomes from FIFO research studies. With this information, students conducted empathy-mapping exercises to chart their first-hand research against published information and media representations of FIFO lifestyles. This research strategy allowed students to understand the issue from both a micro and a macro perspective. For example, through empathy-mapping exercises, students who had little knowledge about the challenges facing FIFO families were able to understand the emotional states of family members at various stages of the FIFO cycle.

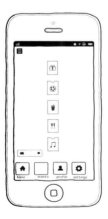

teen's home page

teens events tab and calendar

coupon page

2.68 Melanie Tarr's app design that functioned as a secured communication system between teenagers and their FIFO parent. It included a countdown reminder of the returning dates of FIFO parent, and a competition to win vouchers that promote teenagers to engage with FIFO parent when they are at home. These functions were the outcome of the co-creation workshops. *Design: Melanie Tarr.*

User-centered approach: Students were encouraged to consider a product or service from a bottom-up approach—to prioritize end users' experiences in the design process rather than assuming a "designer knows best" stance. This focus produces design outcomes that empower end users and their broader community.

Co-design and co-creation: Students developed their design based on a "design with people" perspective. While students did not have ethics approval to engage with stakeholders, co-creation methods were achieved through engaging the researchers who are experts in FIFO lifestyles. Students were able to use methods such as persona and storyboarding to include users in their design processes.

CHALLENGES The main challenge of this project was for students to understand the emotional needs of FIFO family members. For some students, a FIFO lifestyle is a new concept and they struggled to see the reason why this is a social issue. For example, students from Asian countries were accustomed to living with extended family, including grandparents, a practice that provides support if one parent, or both, need to travel for work. The sense of loneliness and isolation might not be as intense as those experienced in Australian communities, where families are units independent of extended family. Empathy-mapping and persona methods allowed students to see situations from the stakeholders' perspectives.

STRATEGY Challenges facing FIFO families are complex and multifaceted. Students needed a holistic understanding of the situation while exploring ideas and prototypes. They were led through the stages of redefining challenges, exploring and creating prototypes, and refining and proposing ways to implement their ideas:

Redefine challenges: Weeks 1–4 were dedicated to understanding and unpacking the challenges facing FIFO communities. Based on literature searches, and a summary of research outcomes from clients, students were instructed to adopt a persona in order to see situations from stakeholders' perspectives. Students were asked to act as a FIFO family member, and map what they would do, see, think, hear, and say at different stages of their daily lives. In some situations, students were asked to map the lifestyle

of a stay-at-home partner of a FIFO worker, to experience their life while the worker was at home and away, and the transitions in between. This design stage allowed students to thoroughly understand the challenges from stakeholders' perspectives.

Explore and prototype: In weeks 5–9, students were introduced to visual thinking tools for ideation and prototyping. They were encouraged to utilize visuals not just as presentation tools but as thinking tools. Methods such as storyboarding and business model visualization were introduced. Students were able to utilize these tools to visualize users' experiences in a cohesive manner and to prototype their proposed design through iterative processes. For example, students used storyboards to visualize a stakeholder using a proposed app that aimed at developing closer relationships between children and the FIFO parent in daily life. Business model visualization techniques were used to examine if the proposed ideas had relevance to the community, were appropriate to be delivered, were feasible, and were valued by partners such as mining companies and broader FIFO communities. Each student documented these processes in their development journal for reflection, allowing them to identify the strengths and weaknesses of their ideas, and be able to improve them through iterative design. Students were encouraged to have at least three rounds of iterative processes through the semester.

Students were encouraged to consider a product or service from a bottom-up approach—to prioritize end users' experiences in the design process rather than assuming a "designer knows best" stance."

——

Jamie's Dad sat a "introductory to FIFO" workshop with the companies occupational therapist. He is informed of different situations that occur with FIFO teens. He is given many ways to communicate with Jamie.

Rob really wants to make sure that Jamie is OK while he is away. He buys him a new mobile phone and installs the FIFOteen app.

Rob can't go paintballing on the 30th September as its the day after he gets home and he will be tired.

He reschedules.

Jamie's Dad works in the heat but in an airconditioned truck. He misses his family but knows they will be better off financially. He sends them a photo of the mine pit he is working and updates his location. That way when Jamie logs in he can keep track of Dad through the gallery. Dad's gallery forms a visual diary that's continually updated.

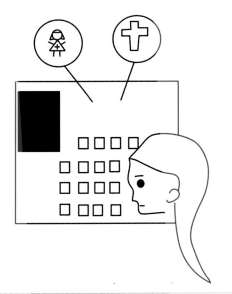

Jamie's teacher notices he is a little quiet this week and checks the calendar she has been given permission to access by Jamie's parents. This is the FIFO workers roster. She is aware he is without his Dad this week and keeps an eye out. The school chaplin also has access to Jamie's Dad's calendar. He makes a point of kicking the footy with Jamie this week.

2.69 Melanie Tarr's storyboard that visualized the ways teenagers and parents would use the proposed app. *Design: Melanie Tarr.*

2.70 Melanie Tarr conducting persona and prototype methods to develop her project, FIFOteen.

Refine and implement: Weeks 10–12 were for students to refine their proposed strategies. Students had two opportunities to present to the clients. The first was a mock presentation, in which clients gave feedback on working ideas with draft prototypes. Students then had 2 weeks to take on the feedback and improve on their design. Final designs were then presented to clients for assessment during the final week.

EFFECTIVENESS The introduction of a design thinking framework to encourage students to see design as a holistic and empathic thinking process was a success. Most students demonstrated good understanding of innovative design for social purposes through bottom-up methods. The division of the semester into three sections that each focused on one part of a design process worked well in getting students to understand holistic design.

One area that needs improvement is that most students developed and proposed strategies based heavily on technology rather than analogue processes. The majority of outcomes were phone apps and web-based communications. While these could be appropriate, there is a risk of excluding people-centered processes in their search for a solution.

ASSESSMENT This project had a different impact on educators, students, clients, and the community. The introduction of design thinking and empathy-based design methods yielded generally positive feedback from the students. Through the university's online feedback system, students reported that "[the project] really opened my mind to a new framework of thinking and problem solving," and "I want to do it again." These are good indicators that students were able to see the broad contribution of design in a complex social context.

Apart from providing feedback to students' project development, the researchers mentioned that by going through the design thinking framework and process with students, they could see how design could contribute positively to their field of research in child and adolescent health and well-being.

A round table discussion was held in November 2013 with representatives from mining companies and not-for-profit organizations that were involved in FIFO communities. Design solutions from the project were discussed. Feedback was positive and the communities were keen to find ways to develop some ideas further. Clients/collaborators and students involved in this project are currently exploring avenues to realize some of the design proposals.

This two-semester project allowed educators to identify and refine ways to teach design thinking to students. The purpose of the project was not to insert the term "design thinking" in the curriculum, but to expand students' understanding of the practice of design from production-centered to having the ability to (re)define a problem and work on it to develop people-centered innovation. Design educators in the school confirmed that the division of the semester into design stages helped to introduce holistic and people-centered design to students effectively.

CREATING AN IDENTITY FOR THE CAHABA RIVER BLUEWAY

Doug Barrett, Associate Professor, Graphic Design, The University of Alabama, Birmingham, Alabama

Matt Leavell, Project Director, Alabama Innovation Engine, a partnership of The University of Alabama and Auburn University, Auburn, Alabama

CLIENTS

Alabama Innovation Engine: A design-based economic development partnership of Auburn University and The University of Alabama. Alabama Innovation Engine was created to facilitate collaboration between designers, non-profit organizations, and governmental entities. www.uaced.ua.edu/.

Cahaba River Society: A Birmingham, Alabama-based watershed advocacy organization working to protect and restore the Cahaba River watershed and its rich diversity of life. www.cahabariversociety.org

The Nature Conservancy: A national organization engaged in environmental conservation efforts. In Alabama, a portion of their work includes freshwater restoration efforts. They also own several tracts of land along the Cahaba River. www.nature.org.

PROJECT TITLE
Creating an Identity for the Cahaba River Blueway.

DURATION
12 weeks, summer 2012.

BUDGET
Design efforts were pro bono.

TEAM
Doug Barrett, University of Alabama at Birmingham (UAB); **Matt Leavell**, Alabama Innovation Engine; **Nisa Miranda**, The University of Alabama Center for Economic Development; **Cheryl Morgan**, Auburn University's School of Architecture Urban Studio; **Dan Monroe**, Cayenne Creative; **Marion Powers**, Cayenne Creative; **Samantha Gibbons, Amy Clark, Daniel Twieg, Jenny Waycaster**, UAB BLOOM Studios; **Beth Stewart**, Cahaba River Society; **Randy Haddock**, Cahaba River Society; **Paul Freeman**, The Nature Conservancy.

2.71 Sample design for a launch point monument sign that would be seen from the road or entrance to the river.

DESCRIPTION The Cahaba River watershed is a unique natural and economic asset for Alabama. Every day the watershed is home to a diverse set of communities and people representing urban, suburban, and rural lifestyles. One-fifth of the population of Alabama drinks water from the Cahaba River. The biodiversity of life in the watershed includes populations such as mussels, fish, birds, and other wildlife. Significantly, the Cahaba River is in the top 10 US rivers for both snail and mussel diversity.

Several organizations in Alabama are working to preserve this regional asset and integrate it more fully into economic development efforts. These include traditional advocacy organizations, environmental groups, city governments, county governments, federal agencies, academic institutions, and the outdoor industry. Because of geographic, political, organizational, and financial limitations, each group has historically focused on its own portion of work, and efforts have been isolated from one another.

In 2012, a few organizations began exploring how to collaborate more effectively to protect the Cahaba River watershed. Alabama Innovation Engine and UAB proposed a collaborative effort between the professionals of Cayenne Creative and students in Graphic Design at UAB to develop a visual identity for a Cahaba Blueway. The title "Blueway" indicates that this would be more than a simple canoe trail, but instead a comprehensive project encompassing land trails and communicating the area's history. Achieving a "Blueway" designation, one of our long-term goals, would raise the visibility of the region and provide federal recognition indicating that the project is watershed-focused.

Students were participating in BLOOM Studio, an invitation-only class offered by the Department of Art and Art History at UAB. The visual identity proposed would provide a focal point for collaboration between the multiple organizations. The design process would enable the development of relationships between the three organizations and identify opportunities for design and development in the watershed. For this project we visually explored a branding identity system for the river, creating assets such as a logo, wayfinding system, collateral materials, and a sample iPhone app.

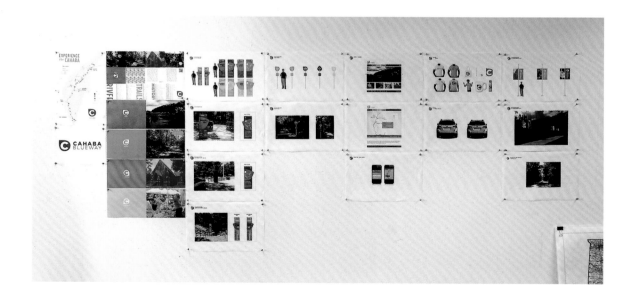

2.72 Items pinned up for an in-process critique include maps, wayfinding signage, T-shirts, and other collateral material.

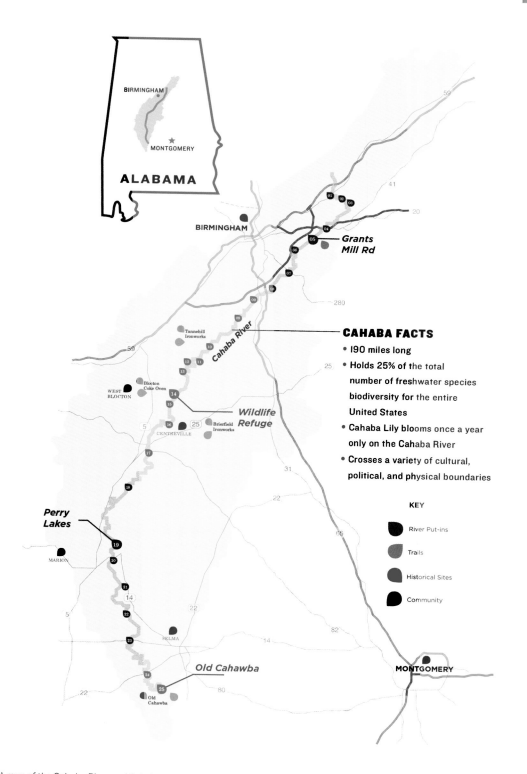

ALABAMA

CAHABA FACTS

- 190 miles long
- Holds 25% of the total number of freshwater species biodiversity for the entire United States
- Cahaba Lily blooms once a year only on the Cahaba River
- Crosses a variety of cultural, political, and physical boundaries

KEY

- River Put-ins
- Trails
- Historical Sites
- Community

Grants Mill Rd

Wildlife Refuge

Perry Lakes

Old Cahawba

2.73 A map of the Cahaba River and Cahaba watershed (in green) showing its relationship to the state of Alabama and to the major metropolitan areas of Birmingham and Montgomery.

RESEARCH Utilizing "design-thinking" methodology to explore the visual language of the river, students worked collaboratively with design and economic facilitators, visited locations along the river, talked with local stakeholders, and gathered assets in the field. A project team was formed to address a broad range of issues that would be encountered when designing a visual identity for such a large geographic feature, especially one that affects such a large area of the state. Issues included conservational land use, physical geology, and rural economic development. The team included student and professional designers, architects, economic development professionals, and conservation and forestry professionals.

A full-day kickoff meeting was held in the format of a design charrette to familiarize everyone with the project objectives as well as the different aspects of the river and the surrounding economies. The charrette was facilitated by Cayenne Creative and provided an opportunity for students to partner with real-world clients to create the basis for design solutions.

During the meeting a nine-square exercise was done to determine the "personality" of the river as a way to get the team to agree upon a common theme. To understand the audience and focus our design decisions, a list of "typical river users" was developed, including:

- adventure/extreme sports enthusiasts, bikers, hikers, campers, canoers, younger audience
- sportsmen, fishermen, hunters, middle-aged to older audience
- RV-ers (staying overnight) who also enjoy, birding, walking, an older audience
- day-trippers, moms and dads, casual tourists, kids, a mixed audience looking for a short one-day trip close to home.

CHALLENGES One of the biggest challenges the group faced was how to create an abstract icon that could easily be recognized as the Cahaba River, a physical place that means so many different things to so many different people. We wanted to create an identity that all the communities and stakeholders along the river can embrace and call their own.

The group felt that this identity and the Blueway designation would help build river pride and stewardship within the state and surrounding communities by providing real and virtual opportunities for people to engage with the Cahaba River and experience her natural wonder and beauty.

Part of this challenge was the creation of a color palette that referenced the natural colors, beauty, and history surrounding the river. The following four colors and their attributes were chosen as a way to break the project up into the four manageable areas: river, trails, history, and community:

1. **River/Blueway** *blue*: cool, water, depth, trust, wisdom, truth, calm.
2. **Trails/Longleaf** *green*: trees, nature, growth, fertility, safety, health, organic, luck.
3. **History/Old Cahawba** *orange:* history, strength, endurance, drawing attention like hunting colors, speaks about age but is attractive to youth.
4. **Community/Yellowhammer** *gold:* warmth, sun, curiosity, naturally bright, joy, happiness, attention, pleasant.

STRATEGY The Cahaba is not only a waterway; it is a figurative artery. We want people to enjoy the river but also engage with the communities surrounding it. For now, the river feeds the land around it, provides drinking water to surrounding communities, and nourishes its own ecosystems. But imagine what the river might nourish if people not only engaged with it in the typical ways—boating, fishing, swimming, and hiking—but also engaged in the surrounding areas and immersed themselves in their rich culture and history. The Cahaba could become a catalyst for community and economic improvement.

2.74 Street banners and signage allow local communities to build recognition and join the overall project by identifying themselves as a Cahaba River community.

> "
>
> *Utilizing "design-thinking" methodology to explore the visual language of the river, students worked collaboratively with design and economic facilitators, visited locations along the river, talked with local stakeholders, and gathered assets in the field."*
>
> ——

2.75 iPhone application mock-up that will allow users to plan a trip, find the nearest canoe launch and points of interest along the river. The application is broken up into areas about the river, trails, community, and history.

The design of an identity, wayfinding system, and collateral elements gave us a starting point to begin the conversation about designating the Cahaba River a National Blueway. A well-conceived and designed campaign provided the professionalism the project needed to communicate its worth to funding sources, and to reinforce the significance of the Cahaba River to a broader audience.

While the story of the Cahaba is best heard by experiencing the river, that is a limited venue for reaching out to the public. The river is also important to people that aren't necessarily paddlers or naturalists. This work broadens the ability of stakeholders to reach out to the people who are affected by water issues but don't necessarily interact with the Cahaba on a regular basis. By giving the Cahaba River a branded identity, we can build interest and support for the Cahaba and the Blueway initiative with local stakeholders and federal funders.

EFFECTIVENESS The object of this design project was to reach potential funding sources: individual donors, foundations, and governmental organizations, while building partnerships with communities, individuals, and governments essential to protect and preserve the Cahaba River.

The effectiveness of the final project can be seen in four major funding initiatives and partnerships that were achieved through the use of the materials generated by this project:

1. Sappi Ideas That Matter grant ($48,000).
2. Community Foundation of Greater Birmingham grant to The Nature Conservancy for the Blueway collaborative ($125,000 over 2 years).
3. Auburn University/University of Alabama funding for Alabama Innovation Engine.
4. Partnership with Fresh Water Land Trust on first Cahaba River launch site at Moon River.

ASSESSMENT The final logo references a compass. As a navigational device, the logo speaks the language of the outdoors, of adventure and wild places that capture the spirit of the Cahaba River. The outcome of this work has raised awareness of the Cahaba River and created recognition that designating the Cahaba River as a National Blueway can be the catalyst for economic and social change in the state.

2.76 Post-it notes were generated during a team brainstorming session and used by the students during the design process.

BALLOT:
A DIGITAL RESOURCE TO ASSIST YOUNG ADULTS WITH THE VOTING PROCESS

Paul Nini, Professor, and **Michael Booher**, Student,
Visual Communication, The Ohio State University,
Columbus, Ohio

CLIENT

The *Ballot* digital resource was developed primarily to serve voters in the 18–25-year-old age group, with the goal of increasing voter turnout during elections. Research indicates that a large percentage of individuals from this demographic in Franklin County, Ohio, only vote during presidential elections, or not at all.

PROJECT TITLE

Ballot: A digital resource to assist young adults with the voting process.

DURATION

Fall 2013–spring 2014. The first semester was devoted to problem identification and generative research with stakeholders to establish design directions. The second semester was devoted to project development and evaluative research with stakeholders to refine design prototypes.

BUDGET

None.

TEAM

First semester advisor: Associate Professor **Peter Kwok Chan**. *Second semester advisor:* Professor **Paul Nini**. *Student:* **Michael Booher**.

2.77 (above), **2.78** (page 252) and **2.79** (page 253) *Ballot* is an entry point for young adults to become more engaged in the voting process. It's envisioned as a responsive web system, allowing users access via multiple devices. *Ballot* would help young adults check their registration status. If registration is needed, the system would walk them through the process, help young adults better understand confusing language by simplifying the message. Once voters have done their research, they could create a checklist of who and what they intend to vote for. The checklist could be accessed while at the polling place, and also to help young adults find their polling place. *Design: Michael Booher.* All iPhone Screen Images

DESCRIPTION Voting is a right, yet it is one that Americans increasingly do not exercise. Whether it's because of confusing ballot language or the perception that these issues don't pertain to a particular voter—the simple fact is that voter turnout is decreasing, especially among young adults. Creating good voting habits at an early stage can make young adults voters for life. *Ballot* is a resource designed to assist young adults through the election process, and is intended to take the guesswork out of voting. It is a tool that gives young adults clear, non-partisan information that allows them to make educated choices during elections.

Voter turnout drops dramatically during non-presidential elections. As an example, in Franklin County, Ohio, 71 percent of eligible voters cast ballots in the 2012 election, when President Barack Obama was reelected. In contrast, only 20 percent of eligible voters cast ballots in the 2013 election, when no presidential election was held. In a survey conducted with 45 respondents aged 18–25, only 21 percent indicated that they vote in almost every election; 55 percent indicated that they only vote during presidential election years; and 24 percent indicated that they never vote. Therefore, 79 percent of the individuals surveyed either don't vote at all or only vote once every 4 years. Clearly, there exists room for improvement.

Conversations with potential users uncovered the following reasons for not voting:

- confusion concerning how to register to vote
- inability to understand ballot language, especially about issues, school levies, etc.
- difficulties with recalling how they wish to vote when going to the polling place
- inability to locate the correct polling place to cast their votes.

To address the above issues, *Ballot* was created as a responsive web platform and digital resource to assist young adults with the voting process.

Function 1: Register By answering some brief questions, *Ballot* can check voters' registration status. If they need to register or change their address, *Ballot* can walk them through the step-by-step process.

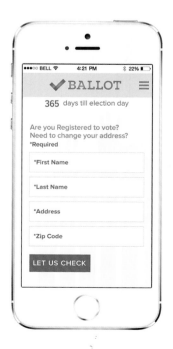
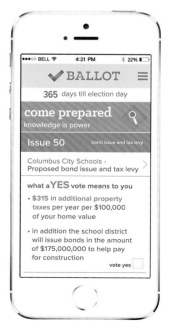

"

Given how difficult it can be to register to vote, find and keep clear information which informs one's votes, and locate the correct polling place, an application such as this stands a good chance of acceptance, if made widely available."

RESEARCH Students are required in the senior thesis process to identify a social and/or commercial problem area that requires a design response. They conduct secondary research to gather sources to better inform them about the various issues surrounding their problem area. Students then engage and collaborate with a variety of stakeholders—such as direct users, audience members, and other interested parties—to generate possible approaches to the problem. Design prototypes are developed, which are then refined via evaluative research with stakeholders to arrive at finished design solutions.

Function 2: Come prepared *Ballot* language is broken down into easy-to-understand text, so that voters know exactly what an issue might mean to them.

Function 3: My checklist Once voters have done their research, they can create a simple list to remind them how they intend to vote. The mobile platform makes it easy for voters to take their checklist into the voting booth.

Function 4: Where to vote Most voters know where their polling station is—but for young adults who may move frequently, voting can be more difficult. The application shows voters exactly where their polling place is and how to get there.

Responsive web platform Most young adults get their news from the Internet, and it's a powerful tool to help them get connected. A responsive web platform means that voters can access *Ballot* on multiple devices, including desktop and tablet computers, and smartphones.

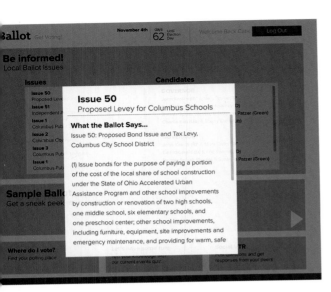

2.80 Wireframes helped with creating the flow of information and how users would interact with the interface. Shown here is a screen concerning a specific ballot issue. *Design: Michael Booher.*

CHALLENGES Access to users was not an issue, as many individuals from the 18–25-year-old age group in the Ohio State University campus community were willing to speak about the voting process and to evaluate design prototypes at various stages. The major challenge was with the local county board of elections, which chose not to participate in the project. Fortunately, the local chapter of the League of Women Voters proved to be very helpful, and provided valuable background information, as well as feedback on the project as it developed.

STRATEGY After the basic functional criteria were established via secondary research and conversations with users, two brand identity directions were developed and applied to sample touch points. The visual direction finally implemented was clearly favored by the various stakeholders, and was then refined. A demonstration walk-through scenario was developed, and wireframe designs were constructed to identify required interactive elements on various screens. The final brand identity elements were applied to all aspects of the project, and a video demonstration of the project was created.

EFFECTIVENESS As the project has not been implemented, there is no way of knowing if it will indeed increase regular voting among 18–25-year-olds. However, feedback on finished prototypes indicates a high level of acceptance from the potential user group. Given how difficult it can be to register to vote to find, and to keep clear information that informs one's votes, and locate the correct polling place; an application, such as this, stands a good chance of acceptance, if made widely available. Virtually everyone who has seen the demonstration of the project has expressed a desire to actually use it, which can be taken as a very good sign.

ASSESSMENT The faculty members and professional designers who evaluated this project favorably assessed its results from both functional and aesthetic standpoints, praising both its ease of use and straightforward interaction design. The student designer had a very good experience with a project created to have positive social impact, and plans to approach organizations such as the League of Women Voters to explore future sponsorship and implementation possibilities.

ADDITIONAL INFORMATION Video demonstration of the project: http://vimeo.com/90110763.

PROSPERITY GARDENS

Brian Wiley, Assistant Professor of Graphic Design, Boise State University, Boise, Idaho and
Eric Benson, Associate Professor of Graphic Design, University of Illinois, Urbana-Champaign, Illinois

CLIENT
Prosperity Gardens is a Champaign, Illinois non-profit that focuses on workforce development and nutrition education through the context of a neighborhood farm. At-risk youth are introduced to career paths in agriculture, marketing, entrepreneurship, nutrition, and the culinary arts.

PROJECT TITLE
Prosperity Gardens.

DURATION
6 weeks, February–March 2013.

BUDGET
$700.00 total: $500 for Little Things Lab's travel expenses to campus; $200 for prototype production.

TEAM
Instructors: **Brian Wiley** and **Eric Benson.**
Prosperity Gardens director: **Nicole Bridges.**
Little Things Lab facilitators: **Josh McManus, Kate Creason,** and **Megan Deal.**
Designer: **Amanda Buck.**
Students: 32 sophomores and juniors from multiple disciplines.

2.81 Promotional poster. *Design: Bryan Lorenz and Scott Durand.*

DESCRIPTION At the University of Illinois, graphic design professors Brian Wiley and Eric Benson introduced the graphic design students to the notion that graphic design practice can be more diverse than only working for corporate clients. Josh McManus, Kate Creason, and Megan Deal from Little Things Lab in Detroit, Michigan and Amanda Buck, senior designer with the 2012 Obama campaign, were invited to help facilitate a weekend immersion project for the local non-profit Prosperity Gardens. This initial component was voluntary for the students, although strongly encouraged, and lasted approximately 48 hours.

The class of 32 students and four facilitators visited Prosperity Gardens' physical site on a Friday afternoon, listened to and helped identify their needs, and collaborated over the next 2 days to tell their story. By the end of the weekend, the team gave the urban garden a complete brand refresh that included prototypes of the new identity applied to a variety of collateral; a social media campaign was created to locate a free/low-cost truck; the team developed a handmade salsa to be sold for economic sustainability; and they identified a host of other great ideas that would be continued in the next component of the project.

RESEARCH The research varied depending on the module students were engaged in. The students who attended the weekend workshop relied heavily on contact with the non-profit director Nicole Bridges to identify needs and challenges that Prosperity Gardens was facing. During the classroom modules, students researched multiple ideas before deciding on any one solution. They identified similar case studies in tertiary fields, did on-site observations, and talked with experts in their field to prepare their final proposals.

CHALLENGES There were several challenges the team faced during the kickoff weekend. The main challenge for the students was committing ample time to a weekend workshop with no predefined outcomes. While a large number of students participated, those students who did not were disconnected from the project. It was also challenging to switch gears from a service provider model—one in which the designer provides only graphic solutions—to a model in which the designer is more of a strategist who creates possibilities.

Another challenge was working this type of project into a vertical studio composed of two sections of students. Unfortunately, this meant that the first section was able to work with Little Things Lab, while the second could not. Since the second section students missed the service design methodologies module, it was a difficult for them to figure out their role.

A final challenge was translating all the design outcomes (such as websites, social media strategies, and identity guides) into practical solutions that the client could understand, and that would not create more work for Nicole Bridges.

We've never seen students work so hard; most of them were putting in 16-hour days over the weekend!"

———

STRATEGY Our strategy was to begin by immersing the students in the world of service design through the guidance of Little Things Lab. We hypothesized that the quick timeline and open-ended assignment might cause initial confusion, but would, in turn, lead to team bonding and enjoyment of the experience of brainstorming and prototyping. The instructors would be there with the students over the weekend at selected times to encourage them and help with the tasks at hand.

2.82 Sign and overview of Prosperity Gardens property. *Photo: Kiki Kolakowski.*

After the immersion weekend, we planned for the continuation of the developing projects to be assigned to teams of students interested in completing the digital or printed artifacts. We hoped those who conceived the project would feel empowered to continue to design the final deliverable, and in the end we found this assumption to be true. We structured the first half of the project to include a presentation for the client to gauge which projects needed refinement, and to gather new ideas for the second group of students. We knew, before the critique, that there would be lingering questions and potentially unfinished projects that the second 3-week module of students would need to answer and complete, so we prepared a strategy of mixing various levels of students based on their skill sets and leadership. The new teams were designed to be small (two to three people) and were given motivation by a scripted second visit by Nicole Bridges to help kick off the second half of the module.

EFFECTIVENESS Working directly with professionals was great for the students, as was the real-world applicability of the project. Both were incredibly motivating for the students and we think it was one of the most successful facets of the project. We've never seen students work so hard; most of them were putting in 16-hour days over the weekend! There were things that we could have done better, however. We purposely went into the weekend with few expectations about what would come out if it; we didn't want to predetermine the outcomes or deliverables. While we still think that was the best way to proceed into the weekend, more could have been done at our end to prepare the students for that uncertainty.

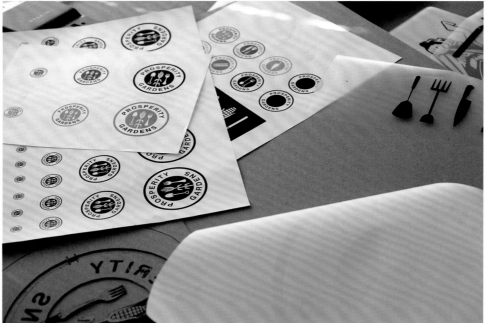

2.83a Business cards. *Design and photo: Kiki Kolakowski.*

2.83b In-progress work from the workshop weekend.
Photo: Eric Benson.

Additionally, we believe the most glaring challenge to the effectiveness of the project was incorporating teams of various years (sophomores and juniors) whose varied dynamics hindered the productivity of the student groups and eventually limited the amount of work completed. In many cases the teams organically became too big (10 +) due to overlaps in mutual interests on projects needing completion. As instructors, we should have stepped in and addressed that issue before it happened, although the number of students in the combined class made that micro-interaction difficult. However, the students' excitement at working outside of the studio and in the "field" was really great to experience!

Overall, one of the most successful decisions we made was to place a summer student design intern with Prosperity Gardens. Too often these partnerships between community and classroom/designers fall flat after the initial creative session; the community partner is left with a lot of great ideas but little direction as to how to implement them. Prosperity Gardens' design intern, Catherine (Kiki) Kolakowski, has been able to put all those great ideas into practice through hard work.

At the end of the 6 weeks we:

- hired a summer design intern for Prosperity Gardens
- designed a series of presentations for the founder for donor pitches
- created a social media strategy for the client Facebook page
- produced two videos for promotion and fundraising: www.youtube.com/watch?v=PVbFzk9H3Y0, www.youtube.com/watch?v=Uabco6xLp1o
- devised and implemented farm signage (entry sign and smaller educational signs for the raised beds) that was originally designed during the weekend session
- designed a downloadable media kit
- coded a custom website with WordPress as a content management system: www.prosperitygardens.org

- illustrated an online children's comic book and created a cookbook of easy five-ingredient recipes to encourage further community engagement
- conceptualized a Farmer's Market stand/informational booth
- conceptualized an end-cap for grocery store salsa sales
- produced a series of practical designs for a future mobile market trailer
- proposed a variety of collateral pieces, such as posters, tote bags, and shirts for fundraising campaigns.

ASSESSMENT In our experience with similar assignments, students understand what they accomplished and learned when faced with a challenge in the workplace or an ethical awakening. Many of our students are hired at a studio or agency and feel a sense of pride when their design is placed in a portfolio (or better yet, wins an award), but they are usually unaware of their work's direct impact on a person or community. In a more socially focused project like the one at Prosperity Gardens, metrics are less defined, and therefore accurate assessment becomes more difficult. However, it is clear that students' positive interactions with client and community members really drive home the importance of being a citizen designer, not just a consumer.

THE HAPPINESS PROJECT:
TRANSLATING HAPPINESS THROUGH DESIGN

Dr. Stuart Medley, Senior Lecturer, **Dr. Christopher Kueh**, Senior Lecturer, **Dr. Hanadi Haddad**, Lecturer, School of Communication and Arts, Faculty of Education and Arts, Edith Cowan University, Perth, Western Australia

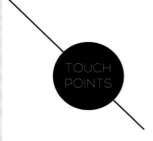

FINDING THE CYCLE ROUTES AND PATHS

A way finding system could be developed, with signage placed along cycle routes and paths letting commuters know distance to Fremantle landmarks and other parts of the city. It may also be useful in promoting the idea of riding to work to non-cyclists.

CLIENT
City of Fremantle,
Western Australia.

PROJECT TITLE
The Happiness Project.

DURATION
13 Weeks, fall 2014.

BUDGET
None.

TEAM
Approximately 100 students across four class groups. Most projects were individual projects, with a small number of small-group projects (two in a team). Nominally these students were in their second year of a 3-year degree. The nature of the School of Communications & Arts (SCA) at Edith Cowan University (ECU), however, allows students from majors as diverse as journalism, languages, public relations, creative writing, arts and design to take the unit as an elective in any year of their studies.

2.84a (above), **2.84b** (opposite) and **2.84c–2.84d** (page 262) With her project Cycle Freo, Natalie Sullivan tackled the challenge of proposing Fremantle as a bike-friendly city. Postcards, brochures, website, and apps allow and encourage users to connect with other riders in ways that ensure the sustainability of the project, which aimed at improving wellbeing by encouraging people to cycle. *Design: Natalie Sullivan.*

DESCRIPTION People change their surroundings, work, interactions, and thinking patterns with the sole aim of achieving happiness. The long history of people striving for happiness inspired a collaboration between ECU Design and the City of Fremantle to initiate the Happiness Project. The design course, DES2101 Design Practices: Identity, aims to use innovative design approaches to inject happiness into the City of Fremantle. Student projects examined areas such as health, the environment, the economy, and community through bottom-up, empathic design approaches—design built on input from the citizens of Fremantle and other stakeholders. The outcomes were to be a range of inspiring and innovative ideas presented through exhibitions and design events in the City of Fremantle. The students' task was to define and research a challenge in the City of Fremantle that could be solved, alleviated, or exposed through communication design. The challenge was to address happiness in the city. Students were to consider a problem in one or more of the following categories:

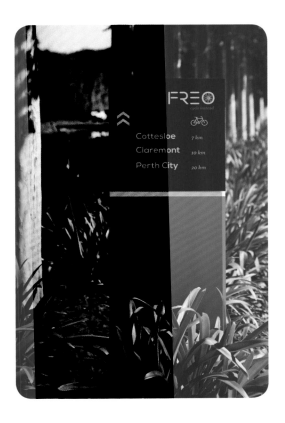

Geography—wayfinding, access issues, public transport

Environment—sustainability, cityscape, re-purposing/efficient use of space, aesthetics vs. function

Culture—arts, festivals, public art, souvenirs, indigenous ownership/heritage, how to impart information about events, celebrating artists

Activity—use of public space, city games, historical and future activities, science and libraries, seasonal events.

Services—ways to improve residents' and tourists' experiences in the city, visual identity for services such as transport, police, water

This project allowed students to understand the contribution of design in using available resources to achieve maximum benefits for community stakeholders. The project process focused on applying design methods to empower people at various levels within the community.

Fremantle is atypical of Australian cities. It is relatively small and walkable, with quite a large number of Victorian-era buildings situated between a working seaport and a fishing boat harbor. Its central retail and recreational zones are also close to the Swan River, and its maritime history has made it a traditionally working class area. For a substantial part of its history it has been a "safe seat" for the Australian Labor Party. This has had the corollary effect of the city being somewhat overlooked for major civil and infrastructure projects during conservative political terms in Western Australia. Its own community has a reputation for tolerance and, at the present time, the local council appears open to experimental projects as a way to frame thinking about the future of the city.

The project is intended to work as an active research investigation which can be revisited annually to improve on earlier proposals, address issues in evolving ways, promote cross-institutional and cross-cultural cooperation, and create sustainable cooperation between design and the local community.

RESEARCH The project focused on designing through empathy. Students were directed to identify and understand the needs of the community as the foundation to their design. According to Kouprie and Visser (*A Framework for Empathy in Design: Stepping into and out of the User's Life*, 2009), there are three ways to achieve empathic design: have direct contact with users to embed oneself into the user's life; analyze raw data such as photographs of users in their natural environment, users' diaries and drawings; and role-play to understand users' experience. In the Happiness Project, students were encouraged to develop empathic design through the following techniques:

Observations and empathy mapping: In week 4 of the project, students took field trips to the City of Fremantle. During the trips, students were to adopt the persona of a tourist with children, a person who lives outside of the city but works in the city, a backpacker on a tight budget, or a small business owner running a shop in the city. Students were asked to observe and note down what they heard, saw, felt, and thought, through the persona's point of view, while walking around the city. This technique allowed students to explore the city from a user's perspective, and hence build an empathic perspective for identifying design problems and developing design solutions.

Role-play and storyboarding: In week 7, students were introduced to role-playing and storyboarding as a means to evaluate their design ideas. At this stage, students had developed some ideas for their final design. They were asked to think of themselves as one of the stakeholders in their design scenario, to draw a storyboard showing how that person might use their design, and to identify aspects of the scenario that would not work. This again allowed students to build empathy into their design solutions.

TOUCH POINTS

Fig 8

POSTCARDS / BROCHURES

Postcards and other printed materials could be created to promote and support the website and the application.

CYCLING MAP APP >>>

A map and navigation application would be available from the website. Users could map out their routes, connect with other riders via Facebook and keep track of the kilometres they have cycled.

Fig 9

WEBSITE

Central to the communication plan is **www.cyclefreo.com**. It will be a hub of information for cycling in Fremantle. The website will include a trip planner for new commuters along with links to download an app with cycling routes and maps. An events calendar and blog could also be incorporated to the design.

Fig 10

2.85 In her project, Access Fremantle, Caitlin Brass identified that heritage and cultural trails in Fremantle were very limited for wheelchair, stroller, or pram access. Through empathy mapping Caitlin proposed inclusive design, benefiting people with a disability, the elderly, and children with their parents, as a way to improve heritage trails for everyone. *Design: Caitlin Brass.*

CHALLENGES For academics, the main challenge was to make clear to students that design processes are as important as producing any design outcome. In the design stages of *discovery*, *define*, and *develop*, there was confusion among students regarding the relevance of the exercises—such as empathy mapping and storyboarding—to the physical design outcome. Many had difficulty drawing the connections between the macro and micro perspectives of the project: What was the bigger picture and how did it connect to the finer details? What was the relationship between value, vehicle(s), and audience? The focus on design process and research was an obvious challenge for students who were used to focusing from the beginning on producing a design solution.

Academics facilitated the drawing of these connections by encouraging students to undertake "stop, review, question, and reflect cycles," individually and in groups, as often as possible. Students found that applying reflective techniques to examine precedent studies, selected by the academics, a particularly effective method. For example, students were asked to discuss in class and reflect in their journals about video clips shown, such as the TED talk by Emily Pilloton, and the Volkswagen Fun Theory projects. These exercises allowed students to examine and understand process-driven design. In addition, part of the assessment required students to research and select local and international exemplars pertinent to their chosen perspective on the Happiness Project and apply critical analyses to these. Pulling back from their own projects allowed them to gain perspective and focus on refining their project statements down to the core design problem and key issues.

STRATEGY This was a semester-long project. At ECU, semesters are 14 weeks long with 12 weeks of contact of 3 hours per week. Adapting the British Design Council's four-steps design process, the 12-week project was broken down into the following:

Discover Weeks 1–4 were dedicated to research, allowing students to build a background understanding of the project. Activities during this period included a guest lecture from the Mayor of the City of Fremantle, a guest lecture from a designer renowned for his social focus, and field trips to Fremantle to conduct first-hand research such as empathy mapping, observations, and photo-ethnography. Students were also encouraged to conduct precedent studies of similar initiatives in other cities, and to analyze the approaches applied in these examples.

Define In weeks 4–5 students developed a design brief based on their people-centered research outcomes. This step encouraged them to develop a critical and analytical mindset in order to identify challenges and make concrete design proposals. In the light of empathic design, the students were asked to focus on defining the design problem and challenges rather than settling on a solution at this early stage. This was to encourage organic development of outcomes and prototypes in the next stage.

Develop In weeks 6–9 (including 2 weeks' mid-semester break), students developed and prototyped their ideas through experimentation. Methods such as persona, storyboarding, rapid prototyping, and mapping were introduced. These are critical design methods that allowed students to develop bottom-up outcomes to reflect the sentiments of Fremantle locals, rather than conventional, top-down design methods that exclude locals from the design process.

Deliver During weeks 9–12, students were shown ways to present ideas through appropriate visualization techniques.

2.86 Access Fremantle mock-up of prototype in situ. *Design: Caitlin Brass.*

"

*Students really responded
to a live brief, with a real
set of issues to address
in a real town that many
of them have strong
opinions about."*

——

Through these steps, students were required to submit exercises embedded in the discovery stage, a research and development journal, and final design consisting of two A0 posters and a rationale booklet. Finally, projects were selected for a presentation and, ultimately, public exhibition at the City of Fremantle.

EFFECTIVENESS Students really responded to a live brief, with a real set of issues to address in a real town that many of them have strong opinions about. The "concreteness" of the project was strengthened by visits to the school in the first weeks of the project by the Mayor of Fremantle, Dr. Brad Pettitt, and site visits where students role-played in order to understand the city from different points of view.

Students were encouraged to form their own teams. On occasion these teams involved students from different disciplines. This mix can make for a compelling outcome when the project has rigorous writing (from a public relations or journalism student) combined with engaging visual explanation (graphic design students) and strong model-making skills (environmental and spatial design students).

Where the projects excelled was in the realization that a process or project proposal can be explained through design; for example, that graphic design can be used to suggest a way ahead for the city, rather than having to be a finished artifact in itself.

ASSESSMENT Open briefs always carry some risk of confusion and even resentment among students through the lack of any obvious direction being supplied by lecturers or tutors. The biggest challenge is to get students to understand that the design research process *is* design itself, and that design doesn't need to be weighted toward an object-based outcome. Despite an introduction to service design methods (such as empathy mapping) and design thinking generally, many students will get into the "design mode" late in the project and their outcomes may have little to do with their empathy maps and field trips.

Socially focused design projects need to be more widely available in the whole design curriculum, rather than being just the focus of this one course, in order for students to understand that this is a process that can be applied in many projects. We can encourage students to think about "heuristic" tasks that focus on building new relationships between people and place.

PART 3

MAKING A DIFFERENCE

" Interestingly, for some time now, I've watched the emergence of a generation of design students and young designers who don't want to become the agents of commercial seduction. They are looking for a new role—one where social value is the new capital, not the sales charts of brand owners. Suddenly, they seem like the only acceptable future for design."

Adrian Shaughnessy, Designer, Author, Scratching the Surface

———

" A generation of 20-year-olds is about to take the industry by storm and demand new paradigms. It may be naiveté, or it may be that there is so much in the world that needs fixing, but our generation, whether we're designers or doctors or lawyers, wants to know that our skills are going toward global problems rather than superfluous indulgences."

Emily Pilloton, Founder, Project H, Just Design

———

" Designers are tackling local and global issues they feel passionate about, using design as their tool. Whether it be access to clean water in a foreign country, or public health and safety in our own communities, designers are making the time and finding the funding to engage in meaningful work outside of their day jobs."

Alice Bybee, Designer, Just Design

———

" The great problems, the ones really worth solving, aren't already on the agenda. If we are curious, open and empathetic, the great problems will find us."

Brian Collins, Founder, Collins:, Just Design

———

3.1

SECTION 1

GETTING INVOLVED

DESIGNING SUSTAINABLE AND EQUITABLE RELATIONSHIPS WITH COMMUNITIES

Eric Benson

How do you create sustainable engagement with the community you wish to serve? Designers all over the world have explored this question with mixed results. Despite a lack of funding for such philanthropic initiatives, individual designers interested in this question forge ahead in an attempt to better design for people in communities in hope of the greater good. The lessons learned from these trailblazers are the subject of this essay. The first and most important lesson learned from the field is that the notion of "sustainable" in the question is paramount to success. Sustainable by definition demands that people, profit, and planet are all kept top of mind and ideally balanced. Megan Deal, co-founder of the Cincinnati, Ohio-based social design studio Tomorrow Today has found in her community work that:

The best work starts by building strong relationships. In our work, we're very intentional about seating the right people at the table from the beginning. It's vital to have both a local connector and an inspired patron in place. Without an on-the-ground partner, the work won't stick. Without a revenue source, the work won't last. Managing these relationships and setting expectations is key. The process is never easy, rarely cut and dry, and requires a skill most designers don't learn in school. But it's a crucial component to designing in/with/for community. (Deal, 2014)

Bernard Canniffe, an advisor to the social change organization Project M and Chair of Graphic Design at Iowa State University, has also found that building a strong relationship with the community first is the key for the project to work:

Sustainability and commitment are the heart of the citizen designer when one engages with a community. This has very little with designing a T-shirt for the community and then leaving. It has everything to do with staying with the project and in the community until the community feels confident to continue to sustain the project on their own. (2014)

LISTEN NOT HEAR Unpacking both of these quotes together is revealing in regards to how to build a sustainable relationship with a community. The two experiences inform us that creating a personal and equitable bond with the right community member or organization is the first step toward a successful project and partnership. Building relationships requires listening.

It is important to put the community interests and needs above that of the designer. We all want to get something out of a creative project individually; however, when it comes to working with a community, listening to their desires is crucial and necessary. Professor Canniffe elaborates on the importance of listening:

There is a fundamental difference between listening and hearing when engaging in and with communities. Designers are trained to hear more than listen and it is in the listening that the community advocates and the designer includes the community as an equal participant. (2014)

JOIN THE COMMUNITY Delving further into the quotes by both Deal and Canniffe demonstrates that building a relationship through listening to a community should help the designer become a valued new member of that community. Showing dedication to, empathy for, and genuine interest in their concerns lays the foundation of trust that eventually enables the designer to sew him- or herself into the fabric of the community. An invested member of the community understands what that group needs and wants. This is necessary in any well-informed design process: to understand user needs. In this case, however, it seems that creating a sustainable relationship with a community is not just knowing what the needs are, but also for the designer to share or feel empathy for those aspirations.

Embedded in all these lessons is research. Talking with one community member reveals what he or she desires, but is not necessarily representative of everyone's thoughts. In any good study, getting a representative sample is vital. Using only one or two sources of feedback, although important on their own, will create assumptions, which will skew project successes. For the social designer, asking many people and listening with empathy is the key to understanding.

In order to have these types of conversations, trust is required. This is sometimes difficult to achieve in communities where socioeconomics and racial histories have created strong divisions and mistrust between people within the community and outside of it. In these challenging situations, designers should, as Megan Deal suggests, "seek wise counsel." Designers are usually good facilitators, but we don't know everything—and we should not pretend we do. Finding support and guidance from those experienced in these types of challenging conversations is the right path for building confidence in the project and consequently a stronger relationship.

DESIGN WITH NOT FOR Frog Design has been active in the world of participatory design (or co-design) where the key stakeholders of the project are earnestly involved in the process and solutions. They have created a "Creative Action Toolkit" that details their research into creating positive social impact. Their hypothesis is simply that "groups make change." Similarly, Project H, run by designer Emily Pilloton, put together a comparable field guide entitled *The Design Revolution Toolkit* which provides a list of concepts to think about to "design better solutions for the greater good: for people instead of clients, for change instead of consumption." With participatory design, the act of community involvement in a collaboration should activate the ownership of a project and its results by the participants. This ownership will hopefully help build a sustainable path toward implementation as community members feel they had a say in an outcome as opposed to having the solution imposed upon them. The overriding principle here is to design with, not for.

Professor Canniffe further argues that "[t]he social designer is not a design missionary. It is essential the designer both engages and activates the community to own and sustain the project." Designers should not go into a community or neighborhood uninvited or without prior knowledge of the issues and deliver solutions based on what is felt to be best. Instead honest and humble discussions are needed to create a knowledge base and build trust. Community members deep in the design process are actually better described as a team of specialists invested in a problem to help propose and create solutions. Each individual is not only an expert on him- or herself and connected needs within the community, but also someone that provides different views on the issues of the group itself. For a sustainable relationship to be forged, different community perspectives should be discussed and listened to, and time ideating with willing civic members must occur prior to any physical project realization.

Project completion requires funding and for a designer to dedicate his or her time to the community requires some form of economic payment for full focus. This has been and still is a real challenge for many designers working for the greater good. Grants, fellowships, and endowments have been vital catalysts to aid in these types of community collaborations; however, to encourage more progress, some economic model is needed for this type of work to be truly sustainable. Potential solutions investigated by design studios like WorldStudio and Rule29 explored how, when appropriate, prospects for entrepreneurial and social entrepreneurial opportunities could arise allowing all parties to share in the economic benefits. A designer, in payment for his or her help, could share in the royalties of sales of goods and services from the community-led solutions.

FINISH WHAT YOU START Megan Deal firmly believes in the notion that you should "finish what you start." The end of a social design project should be defined as where the community feels confident enough to continue with what they helped create. However, it is important to remember that as part of the project the designer, to some degree, becomes a member of the community. The designer will also have a sense of pride and ownership in the process and results, which should be the bond that forms a sustainable community partnership. The joint investment is a bond that, if done well, is hard to break. It is the last step in a process that is not prescriptive but has loose guidelines for success. Deal eloquently puts the social design practice not into 10 steps, but instead 10 points to remember:

1. Simplify.
2. Lead by example without imposing answers.
3. Work on what you are.
4. You can do anything, but you can't do everything.
5. Invest in individuals.
6. Flirt with failure.
7. Be relentlessly organized.
8. Invention cannot be crowd-sourced.
9. If you want to change the world, stop trying to change the world.
10. Finish what you start.

DESIGNING FOR THE GREATER GOOD Even though we are designers, we are also citizens in the world in which we live. We have an obligation to create for our planet, for our neighbors, and for our economy. For too long we have focused on creating larger profits for already extremely wealthy corporations. Jorge Frascara argues that designers should exclusively "design to support life, design to facilitate life, and design to improve life" (*The Dematerialization of Design*, 2001). The Design Academy Eindhoven states on its Master's of Social Design website: "There is no such thing as social design! As a designer you are obliged working with the social aspect. You ask yourself continuously: why do I design, what impact will my design have, whom will it affect and what do I achieve with my body of work."

Forging any sustainable relationship is hard to do. Whether it is with your spouse, friend, client, or community, it takes time and dedication. However, in the case of designing for the greater good, it's an investment all should embrace.

Eric Benson is Associate Professor of Graphic Design at the University of Illinois, Urbana-Champaign campus. His research at www.re-nourish.com and teaching laid the foundation to create the Fresh Press Agri-Fiber Paper Lab. Fresh Press explores the potential of papermaking to be zero waste, environmentally sustainable, and a catalyst for a thriving local economy. His forthcoming book Design to Renourish: Sustainable Graphic Design in Practice *co-authored with Yvette Perullo, will be published by Focal Press in 2016.*

FIVE QUESTIONS TO
KENJI NAKAYAMA

1. What were the most important influences that shaped you as a designer?
The everyday. I think that living life, and a lot of the things surrounding me, the people that I came across, have the biggest influence on me. Every day I find things that are interesting, unique, and thoughtful. It has been like that since I was young, and, over time, I have built up a pool of inspiration and information that led me to a career in design.

2. Do you agree or disagree with this statement: Designers have a social and ethical responsibility to create and transmit meaningful forms of communication that benefit society and culture. Why?
Yes, I agree. I believe that good design tends to have the power to attract people, and, sometimes, it can be more universal and powerful than words.

3. Your project with Christopher Hope, "Signs for the Homeless," is an exchange of handwritten panhandling signs for colorfully illustrated, eye-catching recreations that aim to give the homeless a power that most of us take for granted: the power to be noticed. Can you talk about your involvement with "Signs for the Homeless" project and why it is important to do this type of work?
In 2006, when I was working for a sign shop, I used to walk by a homeless woman who would sit around the corner from the shop. She was an artist and she was always making poems and watercolor paintings to sell. One day she asked me to make her a professional-looking sign to help her sell artwork. My boss was not supportive of her request because he thought it would attract more homeless people. So I didn't do it. But I kept wondering why I just didn't do it on my own time.

I started the project "Signs for the Homeless" in 2010. My intention was to provide homeless people more visual signs to raise awareness. After meeting more homeless people, and while the project was getting more exposure, the perspective of this project might have changed. While it is important to have the signs as the starting point of the conversation between us (the artists) and homeless people, our real goal is to enable that their story be told—to introduce who they are, to humanize them—and the most important goal is to raise awareness—more awareness, more opportunity for change.

4. New roles are emerging for design professionals as their function is increasingly changing from that of generators to facilitators of ideas. Can you comment on this?
When I was working as a designer for a large company, I sometimes felt like I was a facilitator of ideas. Even though the company was design-driven, there was always a creative process—design teams would brainstorm concepts for every new season, and then they would design around the concepts. Unfortunately, the reality was that marketing often drove the final results.

5. What advice would you give a student studying visual communication today to help them prepare for contemporary professional practice?
Design has the ability to increase the potential of things— the homeless sign project is one such example. I agree that design can be a way that young people can participate in changing society. But it should be done exactly the way the designer wanted, and the design or visual shouldn't be compromised.

3.1a–3.1b Susan J. holding her old sign and her new sign in Harvard Square, Cambridge, Massachusetts, March 2013. *Photo: Kenji Nakayama.*

Today we have easy access to all sorts of information through the Internet, including design sources, latest design trends, etc. Since the majority of us—who have access to the Internet, especially social media—can communicate to a larger group of people spontaneously, sometimes the message spreads out epidemically, and travels beyond the group (e.g., by retweets and reposts). This enables us to easily communicate to others and such communication doesn't always require much of an effort. Therefore, this "habit" could reflect on visual communication as well, as some people refuse to learn the fundamental part of communication skills (design skills) or they underestimate the basics (knowledge and skills), which limits their ability to communicate and express their ideas to others.

Kenji Nakayama is a professional sign painter and visual artist, and a 2014 recipient of the St. Botolph Club Foundation—Emerging Artist award. He was a former mechanical engineer in Japan, also a former footwear designer at Converse Inc. His unique career path clearly reflects his work ethic, as he dedicates his time and energy to his craft trade and art making. He currently lives and works in Boston, Massachusetts.

3.2a Rudolph West holding a new sign in Central Square, Cambridge, Massachusetts, February 2013. *Photo: Kenji Nakayama.*

3.2b–3.2c Angela holding her old sign and her new sign in Central Square, Cambridge, Massachusetts, February 2013. *Photo: Kenji Nakayama.*

TEACHING SOCIAL LITERACY

Myra Margolin

I am a community psychologist. I teach social design students basic frameworks for "reading" the social world and understanding social issues and social problems. The need for this stems from my observation that social design projects are often not grounded in the realities of communities. As a result, many projects are less effective than they could be. Although the idea of "design with" and participation are fairly common amongst social designers, many people setting out on this path have not done the work themselves to know how to understand social phenomena. This means that, even if one has a community-based, participatory process, one still might be lacking tools to create a meaningful social intervention.

THE FRAMEWORKS The following are the six basic frameworks and tools that I introduce to my students, which can be used throughout the social design process.

1. Levels of analysis: The idea of levels of analysis is that social phenomena occur and have causes at multiple "levels." The levels I teach are the individual, the micro (relational), the organizational, the local (e.g., neighborhoods, cities, or rural areas), and the macro (national or global).

2. Problem definition: For me, problem definition is the most crucial concept for the social designer. Many projects fail because they get problem definition wrong. Problem definition, essentially, is the identification of an undesirable social phenomenon and an explanation for why it exists. The phenomenon itself should be grounded in empirical evidence. So, for instance, one might talk about violent crime. One should be able to provide data showing that violent crime actually occurs. The explanation for why there is crime can be a hypothesis. Perhaps one thinks there are not enough police. Or one thinks that violent crime is due to youth disengagement in school. Together, the empirical evidence and the hypothesis form one's problem definition.

3. Victim blaming: "Victim blaming" is a common term that is often misused. My explanation for victim blaming, based on Ryan's (*Blaming the Victim*, 1976) original proposal, is an individual-level intervention with a macro-level problem definition. For instance, one might say that there is violent crime because of irrelevant, nationally mandated curricula in schools that alienate young people, leading them to drop out of school and get involved in the streets. In this case, the explanation for the problem is a macro-level one: nationally mandated curricula is irrelevant to youth, particularly those in poor neighborhoods who carry a lot of stress. A victim-blaming intervention might acknowledge this, but still create an individual-level program to "fix" the kids. Maybe the program would build life skills for low-income youth. A non-victim blaming intervention for this problem definition would be to address the macro-level policy and to advocate for more culturally relevant curricula.

4. Five whys as a tool for uncovering problem definition: "Five whys" is a very useful tool for "unpacking" the causes for social phenomena (Kohfeldt and Langhout, *The Five Whys Method: A Tool for Developing Problem Definitions in Collaboration with Children*, 2012). Essentially, one starts with a social phenomenon and asks, "Why is this happening?" and lists every possible explanation one can think of. Next, one looks these explanations and, for each one, again asks, "Why?" and so on until one has exhausted one's knowledge of an issue. This process cannot be done if one does not know anything about the issue at hand and requires prior research and engagement. It can also be used to reveal gaps in one's knowledge. One might ask, "Why?" and answer, "I don't know." This, then, would indicate future areas to explore.

Once my students have created these Five Whys charts, I ask them to look at each "why" and label whether it is an assumption (not grounded in any evidence), a hypothesis (grounded in some evidence), or personal experience (grounded in one's lived experience with the issue). The reason to break down these distinctions is that many students will revert to assumptions on the first go around and assumptions, in general, are not useful for shaping social intervention.

When a compelling Five Whys chart has been created, I ask students to identify the levels of analysis of their "whys." This can help them identify individual-level explanations. In general, these are not very helpful. If one is dealing with a social phenomenon, it means that it is happening in a patterned way that impacts many people. Therefore, at least part of the explanation must be at the organizational level or higher.

5. Theory of change: In shaping an intervention, students must choose which "why" to address. They should assess which explanation they feel will have the most leverage for creating positive change. Once they have picked a why, they can easily identify their theory of change. For instance, if people believe that violent crime is happening in their city because of disinvestment in poor neighborhoods by the local government, then their theory of change would be: if there is more investment in poor neighborhoods, then crime will decrease. Many social design projects are created without theories of change. Having a clear theory of change not only grounds a student's project, but provides a very simple way to assess whether the project is having the desired impact.

6. Transformative and ameliorative interventions: The last core framework is the differentiation between ameliorative and transformative interventions. Both types are grounded in the understanding that the social system is not working well for everyone and, as

a result, some people are suffering. An ameliorative intervention attempts to alleviate some of this suffering while a transformative one attempts to change the social system so that the suffering does not occur in the first place. Both types of intervention are important, but students should understand the nature of the intervention that they create.

If one is creating a transformative intervention, one must have a problem definition that is not exclusively at the individual or micro level. That is, when you ask, "Who or what is expected to change?" the answer should not be grounded in individuals' psychology (i.e., their thoughts or behavior). A transformative intervention has the explicit intent to create a fundamental shift in power dynamics. It reallocates resources or shifts the control that a particular group has over significant decisions impacting their lives. One cannot create transformation without shifting power. Therefore, if one is interested in transformative change, one would use these criteria to identify which "why" to address. One should choose an intervention point that addresses power and has a systemic or institutional root.

Many students come to the practice of social design with strong design skills. The intent of my lessons is to also give them skills to work with the social world. Ultimately, the skill of engaging meaningfully with the social world is one that must be learned through experience and over a long period of time (Kieffer, *Citizen Empowerment: A Developmental Perspective*, 1984). But having some basic tools and frameworks can help students begin this process as they shape social design projects.

Myra Margolin was trained in filmmaking and community psychology. For many years she worked in the field of community-based media, training people in video and photography to tell stories of their lives and communities. She teaches principles of social change and intervention at Maryland Institute College of Art and Design (MICA) in their MA program in social design.

CULTURAL RESPECT, NOT SOCIAL RESPONSIBILITY:
THE SEVEN PRINCIPLES OF DESIGN ANTHROPOLOGY

Elizabeth Tunstall

In Steven Heller and Veronique Vienne's 2003 edited volume, *Citizen Designer*, they state that "A designer must be professionally, culturally, and socially responsible for the impact his or her design has on the citizenry." Yet, how does one become such a designer? While there are many guides on professional and socially responsibility, providing guidance on "cultural responsibility" is more challenging because the cultural offers a critique of fundamental ways of being in the world that can upset contemporary power structures. Culture demands respect, not responsibility, which sometimes means stopping the design process where it might be considered disrespectful. Design anthropology is a discipline focused on how design translates values into tangible experiences. Through the seven principles of design anthropology, I seek to assist students and practitioners in developing design approaches based on cultural respect, not just social responsibility.

Many guides exist that assist designers in becoming professionally responsible for the impact of their designs. Nearly every major professional design organization in the world has a professional code of ethics, including Icograda's Code of Conduct and ICSID's Code of Professional Ethics. The organizations use these codes to endorse individual designers as well as events to ensure that designers reflect positively on the discipline. In terms of social responsibility and impact, design's reach beyond the for-profit sector into the not-for-profit sector has accelerated over the past 15 years. Large design organizations, such as IDEO, have even established their own not-for-profit organizations to capitalize on this shift. Thus, design for social responsibility has become its own industry of books, conferences, toolkits, and digital platforms. But cultural

responsibility remains another matter. One finds very few guides on cultural responsibility in design. In fact, the majority of people conflate the social and the cultural. When one reads or hears about cultural responsibility in design, it is often within the statement "social and cultural responsibility." Yet, having been trained in the American tradition of anthropology, I find it important to distinguish between the social and the cultural.

In the book *History and Theory in Anthropology* (2000), Alan Barnard describes the differences between the social and the cultural. The social concerns itself with society as a unit of analysis. It is focused on the "relations between individuals, relations between social institutions [e.g., religious, political, familial, and economic institutions], or relations among social categories." Yet, the social also represents the imposition of European categories on the rest of the world. Concepts such as religion, politics, family, and economics were based on European models of those institutions. Other peoples were benchmarked against those European models with the result of being lesser than Europeans— something I have discussed in more depth in my 2013 book chapter, "Decolonising Design Innovation." Because social responsibility does not directly challenge European, or Euro-American, dominant ways of being in the world, large corporations, NGOs, or foundations find it easy to sponsor social responsibility. Thus, it is easier to create a design industry around it.

Barnard goes on to describe how the cultural concerns itself with shared sets of "ideas, skills, objects" among a group of peoples. It is focused on the holistic values, beliefs, and practices from which people construct meaning. The cultural recognizes that the established social categories may not make any sense to other people who have their own ways of being in the world. Thus, the cultural offers alternative ways of being in the world that redefine and decenter the very notion of the "human" in, for example, human-centered design. For instance, design has yet to specialize in design for supernatural beings, which for many cultures is a fundamental aspect of being human.

Design anthropology is explicitly concerned with the cultural—how design translates values into tangible experiences, such that it respects other ways of being in the world. It is a methodology of respectful design, which, in the 2011 Icograda Design Education Manifesto, I have defined by combining Richard Sennett's definition of respect ("the mutual recognition of intrinsic worth") with Herbert Simon's definition of design ("the creation of preferred course of action") as: "The creation of preferred courses of action based on the mutual recognition of the intrinsic worth of all human, animal, mineral, fauna and flora creatures and the treatment of them with dignity and regard."

Design anthropology proposes a set of seven principles regarding how one understands and positively impacts (1) value systems, (2) the processes and artifacts of designing in making value systems tangible, and (3) the aligning of people's experiences with the values they prefer—all under conditions of unequal power relations.

The first three key principles of design anthropology are influenced by the concept of transculturation as defined by Cuban anthropologist Fernando Ortiz, in his 1945 book, *Cuban Counterpoint: Tobacco and Sugar*. He defines transculturation as "the process of transition from one culture to another" that includes acquiring another culture (acculturation), the loss or uprooting of a previous culture (deculturation), and new cultural phenomena (neoculturation). The first three principles inform a respectful approach to the understanding of value systems:

1. Accept value systems and cultures as dynamic, not static. Each generation goes through the process of negotiating the elements that make up their value systems and cultures.

2. Recognize the mutual borrowing that happens among value systems and cultures, and seek to mitigate or eliminate the unequal circumstances in which that borrowing takes place.

3. Look simultaneously at what is expressed as that to be gained, lost, and created new, in the recombination of value systems and cultures by a group of people.

The fourth principle of design anthropology emerges out of the critical dialogue of designers in India, Africa, China, the Pacific Islands, Latin America, the Middle East, as well as various indigenous and "minority" designers:

4. Eliminate false distinctions between art, craft, and design, in order to better recognize all culturally important forms of making as a way in which people make value systems tangible to themselves and others.

The distinctions between art, design, and craft that define European design history do not exist in other cultures. The hierarchies ascribed to art-design-craft have significant impact on the cultural and economic wellbeing of communities whose work has been designated as craft, and thus ascribed a lower economic value. The fifth principle of design anthropology draws upon the practices of Scandinavian cooperative design (see Susan Bødker et al.'s *Co-Operative Design—Perspectives on 20 Years with 'the Scandinavian It Design Model'*). It informs how one respectfully approaches the process of design making:

5. Create processes that enable respectful dialogue and relational interactions such that everyone is able to contribute their expertise equally to the process of designing and those contributions are properly recognized and remunerated.

The final two principles related to design's role in dismantling the value systems that bolster imperialism and creating conditions of compassion and harmony:

6. Use design processes and artifacts to work with groups to shift hegemonic value systems that are detrimental to the holistic wellbeing of vulnerable groups, dominant groups, and their extended environments.

7. Define the ultimate criteria for success of any design anthropology engagements as the recognized creation of conditions of compassion among the participants in the project and in harmony with their wider environments.

The seven principles of design anthropology provide practical guidance for how a citizen designer might become more culturally respectful. In using them, one can see how the professional designer is not separate from being a culturally informed human being. One can see in which contexts one should not design because the design's impact may have negative consequences for a culture. This is what makes being culturally respectful very difficult, because it means listening deeply to a group's call for self-determination and self-definition. But because of design's great impact, it is crucial that it avoids becoming another form of cultural imperialism through the guise of social responsibility.

Elizabeth (Dori) Tunstall is an Associate Professor of Design Anthropology at Swinburne University of Technology, Melbourne, Australia. She received her PhD and MA in Anthropology from Stanford University and BA in Anthropology from Bryn Mawr College. Since 1999, she has worked professionally at the intersections of design and anthropology including stints as a high tech consultant at Sapient and Arc Worldwide and managing director of AIGA's Design for Democracy Initiative.

I made her
favourite dinner
last night.

046 902 3718
amen.ie

AMEN Supporting male victims
of domestic abuse

Cosc

/amensupportservices

3.3 Amen: Dinner. Project team: Lauren Flynn, Michelle Geoghegan, Deividas Dvylaitis, Ben Salveta, Joseph Egan, Alan Harbron, Orla Flanagan. *Concept and design: Lauren Flynn. Photography: Michelle Geoghegan.*

3.2

SECTION 2

RESOURCES

ASSESSMENT CONSIDERATIONS FOR SOCIAL IMPACT DESIGN

Audra Buck-Coleman

Social impact design is gaining popularity and credence in the design profession. Academic programs and design firms are increasingly emphasizing social aspects of their design work. They are also touting their successes—unfortunately, many times without rigorous post-implementation assessment. Without assessment, design cannot clearly articulate its benefits and nor can it be sufficiently appreciated and understood. Assessment is a key factor in social impact design, and yet it seems to be the one about which more designers want knowledge.

I've heard multiple calls for the need for assessment and laments regarding its deficiencies in methods from fellow design educators and practitioners. However, assessment does not need to be created from scratch nor be overly complicated. Designers can employ and modify approaches from other disciplines including the social sciences. Qualitative and quantitative research methods including surveys, interviews, time-use diaries, ethnographic studies, media studies, and focus groups are but a few possibilities. In addition, artistic methods such as cultural probes can also be used. The issue is not a lack of methods but valid application of them. The right assessment method depends upon what you are trying to achieve and how you are trying to achieve it. Designers must carefully consider their research method, assessment method, the population sample, and other factors that can invalidate findings.

Implicit in social impact design projects is the assumption that design can create change. Establishing causality is key. Social science research requires three conditions to establish cause and effect, and these should be applied to social impact design as well. Weakness in any of these three can invalidate claims of social change.

The first condition is temporal precedence. Designers need to be able to show that the factors they are changing were not happening before a design response was employed and that they are happening during and after the design treatment. To do this requires capturing pre- and post-implementation data of the social conditions the design treatment seeks to change.

A second requirement—covariation of cause and effect—is the need to establish design's role in the situation it seeks to alter. Designers need to establish that change happens when the design response is in place and that change does not happen when the design response is absent. Temporal or physical proximity does not automatically mean there is a causal association. Designers must establish that changes are due to the design response rather than coincidence.

The third and most challenging requirement is to eliminate other likely explanations that might be creating change. Designers need to verify that the social change we measure is due, at least in part, to the design response. What degree of change, if any, happens in one population versus another? Incorporation of controls can build support for a project's impact and simultaneously rule out, or at least diminish, other possible triggers.

As designers incorporate these requirements, we also need to alter the verbs we use to describe the impact of our projects. The problems and issues social impact design seeks to address are often complex and entrenched. We want to heal communities, eradicate hunger and poverty, cleanse impure water, and resolve environmental quagmires. Although it is highly unlikely a design project can singlehandedly untangle a complex problem, social impact design can contribute to minimizing and redirecting negative effects. With this, we need to replace the overstating verbs we have been using, such as "solve" and "eliminate," with more pliable ones, such as "contribute," "support," "minimize," and "build." Social scientists are cautioned against using words such as "prove," replacing them with "support" for good reason. This approach can seem frustrating and unsatisfying; however, designers risk invalidating their projects' impact when we overpromise the possibilities and overstate the outcomes.

Incorporating assessment involves changing outdated design mindsets. Too many design books begin the design process with thumbnails and sketches and conclude it with the final product delivery, such as the launch of a package design or the execution of a branding campaign. Assessment, if mentioned, is an afterthought. Instead it should bookend—and even to some degree guide—the creative process. How will you know if social change has happened? What would this look like? What impact might the project have on social, economic, environmental, and/or political conditions? How long will the change take? What is the magnitude of the change we might expect? How can you capture representative data? What data could show temporal precedence? How can you rule out other potential stimuli? In addition to these questions there should be ones addressing design's role in this change. Having answers—or at least a sense of direction—for these questions can help focus the "normal" design process choices of form and content.

Admittedly, incorporating assessment into the design curriculum is not as easy as it sounds. Multiple impediments can slow project progress and deflate enthusiasm. One possible barrier is the misguided expectation that now you have to be an expert social researcher in addition to all of the other expected teaching, service, and scholarship duties. Designers and design educators already have way too many things on their "to do" lists, and adding canons of knowledge and expertise to those lists can be daunting to say the least. However, you don't have to go it alone. Reach out to on-campus or nearby colleagues in the disciplines you would like to engage for your project. Through collaboration you can impart and receive insight in the process.

Conducting surveys, interviews, and other research methods also requires expertise and awareness of the pitfalls that can invalidate findings. Again, just as this idea of adding all of this expertise to your educator toolkit can seem overwhelming, collaboration is an effective way to incorporate that knowledge and add precision to the research process. If a collaborator is not a possibility, try building from existing research and scholarship. If a sufficient body of knowledge has not yet developed within the design canon, look to other disciplines for precedents. Designer educators can also engage their students to supplement the overall project knowledge. Grants and other funding sources can also help finance assistants to capture and assess data. Look for funding opportunities through your project's associated disciplines as well as campus and area organizations. Time limitations also create multiple stumbling blocks. Incorporating assessment into an existing semester or quarter curriculum will most likely mean forgoing other assignments and content. Different programs have different levels of curriculum flexibility, so start by selecting the most appropriate course or series of courses.

Admittedly, conducting assessment is not as exciting as creating the design project. Students prefer creating their own, fresh portfolio-generating projects rather than assessing others'. One possible response to this is to have the students redesign the project to address any shortcomings of the original based on assessment findings. Consider assigning a written component that incorporates the resulting data as well as the students' critical thinking about how to improve the existing design. In addition, design educators can assign students to create information designs that map the research data and assessment. This "fresh" portfolio piece calls upon students to synthesize, prioritize, and visualize the data. "Before" and "after" results can add more complexity and depth to these assignments.

It is also important that students understand why assessment is important and how they represent this in their portfolio and to prospective employers. This can help minimize students' grumblings about assessment until this component becomes the "new normal" for your curriculum.

Designers are accustomed to the instant gratification of immediate website updates, the sight of printed works and the like. Long delays in a project's conclusion due to necessary longitudinal assessment can also be met with protests. However, social design works within a complex network of economic, political, technological, and cultural systems. True social change rarely happens in a semester, let alone a quarter. Many projects will need longitudinal data to inform the temporal precedence as well as to evaluate the design response implementation. If a lengthy study is the best way to assess a project's impact, consider stretching the process out over multiple terms. Long-term investment in a community can foster more trust and better relationships with stakeholders, yielding more insights to inform the design response. One year's students can create a project and the next few years' can conduct longitudinal assessment. Again, grants and other funding can provide assistance in conducting large surveys and in reporting the resulting data.

Finally, if you cannot find ways to satisfy the assessment component, then ask if your curriculum is an appropriate fit for this type of design work. Well-intentioned projects can go astray. Social design projects can be harmful to individuals and communities. While we can learn from failures as much as successes, the former should be kept to a minimum. As designers it is easy for us to be seduced by beautiful typography and smart content. However, we need to think more critically about how that beautiful design fits with the aesthetic of the targeted community, and if that content really speaks to their needs and provokes the change it intends without causing harm.

Undeniably, assessment isn't as nearly as sexy and exciting as creating original designs. Trading projects for assessment assignments will most likely not be met with cheers from students. However, assessment is a necessary component of design projects and a core competency for the designer of the future. We don't have to invent the assessment wheel. We can borrow from the other models and then make modifications as appropriate.

Climate change. Poverty. Water shortages. Drug trafficking. AIDS epidemic. Social injustice. These and other wicked problems were years in the making, and we cannot realistically expect one design project to "solve" them. However, thoughtful, well-executed design projects can make a difference. We just need data to support it.

Audra Buck-Coleman is an Associate Professor and director of the Graphic Design program at the University of Maryland. She holds an MFA from Cranbrook Academy of Art and a BA in Journalism from the University of Missouri. She is currently pursuing a PhD in sociology at the University of Maryland. Her design research focuses on social design, design pedagogy, and the ethical considerations of today's design practice. She has collaborated on numerous design projects including Sticks + Stones, an international multi-university collaborative graphic design project that investigates stereotyping and social issues.

THE CITIZEN DESIGNER:
A CAUTIONARY NOTE

Cinnamon Janzer and Lauren Weinstein

Social change is necessary. Frankly, it's unavoidable. The fact that a vested interest in solving social problems has expanded beyond the traditional social change disciplines—and into those like design—is evidence of a collective acknowledgment of the increasingly pressing problems our contemporary global society faces. This recognition represents an important intellectual shift among the new generations of leaders and problem solvers: a commendable new focus that elevates the importance of social good at least alongside, if not ahead of, profit.

However, there is a downside to the current trend toward social change. Simply having an interest in solving social problems doesn't simultaneously grant the skills and theoretical equipment to be an effective, or even relevant, implementer. Unfortunately, many practitioners in the social design space are working toward social change without the ability to consider the impact of their design decisions, without fully understanding the situation(s) they intend to change.

THE RISKS OF TRADITIONAL DESIGN PROCESSES IN THE SOCIAL REALM In its migration toward social change, design has taken with it, and continued to employ, traditional creative and design-based processes as primary methodologies—the two most ubiquitous are human-centered design (HCD) and design thinking. Both of these processes have been given significant credit and credibility within the world of social design—they are considered to yield innovative and user-driven results. However, the efficacy of these processes within the social realm, and any other realm outside of design, remains questionable and understudied.

HCD and design thinking are applicable methods for designing products that will be used or consumed by humans. However, with its transition away from traditional design and into social design, the discipline is now functioning in an almost wholly different environment—the social, which is a multidimensional, complex, and delicate space whose expansive and nuanced nature is not adequately understood through "human centered." Design thinking and HCD are considered to be able to generate transformative social change by combining the creative nature of these processes with practices from areas like the social sciences. However, these processes lack critical emphasises on thorough research and careful approach to problem definition prior to design.

THE RISKS OF ADAPTING METHODOLOGIES AT LEISURE A number of popular social design toolkits regarding the practice of HCD (e.g., *Collective Action Toolkit* by frog, *Human Centered Design Toolkit* by IDEO, and *An Ethnography Primer* by AIGA) preach the efficacy of design ethnography: a rapid "research" approach to gather quick insights. However, these practices in their current form are fundamentally callow and critically removed from their social science derivatives. These processes take the goals of ethnographic work but neglect the process required to gather such understanding: rigorous research necessary for meaningful results. HCD and design thinking reduce the act of living and working with another people over the course of years, or even decades, to several interviews or a single overnight stay on a rice terrace in Southeast Asia. This massive deterioration in process quality cannot reveal the same nuances and unbiased information that are illuminated through true ethnographic research practiced in anthropology and sociology, which requires participant immersion over an extended period of time.

When practices from varied disciplines are applied to unfamiliar contexts or modified freely, important findings around the needs of end users end up neglected or lost, even when practitioners have the best intentions. These methodologies (HCD and design thinking) alone are not sufficient for understanding and creating social change—complementary knowledge and significant research will likely be necessary: a rigorous study of political science, social theory, development history, and investment in understanding the user's local situational context (from the perspective of the user).

In this way, designers remain at a critical and problematic distance from those who actually constitute the population (the "user") for whom they are trying to design change. Designers seeking to do this kind of work often neglect to collaborate with and learn from "the very actors within the domains they seek to improve" (Kimbell, *Rethinking Design Thinking: Part I*, 2011). Designing solutions through traditional design practices, based on personal ideas and sketches, removes concepts from the supremely important context of the environment they would function in. Prioritizing designers' ideas perpetuates a hierarchy of solution making and values. Such an approach implies that people don't know what they want or need for themselves: this is a dangerous attitude to have in making social change. That solution needs meaningful input from stakeholders—the community, the end users—to be relevant, to be a solution.

Operating without such considerations poses a risk of neocolonialism in practice. Despite seemingly beneficial outcomes, negative impacts at the communities' expense often result as well. Social change focused designs that exclude a community's culture, norms, or values essentially serve to erase community and replace it with a "neocolony" of the creator. These negative impacts are why neocolonialism is a force for change that is fundamentally imposing rather than empowering. Solutions created and problems defined in isolation from the community (and their particular social contexts) often exhibit a disconnection between the people involved and the social phenomena addressed. Consequently, designing in this way creates a high risk of cultural bias or, in this case, design neocolonialism: an influence over a population, community, or society in the absence of formal control.

CRITICAL NEXT STEPS FOR THE SOCIAL DESIGN FIELD If social design, as a discipline, wants to craft its practice toward empowerment and away from neocolonialism, then adopting new, more appropriate practices and modifying—even disregarding, if necessary—methods that are unsuitable for designing situations may be the remedy. We believe that social design can create truly transformative social change through reorienting its theoretical philosophy away from traditional human-centered priorities (object-centric) and shifting, instead, toward new, situation-centered (social systems-centric) priorities.

If we, as practitioners, students, teachers, and scholars, begin to collectively create a solid foundation and framework for social design to build upon and within, then we can start to more clearly connect the dots between concept and reality—between social design's intentions and outputs toward, hopefully, a more positive reality than we currently face. If design-based social change is going to be effective and lasting, it must not depend on the designer, but rather, be rooted in the empowerment of the beneficiaries.

"

If design-based social change is going to be effective and lasting, it must not depend on the designer, but rather, be rooted in the empowerment of the beneficiaries."

———

We urge citizen designers to think about why they want to engage in people-focused design, and hold fast to those passions. Prioritizing the user, their local contexts, their challenges, and their needs will help to reduce the designer's personal influence and bias over outcomes and create more impactful designs. If citizen designers remain focused on the success of the project—and that success is defined by the user's benefit—the appropriate methodology and approach will be apparent. Social designers need to acknowledge biases, frequently revisit assumptions, and be humble. Citizen designers have a unique opportunity to make social change, but need to carefully prepare and select the appropriate tools to research users' situations prior to crafting designs.

With a holistic understanding of a situation, citizen designers can facilitate solutions by synthesizing ideas from key stakeholders and celebrating them. The true value of design is not about personal ideas or credit, but rather about empowering the voice of others and sewing together ideas that might never have synergized without the direction and commitment of someone looking at the whole system of complex, delicately interconnected parts.

A fuller version of this essay has been published under the title "Social Design and Neocolonialism," in Design and Culture, 6.3 (2014).

Cinnamon Janzer holds a BA in Anthropology and Fine Art *from University of Minnesota, Twin Cities, and an MA in Social Design from Maryland Institute College of Art. Her experience lies in systems design and community engagement. Her work currently explores how company culture and distributed authority organizational systems can successfully take root and grow within start-up environments.*

Lauren Weinstein holds a BA in Sociology and Environmental Studies *from Bucknell University, and an MA in Social Design from Maryland Institute College of Art. She is a multidisciplinary designer with a special focus on systems and program design, her experience lies in design research and implementation for international development initiatives on rural information communication technology, inclusive governance, and institutional accountability in West Africa.*

MAKING THE TRANSITION:
A PERSONAL REFLECTION

Penina Acayo

When I was a young child growing up in Uganda, my parents made it clear that adults in our neighborhood had the right to discipline us if we were ever found to be in the wrong. And sure enough, if my siblings and I did or said something that was hurtful to another, we were disciplined by whichever parent was in charge that day. Being very quick to listen and slow to speak was paramount. Learning from one's elders was part of the community culture ingrained in us at a very young age—it did not stop at school but extended to home life.

When I was in primary four (fourth grade), I arrived at school one morning and immediately sensed something was amiss. My teachers had students congregate for a quick meeting to announce that we were to have visitors from "outside countries" who came to share important information with us. We were asked to be on our best behavior, listen to what they had to say, and be polite when responding to questions. There was a lot of excitement and much anticipation leading up to their arrival. Not only were we excited to meet these foreign visitors, but also eager to learn about where they came from, and to listen to their presentation about good sanitation and hygiene practices.

After a general conversation about the merits of proper sanitation, we were placed in smaller groups to discuss how to care for our maturing bodies. The session allowed for an interactive, fun discussion that was later followed by a few gifts including some toiletries, a toothbrush, toothpaste, and other sanitary items. Due to the large number of students, the gifts were only given to a select few. This harbored more feelings of resentment than happiness. As exciting as it was to meet the visitors and learn about proper sanitation, we had hoped to develop a mutual friendship, but unfortunately never saw or heard from our visitors again.

BUILDING RELATIONSHIPS FIRST Whenever we received visitors at home, it was the tradition of our culture to share a meal to get to know one another. After a few of these encounters, a relationship would develop and trust was built. The guests were no longer viewed as strangers but as friends with whom you could share information.

It wasn't until I was in secondary school (high school) that I began to observe more keenly a pattern in the way most outside social interventions worked. It seemed like most international humanitarian groups that came to intervene with local communities set out to achieve a specific goal that involved collecting data from the target audience and then, sometimes, leaving them with a "goodwill" offering. This kind of strategy causes more harm than good.

Once, our high school volleyball team was introduced to a group that seemed passionate about encouraging girls in education and sports. We were asked to submit essays about the role that extracurricular activities played in our high school education and, later, to have an open dialogue about our experiences. Upon receipt of our essays, and much to our collective disappointment, we were given T-shirts and a talk from the project's leaders about their goals and their specific mission. This experience left us feeling manipulated and yearning to be apart of the greater conversation, especially since we were part of the target group they were interested in helping. With no follow-up or sign of proactive initiative to continue this conversation, the project was soon forgotten. So, why would anyone ever feel eager about participating and sharing their experiences if they never feel they can equally contribute to the final solution?

After participating in numerous interventions like the one described above, I stopped thinking of these groups as visitors and considered them more like strangers with their own personal agenda. However, the groups or individuals who invested their time and energy in developing close relationships with the communities they wanted to serve made a longer, lasting impact. Building relationships is an important and crucial component for gaining the trust of the people you want to help or serve.

AS AN EDUCATOR LEADING SIMILAR INTERVENTIONS Socially conscious projects, if tackled with sensitivity, respect, and empathy, have the ability to effect change. However, they can also harm the dignity of the people they are meant to serve, especially if they are part of a vulnerable population. Therefore, it is important that we engage in discussions concerning innovative approaches to teaching and include students in sustainable, social design projects.

As designers, we are equipped with skills we can use to creatively solve problems and develop products or services that meet the needs of the intended audience. The process leading up to the final solution involves countless rounds of iterations and user testing. Therefore, when designing initiatives that involve social challenges, more rigor should be put into understanding and empathizing with the people our solutions are designed for. It is imperative that we genuinely consider the long-term impact of these solutions for the audiences we're engaging, if we want to have a sustainable intervention. Empathy demands that we step out of our normal "check-your-bias-at-the-door and step into the shoes of another," which is a lot harder than it sounds. Understanding people and their context takes time, patience, and a desire to listen and learn first, rather than speak or act.

In the summer of 2014, I had the opportunity to help lead a small group of undergraduate design students to Uganda to share—with instructors—ideas they had developed to teach good hygiene practices to primary school children through interactive physical activities. The hardest part of this project was learning how to expunge any current bias, and to develop a stronger sense of empathy for the serious cultural differences between the United States and Uganda. The students wanted to do well and they worried about how the Ugandan teachers would perceive their ideas. One particular aspect we worked on as a group

was to allow for flexibility within our set goals and outcomes of the trip. It was important for the students to determine the success of their prototypes, but it was equally important for them to experience the similarities and differences within this new culture. They needed to focus on developing collaborative relationships through listening and learning from the Ugandan teachers.

Working within the confines of a tight schedule—semester or year-long project—can hinder the ability to fully connect with a given target audience, especially if there is a considerable geographical distance and foreign cultural context that requires a significant amount of time to understand. Encouraging my students to view these "encounters" as opportunities for connection and collaboration rather than personal projects has enabled them to harness the transformative power of socially conscious design.

Penina Acayo holds a BA in Art from Goshen College, and received her MFA in visual communication design from Kent State University in 2013. While at Kent State, she collaborated on an award-winning project that used simplified iconography to communicate ailments associated with the spread, prevention, and treatment of malaria in Kibera, Kenya. She works as a research associate in visual communication design at the University of Notre Dame and continues to focus on projects that utilize a human-centered approach to solving social problems.

SOME THOUGHTS ON EMPATHY

Gunta Kaza

Empathy is a word that has been tossed around a lot lately. We hear it used to communicate care and concern for another person, from politicians to religious leaders, doctors, therapists, teachers, and others who are invested in the human condition. It is a buzzword in marketing and entrepreneurial endeavors. Corporations promote empathy to sell their services or products by donations made to worthy causes. I've come to know empathy through a study of apathy, anhedonia, boredom, and depression. *The Random House Dictionary* defines apathy as "the absence or suppression of passion, emotion or excitement; a lack of interest in or concern for things which others find moving or exciting; freedom from emotion of any kind." Feeling apathetic is easy. It is feeling hopeless. I may not like feeling hopeless, but in feeling this way, I absolve myself of all commitment and responsibility for my actions—or inactions.

Empathy is difficult and complex. To have empathic concern for another requires effort and understanding. It requires that I set aside my own selfish needs and think about the experience someone else may be having. The ancient Greek word *empatheia* means "physical affection, passion, partiality" and was adapted to create the German word *Einfühlung*, a "feeling into" (Maddaloni, *The Meaning of Empathy*, 1961). It asks me to invest precious emotional energy into another, a cause, a social concern that is not directly related to me, or what I value.

Humans are not born empathic. We are born narcissists. Babies are the ultimate narcissists. They cannot meet their own needs, and depend on adults for food, pleasure, and comfort. Empathy requires effort. To have empathic concern for another requires that I invest interest in someone other than myself and give up the expectation of receiving anything in return. To invest in someone other than myself is a maturational challenge. Am I capable of doing so, and at what price? Are infantile needs worth giving up? Can I progress to thinking of someone else, even if my individual needs have not been satisfied? If I can do this individually, can we do it collectively?

Empathy and activism on behalf of social justice requires doing more, working harder. To be socially minded means to go beyond expectations. Going beyond what comes naturally transcends my animal nature. Freud states that,

"The development of the individual seems to us to be a product of the interaction between two urges, the urge towards happiness, which we usually call "egoistic," and the urge towards union with others in the community, which we call "altruistic." Neither of these descriptions goes much below the surface. In the process of individual development ... the main accent falls mostly on the egoistic urge (or the urge towards happiness), while the other urge, which may be described as a "cultural" one, is usually content with the role of imposing restrictions. But in the process of civilization things are different. Here by far the most important thing is the aim of creating a unity out of the individual human beings ... the aim of happiness is still there, but it is pushed into the background." —*Freud,* Civilization and Its Discontents, *1961*

"

*To have empathic
concern for another
requires that I invest
interest in someone
other than myself and
give up the expectation
of receiving anything
in return."*

Do we model empathic behaviors for our students?
Are we empathetic toward causes unrelated to
us? Can we connect with others halfway across
the globe—with different life styles, values, and
religious beliefs? Why should we? The harshness of
this response is not one we would expect, given our
privileged lifestyle. Empathy cannot be forced upon
us, but it can be learned by mimicry or emotional
induction. The global community allows us to see, to
choose and to make connections, but it also creates
separation and distance, and identification with
what is "not me." This choice is the privilege of our
lifestyle. *What do we choose?*

*Gunta Kaza is the Chair of Graphic Design at the
Massachusetts College of Art and Design where
she teaches in both the undergraduate program
and Dynamic Media Institute (MFA program). She
was awarded the Thomas Gonda Award for Social
Responsibility from Rhode Island School of Design.
She is currently an advanced candidate in the
doctoral program in psychoanalysis at the Boston
Graduate School of Psychoanalysis.*

ALL TOGETHER NOW

Scott Boylston

In his book *Blessed Unrest* (2008), Paul Hawken identifies the varied international trends in restorative, regenerative, and resilient activism as parts of a larger social movement unlike any other, likening them to an interconnected immune reaction of global proportions. "The ultimate purpose of a global immune system is to identify what is not life affirming and to contain, neutralize, or eliminate it. Where communities, cultures, and ecosystems have been damaged, it seeks to prevent additional harm and then heal and restore the damage." Hawken goes on to explore how millions of people worldwide are collectively designing alternative solutions that are as aspirational as they are corrective, and defines this global reaction as a movement that celebrates what is beautiful, creative, and holistically oriented within the human spirit.

Richard Farson's book, *The Power of Design* (2008), published at approximately the same time as *Blessed Unrest*, lays out a grand plan for designers' intent to transcend the self-imposed boundaries that have limited our disciplines' scope over the last century. Farson's framing of a *metadesign* defines a way of acting in the world for designers that expands our purview to systematically address all aspects of the human condition. He prescribes a more rigorous level of design professionalism—one where saying "no" to bad ideas is as essential as saying "yes" to ideas that come from the broader social fabric, rather than the bounded rationality of clients. He encourages metadesigners "to discover and develop new professional pathways in a never-ending process

of growth and change," and stresses that the core to such a process resides within personal character traits like courage, optimism, vision, tenacity, humility, and boldness, but most of all within a trait too often absent: wisdom.

If a new breed of designers is aligning itself with an emerging network of global activism, that's a big win for everyone—unless, of course, designers trip over each other in attempting to define the "better" way of addressing massive global problems rather than focusing on the commonalities that exist between the pursuits. Thanks to the groundwork laid over the last 40 years by designers and non-designers alike, new fields of design such as *design for social impact*, *design for public interest*, *design for sustainability*, *design for social innovation*, and *social design* are earnestly redesigning design. And the burgeoning success of this larger trend owes itself, in no small part, to the diversity of methods being applied.

So, how do designers seeking to shift societal levers through such a diversity of means ensure that their collective energy is optimized toward common goals rather than lost to infighting? One way we can do this is to recognize that we're undergoing a social movement within the design field itself, and to open ourselves to the lessons learned by larger social movements of the past. An inspiring and informative resource exists within the Movement Action Plan (MAP) devised by Bill Moyer, in his book *Doing Democracy* (2001). Moyer focuses on movements that take place within participatory democracies, and defines movements as "collective actions in which the populace is alerted, educated, and mobilized, sometimes over years and decades, to challenge the power holders and the whole society to redress social problems or grievances and restore critical social values."

Moyer's MAP, while grounded in grassroots mobilization, emphasizes a systems-based connectivity between communities, organizations, businesses, and governmental bodies in analyzing the way in which complex social dynamics are navigated by those intent on changing them for the betterment of all. As someone who actively participated in major social movements of the past, Moyer is acquainted with the barriers to timely change, and identifies two limiting factors in the quest for streamlined movement progress: the disruption created by movement infighting, and the inability of movement actors to comprehend the long view of real change in open societies.

Moyer's book identifies four general roles that actors play in social movements: *the citizen*, *the rebel*, *the change agent*, and *the reformer*. He delves into great detail about how these roles are played effectively and ineffectively. Such a framework can help designers not only identify the contributions of each of these actors within the larger society, but understand what it means to play these roles themselves, both within the design community and within their practice. Those truly interested in real change can strategically shift their own behavior according to the situation, strategically select actors who are playing certain roles that are most necessary at that particular moment in time, or commit to the mindset of the change agent, who tends to the overall health of the movement through strategic development, organizational learning, tactical agility, and dynamic leadership.

One of the primary reasons for acrimony between designers who are working in the public interest is that change rarely occurs at the desired pace. Here again, Moyer's MAP is helpful in that he provides detailed insight into eight stages of social movements. The fact that these stages are inspired by stages set forth in the 4,000-year-old *Book of Changes* should provide insight into the nature of mankind's relationship with change. We have only a few fleeting moments on this planet, so we expect that change will occur at a pace less related to the existence of our species, and more by the clock on our iPhones. When it doesn't change as fast as we want, we often resort to pointing fingers. And this finger pointing turns inward: Sell-out. Radical. And so on. A better

understanding of how long-term change loops through phases can help all us appreciate the role we're playing at any particular moment: *Normal Times*; *Prove the Failure of Official Institutions*; *Ripening Conditions*; *Take Off*; *Perceptions of Failure*; *Majority of Public Opinion*; *Success*; *Continuing the Struggle*.

Nothing is assured of course, and Moyer is sure to point that out, but some of the principles that MAP adheres to are that people hold the ultimate power, and that once mobilized nothing can stop them. While there is much to learn through a close reading of this book, one of Moyer's key points is that movement goals are met more quickly when there is an understanding between different groups of actors, despite the sometimes intense disagreements over tactics. Our immune reaction to the twentieth century's shortsighted thinking will be stronger if our mindsets remain as parallel to each other as our actions surely are, and a deeper wisdom can be drawn upon if we understand we are all pushing in the same direction. Nature celebrates diversity in all its forms; designers for social impact should celebrate diversity both within their problem spaces and within the acknowledgment of their compatriots' parallel efforts.

Scott Boylston is co-author and program coordinator for the Design for Sustainability *program at the Savannah College of Art and Design, Savannah, Georgia. His is the author of three books including* Designing Sustainable Packaging *(2009), and has published and spoken internationally on design and sustainability. He is also president of Emergent Structures, a non-profit organization that redirects construction and demolition waste into vibrant, community-based projects.*

RESOURCES

AIGA Design Educators Community Professional Standards of Teaching. (2011).
This publication is available to download free of charge: educators.aiga.org/wp-content/uploads/2011/02/AIGA.PSOT-1.0.pdf.

Bennett, A. and Vulpinari, O. (eds.) (2011). *Icograda Design Education Manifesto 2011*. Montreal, Canada: Icograda. This publication is available to download free of charge: http://www.ico-d.org/resources/design-education-manifesto.

Design Can Change. This publication is available to download free of charge: www.designcanchange.org/files/dcc_answers_for_designers.pdf.

Design for America Process Guide. This publication is available to download free of charge: designforamerica.com/dfa-process-guide/.

Design for Sustainability (D4S) manual can be downloaded free of charge: www.d4s-de.org.

The Designers Accord. (2010). *The Toolkit: Integrating Sustainability into Design Education*. This publication is available to download free of charge: edutoolkit.designersaccord.org.

Ethnographic Primer. New York: AIGA. This publication is available to download free of charge: www.aiga.org/interior.aspx?pageid=3079&id=8320.

Firm Foundation. (2013). *Social Design Field Guide: A Handbook from Experiences in Participatory Design in Indonesia*. This publication is available to download free of charge: www.solokotakita.org/firmfoundation.

Frog Design. (2012). *Frog Collective Action Toolkit*. This publication is available to download free of charge: www.frogdesign.com/work/frog-collective-action-toolkit.html.

The GOOD Ideas for Cities Toolkit. (2012). This publication is available to download free of charge: awesome.good.is.s3.amazonaws.com/goodideasforcities/GIFC_toolkit_2013.pdf.

IDEO. (2012). *Design Thinking for Educators Toolkit*. This publication is available to download free of charge: http://www.designthinkingforeducators.com/toolkit/.

IDEO. (2014). *Human Centered Design Toolkit*. This publication is available to download free of charge: www.designkit.org.

Lasky, J. (2012). *Design and Social Impact: A Cross-Sectoral Agenda for Design Education, Research, and Practice* (a white paper based on the Social Impact Design Summit). New York: Smithsonian Institution. This publication is available to download free of charge: http://arts.gov/sites/default/files/Design-and-Social-Impact.pdf.

Pilloton, E. (2009). *Design Revolution Toolkit*. This publication is available to download free of charge: burlington.edu/files/pdf/design_revolution_toolkit.pdf.

Re-Nourish.com. *Sustainable Standards for Print Projects, Digital Projects, Design Studio*. This publication is available to download free of charge: re-nourish.com/?l=casestudies_standards.

Shedroff, N. (2010). *Design Is the Problem Studio Course Syllabus.* This publication is available to download free of charge: http://livingprinciples.aiga. org/design-is-the-problem-a-course-in-sustainable-design-1-0/.

Shedroff, N. (2013). *Sustainability Studio: A Course in Sustainable Design 1.0.* Download free of charge entire curriculum: www.livingprinciples.org/sustainability-studio-curriculum/.

Social Design Glossary. www.impactdesignhub.org/resources/glossary/.

Social Design Pathways Matrix, Winterhouse Symposium on Design Education and Social Change, Winterhouse Institute, 2013: http://www.socialdesignpathways.com/download-the-matrix/.

Transition Design Framework: The School of Design at Carnegie Mellon University has created a new framework introducing new knowledge and skill sets that respond to recent changes in the field of design, *across all levels in the program.* http://design.cmu.edu/content/program-framework.

Transition Design case study template: School of Design, Carnegie Mellon University: https://www.academia.edu/13122377/Transition_Design_Case_StudyTemplate?auto=download&campaign=weekly_digest.

Transition Design Bibliography, 2015: https://www.academia.edu/13108611/Transition_Design_Bibliography_2015?auto=download&campaign=http:weekly_digest.

BIBLIOGRAPHY

Akama, Y. (2009). "Warts-and-All: The Real Practice of Service Design." *Proceedings of the First Nordic Conference on Service Design and Service Innovation.* Oslo, Norway.

Amabile, T (1996). *Creativity in Context: Update to the Social Psychology of Creativity.* Boulder, CO: Westview Press.

American Psychiatric Association. (2000). *Diagnostic and Statistical Manual of Mental Disorders: DSM-IV-TR®.* American Psychiatric Publication.

Armstrong, H. and Stojmirovic, Z. (2011). *Participate: Designing with User-Generated Content.* New York: Princeton Architectural Press.

Armstrong, L., Bailey, J., Julier, G., and Kimball, L. (2014). *Social Design Futures: HEI Research and the AHRC.* Brighton, UK: University of Brighton.

Baeck, A. and Gremett, P. (2011). "Design Thinking." In H. Degen and X. Yuan (eds.), *UX Best Practices: How to Achieve More Impact with User Experience.* New York: McGraw-Hill Osborne Media.

Barkley, E., Cross, K., and Major, C. (2005). *Collaborative Learning Techniques: A Handbook for College Faculty.* New York: Jossey-Bass.

Barnard, A. (2000). *History and Theory in Anthropology.* New York: Cambridge University Press.

Becker, H. (2007). *Telling about Society.* Chicago: University of Chicago Press.

Becker, H. (2008). *Tricks of the Trade: How to Think about Your Research While You're Doing It.* Chicago: University of Chicago Press.

Bell, E. et al. (eds.). (1995). *From Mouse to Mermaid: The Politics of Film, Gender, and Culture.* Bloomington: Indiana University Press.

Bennett, A. (ed.). (2006). *Design Studies: Theory and Research in Graphic Design.* New York: Princeton Architectural Press.

Berman, D. (2009). *Do Good Design: How Designers Can Change the World.* Berkeley, CA: New Riders.

Bernard, P. (2000). "The Social Role of the Graphic Designer." *Essays on Design I: AGI's Designers of Influence.* London: Booth-Clibborn Publishers.

Best, J. and Harris, S. (eds.). (2012). *Making Sense of Social Problems: New Images, New Issues.* Boulder, CO: Lynne Rienner.

Bishop, C. (ed.). (2006). *Participation, Documents of Contemporary Art.* Cambridge, MA: The MIT Press; London: Whitechapel.

Bloemink, B. (2007). *Design for the Other 90%* catalogue. New York: Cooper-Hewitt, National Design Museum.

Bødker, S., Ehn, P., Sjögren, D., and Sundblad, Y. (2000). "Co-Operative Design—Perspectives on 20 Years with 'the Scandinavian It Design Model'." In *Proceedings of NordiCHI 2000.* Stockholm, Sweden: Centre for User Oriented IT Design (CID).

Booth Davies, J. (1997). *The Myth of Addiction*, 2nd edition. Amsterdam: Harwood Academic Publishers.

Boylston, S. (2009). *Designing Sustainable Packaging.* London: Laurence King Publishing.

Brown, T. (2008). "Design Thinking." *Harvard Business Review*, June: 84–92.

Brown. T. (2009). *Change by Design: How Design Thinking Transforms Organization and Inspires Innovation.* New York: Harper Business.

Brown, T. (2011). Design Thinking. Blog, available online: http://designthinking.ideo.com/ (accessed July 12, 2014).

Buchanan, R. (2005). "Wicked Problems in Design Thinking." In V. Margolin and R. Buchanan (eds.), *The Idea of Design*. Cambridge, MA: The MIT Press.

Buchanan, R. and Margolin, V. (eds.). (1995) *Discovering Design: Explorations in Design Studies*. Chicago: University of Chicago Press.

Canniffe, B. (2014). Interview conducted by email. July 7.

Chick, A. and Micklethwaite, P. (2011). *Design for Sustainable Change*. Lausanne, Switzerland: AVA Publishing S.A.

Connell, R. W. (2005). *Masculinities*. Berkeley: University of California Press.

Courage, C. and Baxter, K. (2005). *Understanding Your Users: A Practical Guide to User Requirements Methods Tools and Techniques*. San Francisco: Morgan Kaufmann.

Cranmer, J. and Zappaterra, Y. (2004). *Conscientious Objectives: Designing for an Ethical Message*. Hove, UK: Rotovision Books.

Deal, M. (2014). Interview conducted by email. July 9.

Dorst, K. (2011). "The Core of 'Design Thinking' and Its Application." *Design Studies* 32(6): 521–32.

Dubberly, H. (2007). "Cybernetics and Service-Craft: Language for Behavior-Focused Design." www.dubberly.com/articles/cybernetics-and-service-craft.html.

Dubberly, H. (2010). "Designing for Service: Creating an Experience Advantage." www.dubberly.com/articles/designing_for_service.html.

Dubberly, H. (2011). "A Proposal for the Future of Design Education." www.dubberly.com/articles/design-education-manifesto.html.

Dunne, A. and Raby, F. (2001). *Design Noir: The Secret Life of Electronic Objects*. Basel, Boston, Berlin: Birkhauser Verlag.

Ehmann, S., Bohle, S., and Klanten, R. (2012). *Cause and Effect: Visualizing Sustainability*. Berlin: Gestalten.

Ehn, P. (2008). "Participation in Design Things." In *PDC'08: Proceedings of the Tenth Anniversary Conference on Participatory Design 2008*. Paper presented at PDC'08 10th Biennial Participatory Design Conference, Indianapolis, IN (92-101). Indianapolis, IN: Indiana University.

Farson, R. (2008). *The Power of Design: A Force for Transforming Everything*. Norcross, GA: Greenway Communications.

Flores, J. (2000). *From Bomba to Hiphop: Puerto Rican Culture and Latino Identity*. New York: Columbia University Press.

Frascara, J. (1988). "Graphic Design: Fine Art or Social Science." *Design Issues* 5(1).

Frascara, J. (2001). "The Dematerialization of Design." *TipoGráfica 50: 18–25*.

Freud, S. (1961). *Civilization and Its Discontents*. Translated by James Strachey. New York: W. W. Norton & Company.

Fuad-Luke, A. (2009). *Design Activism: Beautiful Strangeness for a Sustainable World.* London and New York: Earthscan.

Glaser, M. and Ilic, M. (2005). *The Design of Dissent.* Gloucester, MA: Rockport Publishers.

Gore, A. (2006). *An Inconvenient Truth: The Planetary Emergency of Global Warming and What We Can Do About It.* Emmaus, PA: Rodale Inc.

The Guerilla Girls. (2003). *Bitches, Bimbos, and Ballbreakers: The Guerilla Girls' Guide to Female Stereotypes.* New York: Penguin Books.

Hartigan, J., Jr. (2005). *Odd Tribes: Toward a Cultural Analysis of White People.* Durham, NC: Duke University Press.

Hawken, P. (2008). *Blessed Unrest: How the Largest Social Movement in History Is Restoring Grace, Justice, and Beauty to the World.* New York: Penguin Books.

Heller, S. (ed.). (2005). *The Education of a Graphic Designer*, 2nd edition. New York: Allworth Press.

Heller, S. and Ilic, M. (2009). *The Anatomy of Design: Uncovering the Influences and Inspiration in Modern Graphic Design.* Gloucester, MA: Rockport Publishers.

Heller, S. and Vienne, V. (eds.). (2003). *Citizen Designer: Perspectives on Design Responsibility.* New York: Allworth Press.

Hooks, B. (1997). "Selling Hot Pussy: Representations of Black Female Sexuality in the Cultural Marketplace." In K. Conboy et al. (eds.), *Writing on The Body: Female Embodiment and Feminist Theory.* New York: Columbia University Press.

Howard, A. (1994). "There is such a thing as society." *Eye* 13: 72–7.

IDEO. (2014). Human Centered Design Toolkit. Palo Alto: IDEO. Available for free download at: www.designkit.org.

Irwin, T (2015). "Redesigning a Design Program: How Carnegie Mellon University is Developing a Design Curricula for the 21st Century." Available online: http://www.thesolutionsjournal.com/node/237296.

Itkonen, M. (ed.). (2013). *Resolutions: Responsibility in Graphic Design.* Aalto, Finland: Aalto University.

Kalman, T., Hall, P., and Bierut, M. (1998). *Tibor Kalman, Perverse Optimist.* New York: Princeton Architectural Press.

Kennedy, R. (2002). *Nigger: The Strange Career of a Troublesome Word.* New York: Vintage Books.

Kennedy, R. (2008). *Sellout: The Politics of Racial Betrayal.* New York: Pantheon Books.

Khan, S. and Fisher, D. (2014). *The Practice of Research: How Social Scientists Answer Their Questions.* Oxford: Oxford University Press.

Kieffer, C. H. (1984). "Citizen Empowerment: A Developmental Perspective." *Prevention in Human Services* 3(2–3): 9–36.

Kimbell, L. (2011). "Rethinking Design Thinking: Part 1" *Design & Culture* 3(3): 285–306.

Kimbell, L. (2012). "Rethinking Design Thinking: Part 2 " *Design & Culture* 4(2): 129–48.

Klanten, R., Ehmann, S., Bourquin, N., and Tissot, T. (eds.). (2010). *Data Flow 2: Visualizing Information in Graphic Design.* Berlin: Gestalten Verlag.

Klein, N. (2003). *No Logo.* New York: Picador.

Kohfeldt, D. and Langhout, R. D. (2012). "The Five Whys Method: A Tool for Developing Problem Definitions in Collaboration with Children." *Journal of Community & Applied Social Psychology* 22(4): 316–29.

Kouprie, M. and Visser, F. S. (2009). "A Framework for Empathy in Design: Stepping into and out of the User's Life." *Journal of Engineering Design* 20(5).

Kraft, P and Bansler, J. (1992). "The Collective Resource Approach: The Scandinavian Experience." In M. J. Muller, S. Kuhn, and J. A. Meskill (eds.), *PDC'92: Proceedings of The Participatory Design Conference.* Paper presented at PDC '92: Conference on Participatory Design, Cambridge, MA (pp. 127–35). Palo Alto, CA: Computer Professionals for Social Responsibility.

Lasn, K. (2000). *Culture Jam.* New York: William Morrow.

Lasn, K. (ed.). (2006). *Design Anarchy.* New York: ORO Editions.

Lausen, M. (2007). *Design for Democracy: Ballot and Election Design.* Chicago: University of Chicago Press.

Lavin, M. (2001). *Clean New World: Culture, Politics, and Graphic Design.* Cambridge, MA: The MIT Press.

Leadbeater, C. (2014). *The Frugal Innovator: Creating Change on a Shoestring Budget.* Basingstoke, UK: Palgrave Macmillan.

Light, A. and Akama, Y. (2014). "Structuring Future Social Relations: The Politics of Care in Participatory Practice." In the 13th Participatory Design Conference 204 (PDC '14) 6–10 October 2014, Windhoek, Namibia (pp. 1–10). http://nrl.northumbria.ac.uk/17808/ (accessed December 21, 2014).

Lindenfeld, F. (1973). *Radical Perspectives on Social Problems: Readings in Critical Sociology.* New York: Macmillan.

Lupton, E. (2011). *Graphic Design Thinking: Beyond Brainstorming.* New York: Princeton Architectural Press.

Maddaloni, A. (1961). "The Meaning of Empathy." *American Imago*, p. 23.

Malcolm, J. (2010). *Sustainability as an Enhancement Theme for the 21st Century Graphic Design Graduate: Should It Become Invisible?* Instituto Superior de Educacao e Ciencias, Lisbon & IPT–Instituto Politecnico de Tomar.

Maney, G. (ed.). (2012). *Strategies for Social Change.* Vol. 37. Minneapolis: University of Minnesota Press.

Manzini, E. (2014). "Making Things Happen: Social Innovation and Design." *Design Issues* 30(1).

Manzini, E. (2015). *Design, When Everybody Designs: An Introduction to Design for Social Innovation.* Cambridge, MA: The MIT Press.

Margolin, V. (2002). *The Politics of the Artificial: Essays on Design and Design Studies.* Chicago: University of Chicago Press.

Margolin, V. (2007). "Design, the Future and the Human Spirit." *Design Issues* 23(4).

Margolin, V. (2011). "Graphic Design Education and the Challenge of Social Transformation." *Icograda Design Education Manifesto 2011*, pp. 104–6.

Margolin, V. and Margolin, S. (2002). "A 'Social Model' of Design: Issues of Practice and Research." *Design Issues* 18(4): 24–30.

Martin, B., Hanington, B., and Hanington, B. M. (2012). *Universal Methods of Design: 100 ways to Research Complex Problems, Develop Innovative Ideas, and Design Effective Solutions*. Beverly, MA: Rockport Publishers.

Mau, B. with Leonard, J. and the Institute without Boundaries. (2004). *Massive Change*. London: Phaidon.

McCandless, D. (2010). *Information Is Beautiful*. New York: Collins Publishers.

McCarthy, S. (2013). *The Designer as Author, Producer, Activist, Entrepreneur, Curator & Collaborator*. Amsterdam: BIS Publishers.

McCoy, K. (1997). "Countering the Tradition of the Apolitical Designer." *Looking Closer 2: Critical Writings on Graphic Design*. New York: Allworth Press.

McCoy, K. (1998). "Education in an Adolescent Profession." In S. Heller (ed.), *The Education of a Graphic Designer*. New York: Allworth Press.

McCoy, K. (2003). "Good Citizenship: Design as a Social and Political Force." In S. Heller and V. Vienne (eds.), *Citizen Designer: Perspectives on Design Responsibility*. New York: Allworth Press.

McDonough, W. and Braungart, M. (2002). *Cradle to Cradle: Remaking the Way We Make Things*. New York: North Point Press.

McQuiston, L. (1995). *Graphic Agitation: Social and Political Graphics since the 1960s*. New York: Phaidon.

McQuiston, L. (2004). *Graphic Agitation 2: Social and Political Graphics in the Digital Age*. New York: Phaidon.

Meggs, P. B. (1998). *A History of Graphic Design*, 3rd edition. New York: John Wiley & Sons.

Miller, A. et al. (2000). *Global Cultures: Symbols*. Gloucester, MA: Rockport Publishers.

Mirande, A. (1997). *Hombres y Machos: Masculinity and Latino Culture*. Boulder: Westview Press.

Moggridge, B. (2007). *Designing Interactions*. Cambridge, MA: The MIT Press.

Morelli, N. 2007. "Social Innovation and New Industrial Contexts: Can Designers 'Industrialize' Socially Responsible Solutions?" *Design Issues* 23(4).

Moyer, B. (2001). *Doing Democracy: The MAP Model for Organizing Social*. Canada: New Society Publishers.

Nanda, S. and Warms, R. (2009). *Culture Counts*. Belmont, CA: Wadsworth.

Nelson, G. and Prilleltensky, I. (2005). *Community Psychology: In Pursuit of Liberation and Well-Being*. New York: Palgrave Macmillan.

Nussbaum, B. (2011). "Design Thinking Is a Failed Experiment: So What's Next?" Fast Company blog. Available online: http://www.fastcodesign.com/1663558/design-thinking-is-a-failed-experiment-so-whats-next (accessed December 24, 2014).

Ortiz, F. (1995). *Cuban Counterpoint: Tobacco and Sugar*. Durham, NC: Duke University Press.

Osterwalder, A. and Pigneur, Y. (2010). *Business Model Generation*. Hoboken, NJ: John Wiley & Sons Inc.

Papanek, V. (1971). *Design for the Real World* (2nd edition, 1984). Chicago, IL: Academy Chicago Publishers.

Papanek, V. (1995). *The Green Imperative: Ecology and Ethics in Design and Architecture*. London: Thames & Hudson.

Pilloton, E. (2009). *Design Revolution: 100 Products that Empower People*. New York: Metropolis Books.

Plate, S. B. (ed.). (2002). *Religion, Art, and Visual Culture*. New York: Palgrave.

Polaine, A., Løvlie, L., and Reason, B. (2013). *Service Design: From Insight to Implementation*. Brooklyn, NY: Rosenfeld Media.

Poynor, R. (1999). "First Things First: A Brief History." *Adbusters* 27: 54–6.

Poynor, R. (2000). "Kalle Lasn: Ad buster." *Graphis* 325: 96–101.

Resnick, E. (2003). *Design for Communication: Conceptual Graphic Design Basics*. New York: John Wiley & Sons.

Resnick, E. (2013). *Graphic Advocacy: International Posters for the Digital Age 2001–2012*. Boston: Massachusetts College of Art and Design. Exhibition website: www.graphicadvocacyposters.org.

Resnick, E. and Cortés, J. (2010). *Graphic Intervention: 25 Years of International AIDS Awareness Posters 1985–2010*. Boston: Massachusetts College of Art and Design. Exhibition website: wwwgraphicintervention.org.

Resnick, E., Maviyane-Davies, C., and Baseman F. (2005). *The Graphic Imperative: International Posters for Peace, Social Justice and The Environment 1965–2005*. Boston: Massachusetts College of Art and Design. Exhibition website: www.thegraphicimperative.org.

Roberts, L. (2006). *Good: An Introduction to Ethics in Graphic Design*. Lausanne, Switzerland: AVA Publishing S.A.

Ryan, W. (1976). *Blaming the Victim*. New York: Random House.

Sanders, E. B.-N. (2013). "Perspectives on Design in Participation." In C. Mareis, M. Held, and G. Joost (eds.), *Wer Gestaltet die Gestaltung? Praxis, Theorie und Geschichte des Partizipatorischen Designs* (pp. 69–73.). Transcript Verlag (www.transcript-verlag.de).

Scalin, N. and Taute, M. (2012). *The Design Activist's Handbook*. Cincinnati, OH: How Books.

Schnapp, J. T. and Michaels, Adam (2012). *The Electric Information Age Book*. New York: Princeton Architectural Press.

Seidman, E. and Rappaport, J. (1986). Framing the issues. In *Redefining Social Problems* (pp. 1–8). New York: Springer.

Sennett, R. (2003). *Respect: The Formation of Character in an Age of Inequality*. New York: W. W. Norton and Company.

Shaunghnessy, A. (2013). *Essays: Scratching the Surface*. London: Unit Editions.

Shay, A., Haggerty, M., and Kennedy, S. (2013). *Social Design Field Guide: A Handbook from Experiences in Participatory Design in Indonesia*. New York: Van Alen Books.

Shea, A. (2012). *Designing for Social Change: Strategies for Community-Based Graphic Design*. New York: Princeton Architectural Press.

Shedroff, N. (2009). *Design Is the Problem: The Future of Design Must Be Sustainable*. New York: Rosenfeld Media.

Shepard, B. (2014). *Community Projects as Social Activism*. Thousand Oaks, CA: Sage.

Sherin, A. (2008). *SustainAble: A Handbook of Materials and Application for Graphic Designers and Their Clients*. Beverly, MA: Rockport Publishers.

Simmons, C. (2011). *Just Design: Socially Conscious Design for Critical Causes*. Cincinnati, OH: How Books.

Simon, H. (1969). *The Sciences of the Artificial*. Cambridge, MA: The MIT Press.

Stairs, D. (2010). "Citizen Designer: 21st Century Ethics for Graphic Designers." In *I Don't Know Where I'm Going But I Want To Be There* (pp. 48–9). Amsterdam: BIS Publishers.

Stickdorn, M. and Schneider, J. (2012). *This Is Service Design Thinking*. New York: John Wiley & Sons.

Tapia, A. (2009). *The Inclusion Paradox: The Obama Era and the Transformation of Global Diversity*. Lincolnshire, IL: Hewitt Associates.

TED. (2009). Tim Brown Urges Designers to Think Big. Talk at TED Conference, Oxford, July. www.ted.com/talks/tim_brown_urges_designers_to_think_big.html (accessed December 24,14).

TED. (2010). Emily Pilloton: Teaching Design for Change. Retrieved from Talk at TED Global in July. www.ted.com/talks/emily_pilloton_teaching_design_for_change.

Thackara, J. (2005). *In the Bubble: Designing in a Complex World*. Cambridge, MA: The MIT Press.

Triggs, T., McAndrew, C., Akama, Y., and Choukeir, J. (2011). "Telling Your Story: People and the Aylesbury Estate." *Include 2011: Online Proceedings*, RCA, London, 2011, pp. 1–10.

Tunstall, E. (2011). "Respectful Design: A Proposed Journey of Design Education." In A. Bennett and O. Vulpinari (eds.), *Icograda Design Education Manifesto 2011*. Montreal, Canada: Icograda.

Tunstall, E. (2013). "Decolonizing Design Innovation: Design Anthropology and Indigenous Knowledge." In W. Gunn, T. Otto, and R. Smith (eds.), *Design Anthropology between Theory and Practice* (pp. 232–50). London: Berg Publishing.

Vago, S. (2004). *Social Change*, 5th edition. New Jersey: Pearson Prentice Hall.

Van der Zwaag, A. (2014). *Looks Good Feels Good Is Good: How Social Design Changes Our World*. The Netherlands: Lecturis.

van Toorn, J. (1998). *Design beyond Design: Critical Reflection and the Practice of Visual Communication*. Maastricht, NL: Jan Van Eyck Akademie.

Vedantam, S. (2010). *The Hidden Brain: How Our Unconscious Minds Elect Presidents, Control Markets, Wage Wars and Save Our Lives*. New York: Spiegel & Grau.

Weinschenk, S. (2011). *100 things Every Designer Needs to Know about People*. New York: New Riders.

Wu, F. H. (2002). *Yellow: Race in America Beyond Black and White*. New York: Basic Books.

INDEX